Historical Sketch and Roster Of The Iowa 9th Infantry Regiment

By John C. Rigdon

Historical Sketch and Roster Of The
Iowa 9th Infantry Regiment

1st Printing – Nov 2015 1/0/1/0/

© Copyright 2015. Eastern Digital Resources. All Rights Reserved. No part of this book may be reproduced by any means without the express written consent of the copyright holder.

Published by:
Eastern Digital Resources
31 Bramblewood Drive SW
Cartersville, GA 30120
http://www.researchonline.net
EMAIL: Sales@Researchonline.net
Tel. (678) 739-9177

Contents

He Died at His Post 5

A Turtle on a Lamp Post 6

Officers 7

Assignments 9

Service 11

Companies 17

Summary of Casualties 18

Historical Sketch 19

Field Staff and Band 37

Non-Commissioned Staff 42

Regimental Band 43

Bibliography 251

IA 9th Infantry Regiment 251

Index 253

For Further Research 283

The Historical Sketch & Roster Series 298

He Died at His Post

by J. W. Holman

A soldier had fallen! 'Tis well that we weep!
O soft be his pillow, and peaceful his sleep!
Far, far from his home, and the friends he loved most,
He fell in the conflict, and died at his post.

When brave ones were summoned their country to save,
He hasted war's perils to share with the brave,
And proudly he stood in the van of the host,
And, like his Great Captain, he died at his post.

No more shall earth's conflicts disturb his repose,
He has gone where the weary are free from life's woes;
There covered with glory, on Eden's bright coast,
'Twill be sweet to remember he died at his post.

Farewell youthful soldier! we ne'er will forget,
The life thou has offered, the death thou has met!
Of thee may our nation in history boast;
And tell the whole world, thou didst die at thy post.

A soldier has fallen; but long shall remain
The star-spangled flag which he died to sustain;
For, sooner than let our loved country be lost,
A nation of freemen will die at their post!

A Turtle on a Lamp Post

If You ever see one, you'll know he didn't get there by himself.

This work has been compiled from a number of different sources. I have concentrated on first hand accounts and primary sources when available. It is my hope that this sketch will help in your research and become the basis of future in depth research into this regiment and the men who served.

If you have additional information on the men who served in this unit, or the regiment's actions in battle, drop me a note at JRigdon@researchonline.net. I will incorporate them into future editions.

Officers

Cols., William Vandever, David Carskaddon; Lieut. -Cols., Frank G. Herron, William H. Coyle, Alonzo Abernethy; Majs., William H. Coyle, Don A. Carpenter, George Granger, Alonzo Abernethy, Joseph G. Inman.

William Vandever. Residence Dubuque. Appointed Colonel Aug. 30, 1861. Mustered Sept. 24, 1861. Promoted Brigadier General, March 16, 1863. Resigned March 16, 1863. Brevet Major General June 7, 1865[5]

Francis J. Herron. Residence Dubuque. Appointed Lieutenant Colonel Sept. 10, 1861. Mustered Sept. 24, 1861. Wounded March 7, 1862, Peas Ridge, Ark. Promoted Brigadier General July 30, 1862; Major General Nov. 29, 1863.[6]

David Carskaddon. Residence Marion, nativity Ohio. Enlisted Sept. 14, 1861. Appointed Captain Sept. 24, 1861. Mustered Sept. 24, 1861. Promoted Colonel March 19, 1863. Wounded slightly July 29, 1864, Atlanta, Ga. Discharged for disability Dec. 29, 1864.[7][8]

William H. Coyl. Residence Decorah. Appointed Major Aug 30, 1861. Mustered Sept 24, 1861. Wounded in shoulder severely March 7, 1862, Pea

Ridge, Ark. Promoted Lieutenant Colonel July 1, 1862; Brevet Lieutenant Colonel March 13, 1865; Major and Judge Advocate May 18, 1865[9]

William Scott. Residence Independence, nativity England. Appointed Adjutant Sept 2, 1861, from Second Lieutenant of company C. Mustered Sept. 24, 1861. Wounded in leg March 7, 1862, Pea Ridge Ark. Resigned for ill health Oct. 11, 1862[10]

Ferdinand S. Winslow. Residence Marion. Appointed Quartermaster Sept. 4, 1861. Mustered Sept. 24, 1861. Promoted Assistant United States Quartermaster, with rank as Captain, Jan. 30, 1862.[11]

Jerome Bradley. Residence Dubuque, nativity Massachusetts. Appointed Quartermaster March 16, 1862 from Second Lieutenant of Battery. Commission declined March 16, 1862. Appears to have been appointed Captain A.Q.M. Volunteers Feb 19, 1863. See Official Army Registers, 1861-1867[12]

Benjamin McClure. Appointed Surgeon Sept. 19, 1861. Mustered Oct. 11, 1861. Promoted Assistant Surgeon of Volunteers Feb 4, 1864; Surgeon of Volunteers Sept. 30, 1864.[

Assignments

Organized at Dubuque and mustered in September 24, 1861.

Ordered to St. Louis, Mo.

Attached to Dept. of Missouri October, 1861, to January, 1862.

Unattached, Army of Southwest Missouri, to February, 1862.

2nd Brigade, 4th Division, Army of Southwest Missouri, to May, 1862.

2nd Division, Army of Southwest Missouri, to July, 1862.

District of Eastern Arkansas, Dept. of Missouri, to November, 1862.

3rd Brigade, 1st Division, District of Eastern Arkansas, Dept. of Tennessee, to December, 1862.

3rd Brigade, 11th Division, Right Wing 13th Army Corps (Old), Dept. of Tennessee, to December, 1862.

3rd Brigade, 4th Division, Sherman's Yazoo Expedition, to January, 1863.

3rd Brigade, 1st Division, 15th Army Corps, Army of Tennessee, to September, 1863.

2nd Brigade, 1st Division, 15th Army Corps, to September, 1864.

3rd Brigade, 1st Division, 15th Army Corps, to July, 1865.

Service

Moved to Franklin, Mo., October 11, 1861, and duty there guarding railroad until January, 1862.

Curtis' advance on Springfield, Mo., January 23-February 12, 1862.

Pursuit of Price to Cassville, Ark., February 13-16. Sugar Creek February 17.

Battles of Pea Ridge, Ark., March 6, 7 and 8.

March to Batesville April 5-May 3, and to Helena, Ark., May 25-July 14.

Duty at Helena until December.

Expedition from Helena to Arkansas Post November 16-21.

Sherman's Yazoo Expedition December 22, 1862, to January 2, 1863.

Chickasaw Bayou December 26-28, 1862.

Chickasaw Bluffs December 29.

Expedition to Arkansas Post, Ark., January 3-10, 1863.

Assault on and capture of Fort Hindman, Arkansas Post, January 10-11.

Moved to Young's Point, La., January 17-23, and duty there until April.

Expedition to Greenville, Black Bayou and Deer Creek April 5-14.

Black Bayou April 10.

Demonstration on Haines and Drumgould's Bluffs April 25-May 2.

Snider's Bluff April 30.

Moved to Join army in rear of Vicksburg, Miss., May 2-14.

Battle of Jackson May 14.

Siege of Vicksburg, Miss., May 18-July 4.

Assaults on Vicksburg May 19 and 22.

Advance on Jackson, Miss., July 5-10.

Siege of Jackson July 10-17.

Brandon Station July 19.

At Big Black until September 22.

Moved to Memphis, thence march to Chattanooga, Tenn., September 22-November 20.

Operation on the Memphis & Charleston Railroad in Alabama October 20-29.

Cherokee Station October 21 and 29.

Cane Creek October 26.

Tuscumbia October 26-27.

Battles of Chattanooga November 23-27; Lookout Mountain November 23-24; Mission Ridge November 25; Taylor's Ridge, Ringgold Gap, November 27.

March to relief of Knoxville November 28-December 17.

At Woodville, Ala., until April, 1864.

Atlanta (Ga.) Campaign May 1-September 8.

Demonstration on Resaca May 8-13.

Battle of Resaca May 14-15.

Operations on line of Pumpkin Vine Creek and battles about Dallas, New Hope Church and Allatoona Hills May 25-June 5.

Operations about Marietta and against Kennesaw Mountain June 10-July 2.

Assault on Kennesaw June 27.

Nickajack Creek July 2-5.

Chattahoochee River July 6-17.

Battle of Atlanta July 22.

Siege of Atlanta July 22-August 25.

Ezra Chapel, Hood's second sortie, July 28.

Flank movement on Jonesboro August 25-30.

Battle of Jonesboro August 31-September 1.

Lovejoy Station September 2-6.

Pursuit of Hood into Alabama October 1-26.

Snake Creek Gap October 15.

Ship Gap October 16.

March to the sea November 15-December 10.

Griswoldsville November 22.

Ogeechee River December 7-9.

Siege of Savannah December 10-21.

Campaign of the Carolinas January to April. 1865.

Reconnaissance to Salkehatchie River January 25, 1865.

Salkehatchie Swamps, S.C., February 3-5.

South Edisto River February 9.

North Edisto River February 12-13.

Congaree Creek February 15.

Columbia February 16-17.

Battle of Bentonville, N. C., March 20-21.

Occupation of Goldsboro March 24.

Advance on Raleigh April 10-13.

Occupation of Raleigh April 14.

Bennett's House April 26.

Surrender of Johnston and his army.

March to Washington, D.C., via Richmond, Va., April 29-May 20.

Grand Review May 24.

Moved to Louisville, Ky., June.

Mustered out July 18, 1865.

Companies

Company A - enrolled in Jackson County

Company B - enrolled in Jones County

Company C - enrolled in Dubuque County

Company D - enrolled in Jones County

Company E - enrolled in Clayton County

Company F - enrolled in Fayette County

Company G - enrolled in Black Hawk County, Bremer County &c.

Company H - enrolled in Winneshiek County

Company I - enrolled in Howard County

Company K - enrolled in Linn County

Summary of Casualties

Total Enrollment	1440
Killed	84
Wounded	385
Died of wounds	64
Died of Disease	210
Discharged for Disease, wounds & other	299
Buried in National Cemetaries	139
Captured	32
Transferred	30

Historical Sketch [1]

The ten companies of the Ninth Regiment of Iowa Volunteer Infantry, were ordered by Governor Samuel Kirkwood to rendezvous at Dubuque, as a part of the quota of the State under the proclamation of the President dated July 23rd, 1861, and were mustered into the service of the United States on dates ranging from Sept. 2d to Sept 24th, 1861 by Captain E.C. Washington, Unites States Army.

The Honorable William Vandever, then a member of Congress from Iowa, was given authority by President Lincoln to organize this regiment from the counties composing his district, and he was commissioned by Governor Kirkwood as its first Colonel.

The last company was mustered in September 24, 1861 and 2 days later, the regiment, with a strength of 977 officers and enlisted men, were put on steam boats at Dubuque and transported to St. Louis. Upon arrival, they were marched to Benton Barracks, where it received its first supply of arms, clothing and camp equipment. The 9th remained until October 11th,

---

[1] Adapted from Roster and Record of 9th Iowa Vol. Infantry Regiment in the War of the Rebellion.

1861, receiving such instruction in military drill as could be given in so short a period of time. It was then ordered to proceed to Franklin, Missouri, where regimental headquarters were maintained, while companies were detached to different points for the purpose of guarding the railroad from Franklin toward Rolla, Missouri. During the 3 months in which the regiment remained on this duty, it suffered greatly from exposure the the inclement winter weather, and like all new regiments, was subjected to much sickness on account of exposure. On December 31, 1861, the official returns showed a death loss of 17, and 7 discharged from duty because of disability, total of 24 men; but on that same day, it gained 38 by additional enlistments, and 4 by transfer, for a net gain of 18, grand total officers and men, 995.

However, many were on the sick list, and the hardships the regiment had to endure during the active winter campaign which followed, further reduced its strength by roughly 1/2. On Jan 21, 1862, the detached companies of the regiment were consolidated. The regiment was taken by rail to Rolla, Mo. and from there began its first real campaign against the enemy. It marched from Rolla to Lebanon, Mo., where it joined the Army of the Southwest under the command of General Curtis. Colonel Vandever was placed in command of the brigade to which his regiment was attached. Lieut. Col. Frank J. Herron was then in command of the 9th Iowa.

Confederate General Price evacuated Springfield in advance of the approaching Union troops retreating toward the Ozark Mountains. The Army of the Southwest pursuing left Springfield on Feb 14, 1862 and in less than one month, marched over difficult road, in severe weather of alternating snow and rain, a distance of 250 miles. When they reached Cross Hollows, Arkansas, 300 men of the 9th Iowa Reg't was sent on expedition to Huntsville, 40 miles away, to surprise and capture a detachment of the enemy stationed there as a guard for commissary stores: but on reaching Huntsville, they found the place abandoned, and learned the rebel army under General Van Dorn was marching to attack General Curtis' army. Curtis had fallen back from Cross Hollows and taken a new position at Pea Ridge. Not wanting to be cut off and taken by a superior force, the detachment of Ninth Iowa at once started to rejoin the command. After a continuous march of 16 hours covering 42 miles, it reached the rest of the regiment at 8:00 pm, March 6th. With only a few hours rest after this grueling march, these men went into battle at Pea Ridge at 10 o'clock a.m. March 7th, 1862.

Pea Ridge Arkansas

The enemy opened by a fierce attack on the Union lines, and the 9th Iowa was in the thickest of the fight. The 1st attack was repulsed by the Union forces and it advanced on the Confederates. But it was compelled to retire under a terrific fire of muskets, grape and canister from cannon. The battle continued the whole day with alternating advantage throughout the day. There were occasional intervals, during which the men of both sides replenished ammunitions and removed the wounded to the rear. The fighting was most persistent and desperate, and in no battle of the war was the valor of the American soldier more splendidly exhibited, on both sides. This was the first time the 9th Iowa met the enemy in battle. Its officers and men showed the steadiness and bravery of veterans. If this had been the only service rendered by this regiment, it would have been entitled to the lasting gratitude of every patriotic citizen of the Union, which the 9th Iowa Regiment was defending against those in armed rebellion.

At night the survivors lay on their arms, ready to renew the conflict at dawn. Then the Union artillery opened on the enemy and the fire was promptly returned. In his official report Col. Vandever says, "At this point, finding ourselves exposed to a raking fire from one of the enemy's batteries on our right, we changed direction to the east. About this time, the First Division coming into position on our left, we joined in the general advance upon the enemy, the whole cavalry force participating, and the artillery co-operating. The enemy here broke into disorder, and the fortune of the day was decided in our favor."

The entire rebel army was soon in full retreat, and the battle of Pea Ridge ended in a brilliant victory for the Union army. At the close of his official report Major General Curtis especially commended Col. Vandever and the gallant troops of his brigade, and says, "To do justice to all, I would spread before you the most of the rolls of this army, for I can bear testimony to the almost universal good conduct of officers and men, who shared with me the long march, the many conflicts by the way, and the final struggle with the combined forces of Price, McCulloch, McIntosh and Pike, under Major General Van Dorn, at the battle of Pea Ridge."

The loss to the regiment was very heavy. Of the 560 who went into battle, 4 commissioned officers and 34 enlisted men were killed, 5 commissioned officers and 171 enlisted men wounded, and 1 commissioned officer and 3 enlisted men captured, making a total loss of nearly 40 % of the aggregate number engaged. [2]

---

[2] The original compiler of this sketch finds this loss statement in the return of casualties of the Army of the Southwest in the battle of Pea Ridge, Ark., attached to the report of Major General Curtis, found on p. 205, Series 1, Vol.8, Official Records. In the history of the Ninth Iowa Infantry by Lt. Col. Alonzo Abernethy, on p. 174 of the Adj. General's report of the State of Iowa, for the year 1866, the aggregate loss in killed, wounded and captured is given as 240, making nearly 44% of the total number. In either

After the battle the regiment had only a brief season of rest. Its next experience was a long, devious and trying march with the army of the Southwest, through Missouri and Arkansas, covering six hundred miles and ending at Helena, July 17, 1862. During this march the weather was very warm and dry, and the troops suffered greatly from the heat, dust and thirst, and , on the latter part of the march from insufficient rations. For five weeks of this time the army was cut off from all communication, but fortunately no considerable body of the enemy was encountered and it at last arrived safely at Helena.

Here the regiment went into camp, and for the ensuing five months enjoyed comparative immunity from the hardships and dangers of a soldier's life. It was, however, rendering valuable service in holding an important post, and the time was not spent in idleness. The officers and men utilized the time to the best advantage, in perfecting themselves in military drill and discipline, and, when they again entered upon the duties of active campaigning, they were splendidly equipped for the hard and continuous service which they were called upon to perform

---

event the loss was far above the average of battle of the War of the Rebellion.

during the remainder of their term of service. While the regiment was in camp at Helena, a most pleasing incident occurred, which deserves permanent preservation in this sketch and is thus described by Lieutenant Colonel Abernethy in his "*History of the Ninth Infantry*".

"At Helena a stand of beautiful silk colors reached us, sent by the hands of Miss Phoebe Adams, in behalf of a committee of ladies of Boston, Mass., as a testimonial of their appreciation of our conduct in the battle of Pea Ridge. They were guarded and cherished while in the regiment with religious care. After having been borne over many a proud field, they were, by the unanimous voice of the regiment, given back, riddled and torn - one to the original donors, the other to Brevet Major General Vandever, our original Colonel, who, by his bravery and decision at Pea Ridge and Arkansas Post, with the regiment, and by his honorable record thereafter in other fields, won the confidence and love of his regiment."

December 18, 1862, the regiment was again called into active service, this time on the lower Mississippi, and was assigned to General Thayer's Brigade of General Steele's Division of the Fifteenth Army Corps. It participated in the battle of Chickasaw Bayou, December 28th and 29th, where it maintained its good record for bravery under the fire of the enemy.

Lieutenant Colonel Abernethy, describing the part taken by his regiment in this battle says, "The regiment, though under fire the greater part of the 28th and 29th, was only engaged about half an hour of the latter day. While the hardest fighting was in progress, we were being transferred from a point above Chickasaw Bayou to where the main army was massed, reaching there only to go into position as others were falling back. We were soon withdrawn beyond the reach of the rebel batteries lining the hills in our front, and next day embarked, the attempt having been given over."

The regiment next went into camp on the Yazoo River above Vicksburg, where it remained until the close of the year 1862.

The official returns show that, during the year, the regiment had gained by additional enlistments 54, and by appointment 2; total gain 56. In the same time it had lost in killed in battle 43, died from wounds 41, and from disease 37; total number of deaths 121; 178 were discharged for disabilities; and 8 had deserted, making a total loss for the year of 307. Its losses up to the 31st day of December, 1861 had been 24 and its gain by additional enlistment 42. It will be seen that, in the one year and three months that the regiment had then served, it had lost 331 officers and men, and had gained 98 by additional enlistment. Its losses thus far had aggregated nearly on-third of those originally mustered and gained by additional enlistment, while it had just entered upon the second year of its three year service.

Early in January, 1863, the regiment was engaged in the movement against Arkansas Post, and on January 11th, when the attack upon the fort was made, it was in the reserve line, waiting for the order to move forward to the assault; but, before the order was given, the enemy raised the white flag in token of surrender, and the regiment had the pleasure of witnessing the fall of that stronghold without loss to itself. January 24th found the regiment again in camp at Young's Point, near Vicksburg. About this time, Colonel Vandever was promoted to Brigadier General, and the officers and men of the Ninth Iowa, while rejoicing in his well deserved promotion, felt that they were parting from one of the bravest and most efficient commanders, and that it would be difficult to determine who should succeed him. There was an excellent list of officers from which to make the selection. Captain David Carskaddon of Company K was elected and became the second Colonel of the regiment.

Lieutenant Colonel Abernethy, in his history of the Ninth Iowa Infantry thus graphically describes the experience of the regiment for the remainder of the winter of 1863:

The history of the regiment for these two months of February and March is a tale of sorrow. The health of many of its members was already undermined by a six months' sojourn in the miasmatic regions of the Mississippi valley, and it seemed that but few could withstand the debilitating and enervating influence of this insalubrious climate. The smallpox came now, for the first time, into our ranks. Scores of our number, hitherto stout and rugged, were prostrated past recovery, and now lie buried in shallow graves about the hospitals which once stood in that sickly region; while others only recovered completely, long afterwards, in the mountains of Tennessee and Georgia, or on the sandy plains of the Carolinas. The ordeal of the unpropitious months was the more grevious because it had all the evils of the battlefield, with none of its honors.

Every true soldier will admit the force and truth of the above statement. The inspiration which comes to men in the midst of battle sustains them in the performance of deeds of valor, but when it comes to the struggle with disease and death, without the tender ministrations of relatives and friends, far from home and all its comforts, the men who endure and die, as well as those who endure and live, must be sustained by a fortitude and courage even greater than that which enables them to perform their whole duty when engaging the enemy in battle.

During the month of April. 1863, the regiment participated in an expedition to Greenville Miss., and farther into the interior, in which it met the enemy in occasional skirmishes, but the object of the expedition was accomplished without severe fighting. Upon its return from this expedition, it entered into the campaign which ended in the surrender of the rebel strongholds at Vicksburg and Jackson. Its movements and operation are described by Lieutenant Colonel Abernethy, as follows:

On the 2d day of May, leaving our tents standing at Milliken's Bend, La., the regiment started in light marching order for Grand Guld, crossed the Mississippi, and commenced on the 8th of May the march in rear of Vicksburg. On the 14th reached Jackson, the State capital of Mississippi, and took part in its capture. Four days later, after some skirmishing, in which we lost three wounded, the regiment took position in the outer works which environed Vicksburg * * *

May 19th, after sever skirmishing, and a final assault, the regiment succeeded in getting and holding an excellent position, about seventy-five yards from the enemy's works. * * *

On the 22nd of May, in line with the whole Army of the Tennessee, the regiment went first up to the assault. Its flag went down a few feet from the rebel works, after the last one of its guard had fallen, either killed or wounded, and its dripping folds were drawn from under the bleeding body of its prostrate bearer. In the few terrible moments of the assault, the regiment lost 79 killed and wounded, nearly one-third of the number in action. But that was not all. The assault had failed, and we found ourselves lying in the ravines, behind logs, contiguous to and partly under the protection of the rebel earthworks, above which no traitor could raise his head, except at the expense of his life. There we were compelled to stay until darkness gave us a cover under which to escape. Here I pause to pay the slight tribute of recording their name, to Captain Kelsey, and Lieutenants Jones, Wilbur, and Tyrrell, who fell while leading their companies to the assault, and to Captain Washburn, who was mortally wounded at the head of the regiment.

Our loss in the previous assault of the 19th of May was 16 men, and when, on the morning of Independence Day, the enemy came out and stacked arms and colors on his works, our total recorded loss in the siege was 121.

After the surrender of Vicksburg, the regiment participated in the siege of Jackson, and after the evacuation of that place, took part in the pursuit of the enemy, and lost one man killed in a skirmish at Brandon. The regiment now went into camp on Black

River, Miss., where it remained until September 22d, when it was ordered to Vicksburg, thence by river to Memphis, and from there by rail to Corinth, Miss., from which point it took up the line of march to Chattanooga, and entered upon another campaign which resulted in great success for the cause of the Union, and a crushing defeat to that portion of the rebel army against which the operation were directed. After a march of three hundred miles, during which the regiment had some skirmished with the rebel General Forrest's troops, it arrived at the foot of Lookout Mountain, November 23, 1863, and on the 24th took part in the battle above the clouds, and, later, in the battles of Missionary Ridge and Ringgold. Although not in the heaviest fighting in these three engagements, the regiment accomplished all that was assigned to ti. Its losses in killed and wounded during the campaign aggregated 22. It now marched to Woodville, Ala., where it went into winter quarters Dec. 29, 1863. During the year the regiment had marched 870 miles, and had been convoyed 1300 miles by water and 100 miles by rail. In the same time, it had met with a total loss of 227 and gained by enlistment 11, leaving an aggregate of 510.

January 1, 1864, 287 men of the regiment re-enlisted as Veteran Volunteers for another term of three years, and under the terms of their enlistment were entitled to a thirty days' furlough, to begin after reaching the State of Iowa. They left Woodville, Ala.,

February 4, 1864 and reached Dubuque, Iowa, February 14, 1864, at which point they separated for their respective homes. March 15th found the veterans of the regiment reassembled at Davenport, Iowa, accompanied by 125 recruits. They reached Woodville, Ala., April 10th, having marched from Nashville, a distance of 125 miles. A new supply of arms, clothing and camp equipage was issued to the regiment, and on May 1st, with Colonel Carskaddon in command, it took up the line of march for Chattanooga. In six days it had again reached the scene of military activity, and entered upon another great struggle for the preservation of the Union. The Ninth Iowa Infantry was constantly at the front, on the firing line, and in the trenches, and had its full share in the fighting during the campaign. The compiler of this sketch is compelled, by the limitation of space to which he is restricted, to omit the detailed account of the operations of the regiment given by Lieutenant Col. Abernethy in his history, from which quotations have heretofore been so freely made. It must here suffice to say that, from the opening to the close of the Atlanta Campaign, the Ninth Iowa Infantry displayed the same conspicuous gallantry which had characterized its career in all the battles in which it had been engaged, from Pea Ridge to Jonesboro. Describing the close of the campaign, Lieutenant Colonel Abernethy says:

At Jonesboro, on the 31st of August, where we were attacked in vain, and for the last time, by the rebel army of Tennessee, we held our position easily, and with comparatively slight loss. The march thence to Lovejoy's Station, and back again to East Point, Ga., by the 8th of September, completed the campaign - a campaign which for hard and continuous fighting, for severe labor and exposure, for long marches in the hottest weather, for the duration and persistent obstinacy, is unparalleled in history. We had marched 400 miles, principally in the night, built 40 different lines of works, crossed three large rivers in the face of a powerful enemy, flanked him away from three of the strongest natural positions in the country, and fought the battles of Resaca, Dallas, New Hope Church, Big Shanty, Kennesaw Mountain, and Chattahoochee River, Decatur, Atlanta, Jonesboro, and Lovejoy. The regiment lost in the campaign since the 1st of May 14 killed, 70 wounded, and 6 captured.

The non-veterans of the regiment were mustered out of the service on the 23d day of September, 1864, the original three years term for which they had enlisted having expired. For the re-enlisted veterans and recruits there yet remained the experience of the closing campaigns of the war, which, in some respects, were more remarkable than any which had preceded them. On the 4th of October the regiment was again on the march with the army which followed the rebel forces under General Hood through Marietta, Rome, Reseca, and across into Alabama, returning to the vicinity of Atlanta on the 5th of November, having marched 354 miles. November 15th, the regiment, then under the command of its senior Captain Paul McSweeney, began the famous march with General Sherman's army to Savannah and the sea. This remarkable military exploit was accomplished in 35 days, the distance covered being 400 miles. During the year, the regiment had marched 1,400 miles, and traveled by steamboat and railroad 1,900 miles. It had gained by additional enlistment 160, had lost in killed 14 and from other causes 214, leaving an aggregate of 442 on December 31, 1864.

The closing campaign - the trip by sea to Beaufort, S.C., and the march through the states of South and North Carolina - was full of interest and most worthy of being recorded in, detail, did space permit. Col. Carskaddon, who had been wounded at Atlanta, returned to the regiment, and was honorably mustered out by reason of expiration of term of service on February 14, 1865. While the regiment was marching through Georgia, Major George Granger had died in hospital at Nashville, Tenn., and Captain Alonzo Abernethy of Company F had been promoted to Major, January 1, 1865, and was now in command of the regiment, which he led successfully during the remainder of its service. After giving a detailed description of the events which transpired during the long and toilsome march, the Major thus describes the closing scenes in the history of his regiment:

Our severe labors, hardships, and exposures were forgotten in the pleasure of having taken part in this most magnificent of all our campaigns. The remaining history is briefly told. On the 10th of April started with the army to Raleigh, N. C., where we found the rebel leader suing for terms. When these had been given, the regiment started for Washington, D.C., via Petersburg, Richmond, and Alexandria, Va. Reached the latter place on the 19th of May, after a march of 293 miles in the last nineteen days, and 360 miles from Goldsboro, N. C. Took part in the military pageant of May 24th, which consisted of the review of Sherman's army in the streets of Washington. The regiment came thence by rail and steamboat to Louisville, Ky., on the 1st of June. Went into camp and awaited further orders, which came July 10th to the effect that the remaining regiments of the army of the Tennessee would be at once mustered out of service.

Lieutenant Colonel Coyl had resigned June 17th on account of his having received the appointment of Judge Advocate of the Department of Kentucky. Major Abernethy was promoted to Lieutenant Colonel, and Captain Inman of Company I to Major. On the 18th of July, the muster out was completed.

The regiment was then sent to Clinton, Iowa, where it was disbanded, and the officers and men returned to their homes.

From the time it started from Dubuque, three years and 10 months from the date of its final muster out, the Ninth Iowa Infantry had marched over 4,000 miles, and traveled by rail and steamboat 6,000 miles. During the year 1865, there had been added by transfer from the Twenty-fifth Iowa 53, by enlistment 15, and from the draft rendezvous of the State 129, a total gain of 197. The total losses had be 45, leaving an aggregate of 594 at muster out.

In closing this brief sketch, the compiler again refers to the subjoined roster for the record of personal service to each officer and man of the regiment, in so far as has been possible to obtain such record. As an organization the Ninth Iowa Infantry has a record of service unsurpassed by that of any regiment which the State sent to the field during the great War of the Rebellion.

Total enrolment was 1,440. Regiment lost during service 12 Officers and 142 Enlisted men killed and mortally wounded and 2 Officers and 230 Enlisted men by disease. Total 386

Field Staff and Band

William Vandever. Residence Dubuque. Appointed Colonel Aug. 30, 1861. Mustered Sept. 24, 1861. Promoted Brigadier General, March 16, 1863. Resigned March 16, 1863. Brevet Major General June 7, 1865

Frank G. Herron. Residence Dubuque. Appointed Lieutenant Colonel Sept. 10, 1861. Mustered Sept. 24, 1861. Wounded March 7, 1862, Peas Ridge, Ark. Promoted Brigadier General July 30, 1862; Major General Nov. 29, 1863.

William H. Coyl. Residence Decorah. Appointed Major Aug 30, 1861. Mustered Sept 24, 1861. Wounded in shoulder severly March 7, 1862, Pea Ridge, Ark. Promoted Lieutenant Colonel July 1, 1862; Brevet Lieutenant Colonel March 13, 1865; Major and Judge Advocate May 18, 1865

William Scott. Residence Independence, nativity England. Appointed Adjutant Sept 2, 1861, from Second Lieutenant of company C. Mustered Sept. 24, 1861. Wounded in leg March 7, 1862, Pea Ridge Ark. Resigned for ill health Oct. 11, 1862. See Company C.

Ferdinand S. Winslow. Residence Marion. Appointed Quartermaster Sept. 4, 1861. Mustered Sept. 24, 1861. Promoted Assistant United States Quartermaster, with rank as Captain, Jan. 30, 1862.

Jerome Bradley. Residence Dubuque, nativity Massachusetts. Appointed Quartermaster March 16, 1862 from Second Lieutenant of Battery. Commission declined March 16, 1862. Appears to have been appointed Captain A.Q.M. Volunteers Feb 19, 1863. See Official Army Registers, 1861-1867

Benjamin McClure. Appointed Surgeon Sept. 19, 1861. Mustered Oct. 11, 1861. Promoted Assistant Surgeon of Volunteers Feb 4, 1864; Suregon of Volunteers Septs 30, 1864.

Col. Alonzo Abernethy.

Alonzo Abernethy was born April 14, 1836, in Sandusky county, Ohio, but lived chiefly at Bellevue in that State, until March, 1854, when he removed with his father's family to Illyria in Fayette county, Iowa. He received his education in the public schools of Bellevue, Ohio, Burlington Academy, Burlington, Iowa, and the University of Chicago, leaving the senior class in that Institution in August, 1861, to enter the service, and returning at the close of the war to graduate in 1866. Enlisting in the Ninth Iowa Infantry, company F, at the organization, he served three years and eleven months with his regiment, going out as private and returning as Lieut.-Col. in command. He was in every battle fought by his regiment, nearly forty in number, including Pea Rulge and Arkansas Post, Ark., Vicksburg, Jackson and Brandon, Miss., Cherokee Station, Barton. Crane Creek and Tuscumbia, Ala, Ringgold, Resaca, Dallas, Big Shanty, Kenesaw Mt., Atlanta. Jonesboro and Savannah, Ga , Columbia, S. C. and Bentonville, N. C. He was twice wounded, once severely at Pea Ridge, March 7, 1862, receiving a gun-shot wound in right ankle, which confined him in the hospital for four months. The Ninth Iowa is said to have lost more men killed and mortally wounded than any other Iowa Regiment, including seventy-four at the battle of Pea Ridge.

Having spent his early life on a farm Col. A. chose to follow the life of a farmer, and on his return from the service at once went to work to improve a small farm bought with the savings of his pay as a soldier, beginning at $11 a month. He has always kept up his interest in farm life with the hope of making it his chief and permanent interest; has always owned an Iowa farm, and still has a 250 acre farm under fine cultivation near Osage, though much of the time since leaving the service he has been called to give his time chiefly to other duties. On returning from the war in 1865, Col. A. was elected to represent his county in the lower house of the Eleventh General Assembly, which convened in Des Moines. January 8, and adjourned April 3, 1866. In 1870, having removed to Denison in, Crawford county, he was elected Principal of the Des Moines Baptist College in which position he served for one year, and has been a member of its board of trustees continuously since. In the Republican State Convention of 1871, Mr. Abernethy was nominated for

Superintendent of Public Instruction of the State, and was elected by a majority of 42,256 over his competitor. He was elected for a second term in 1873, and for a third term in 1875, at a time when there was a strong sentiment in the State and in the Republican party against electing state officers to a third term. During his time of service, the law providing for Teachers' Normal Institutes was enacted, which law has done more for Iowa schools and teachers than any other enactment in the history of the State. The State Normal School was also established during this term.

In September, 1878, in response to a second invitation from the board of trustees of the University of Chicago, he resigned his position of Superintendent of Public Instruction to accept the temporary presidency of that institution. After two gears' service in this position, during which he made a summer's vacation trip to Europe, he returned to his Denison. Iowa, farm. But in July, 1881, Prof. Abernethy was again called to public service as principal of Cedar Valley Seminary, an institution of learning established by the Baptists of northeastern Iowa, at Osage, in 1862. He still fills this position, the Seminary enrolling annually from two hundred to two hundred and fifty students, its property and endowments having increased in the thirteen years from ten to seventy thousand dollars. In January, 1868, Co). Abernethy was married to Miss Louise E. Eaton, daughter of Dr. Sewell R. Eaton, who has ever since made for him a typical Christian home. They have had five children, two of whom only are living, Herbert and Clara, the two youngest. Mr. Abernethy is a man of active temperament, though of studious habits; is over six feet tall, and has never been seriously ill in his life.

~----------

Source: A Brief History Of The Organization, And Proceedings Of The Reunions Of 1886 And 1890. By Pioneer Lawmakers Association of Iowa Reunion.

Non-Commissioned Staff

Floyd W. Foster. Age 22. Residence Sabula, nativity Pennsylvania. Enlisted Aug. 8, 1861. Appointed Sergeant Major Sept. 24, 1861. Mustered Sept. 24, 1861. Promoted First Lieutenant of company G Aug. 5, 1863. See company G.

Samuel M. Pearson. Age 34. Residence Cedar Falls, nativity Illinois. Appointed Quartermaster Sergeant Sept. 20, 1861. Mustered Sept. 20, 1861. Reduced to ranks Oct. 21, 1862. No further record.

Franklin A. Morton. Age 27. Residence Janesville, nativity Ohio. Enlisted July 28, 1861. Appointed Commissary Sergeant Sept. 20, 1861, from company G. Mustered Sept. 20, 1861. Promoted Quartermaster March 16, 1862. Mustered out Jan. 10, 1865, Savannah, Ga.

Robert W. Wright. Age 33. Residence Independence, nativity England. Enlisted July 20, 1861. Appointed Hospital Steward Sept. 26, 1861, from First Sergeant of company C. Mustered Sept. 24, 1861. Promoted Second Lieutenant of company C Jan. 29, 1862. See company C.

John Engreman. Age 31. Residence Dubuque, nativity New York. Enlisted Sept. 12, 1861. Appointed Drum Major Sept. 12, 1861, from company C. Mustered Sept. 24, 1861. Mustered out; no date given.

Thomas J. Barber. Age 30. Residence Dubuque, nativity England. Enlisted Sept. 12, 1861. Appointed Principal Musician Sept. 1, 1863, from company C. Mustered Sept. 24, 1861. Reduced to ranks June 14, 1864. See company C.

Regimental Band

Ferdinand Hepp. Age 24. Residence Dubuque, nativity Bavaria. Enlisted as First Class Musician and Leader. Mustered Sept. 25, 1861. Mustered out March 27, 1862.
Frederick Fischer. Age 41. Residence Dubuque, nativity Germany. Enlisted as First Class Musician. Mustered Sept. 25, 1861. Mustered out March 27, 1862.
Frederick Pittroff. Age 30. Residence Dubuque, nativity Bavaria. Enlisted as First Class Musician. Mustered Sept. 25, 1861. Mustered out March 27, 1862.
Fritz Stahl. Age 25. Residence Dubuque, nativity Germany. Enlisted as first Class Musician. Mustered Sept. 25, 1861. Mustered out March 27, 1862.
Herman Fischer. Age 21. Residence Dubuque, nativity Germany. Enlisted as First Class Musician. Mustered Sept. 25, 1861. Mustered out March 27, 1862.
Frederick W. Bock. Age 40. Residence Dubuque, nativity Prussia. Enlisted as First Class Musician. Mustered Sept. 25, 1861. Mustered out March 27, l862.
Herwich Winderlick. Age 25. Residence Dubuque, nativity Saxony. Enlisted as First Class Musician. Mustered Sept. 25, 1861. Discharged for disability Jan. 10, 1862.
Berthold Gantert. Age 25. Residence Dubuque, nativity Baden. Enlisted as Second Class Musician. Mustered Sept. 25, 1861. Mustered out March 27, 1862.
Jacob Yarnock. Age 25. Residence Dubuque, nativity Switzerland. Enlisted as Second Class Musician. Mustered Sept. 25, 1861. Mustered out March 27, 1862.
John Winderlick. Age 31. Residence Dubuque, nativity Saxony. Enlisted as Second Class Musician. Mustered Sept. 25, 1861. Mustered out March 27, 1862.

Carl Volderlick. Age 31. Residence Dubuque, nativity Austria. Enlisted as Second Class Musician. Mustered Sept. 25, 1861. Mustered out March 27, 1862.
Joachin Kurz. Age 32. Residence Dubuque, nativity Germany. Enlisted Second Class Musician.
Mustered Sept. 25, 1861. Mustered out March 27, 1862.
Bartholomew Seidl. Age 38. Residence Dubuque, nativity Austria. Enlisted as Second Class
Musician. Mustered Sept. 25, 1861. Mustered out March 27, 1862.
Theodore Fischer. Age 14. Residence Dubuque, nativity Germany. Enlisted as Second Class
Musician. Mustered Sept. 25, 1861. Mustered out March 27, 1962

Line Officers

Names of company officers at muster in of their companies. Service record given opposite their
names in the alphabetical roster following.
COMPANY "A"
Andrew W. Drip, Captain. **Florilla M. Kelsey,** 1st Lieutenant. **Alpheus Alexander,** 2nd Lieutenant.
COMPANY "B"
Don A. Carpenter, Captain. **Paul McSweeney,** 1st Lieutenant. **Jacob Jones,** 2nd Lieutenant.
COMPANY "C"
Jared M. Hord, Captain. **Hiram C. Bull,** 1st Lieutenant. **William Scott,** 2nd Lieutenant.
COMPANY "D"
David Harper, Captain. **David F. Magee,** 1st Lieutenant. **Carso Crane,** 2nd Lieutenant.
COMPANY "E"
Alva Bebins, Captain. **DeWitt C. Baker,** 1st Lieutenant. **Andrew F. Hofer,** 2nd Lieutenant.
COMPANY "F"
James W. Towner, Captain. **Abner G. M. Neff,** 1st Lieutenant. **Edgar Tisdale,** 2nd Lieutenant.
COMPANY "G"
Frederick S. Washburn, Captain. **Hinkley F. Beebe,** 1st Lieutenant. **Asbury Leverich,** 2nd Lieutenant.
COMPANY "H"
Martin A. Moore, Captain. **Charles Mackenzie,** 1st Lieutenant. **Edgar D. Monroe,** 2nd Lieutenant.
COMPANY "I"
Julius H. Powers, Captain. **Samuel Fellows,** 1st Lieutenant. **Joseph G. Inman,** 2nd Lieutenant.

COMPANY "K"
David Carskaddon, Captain. **Norman W. Claflin,** 1st Lieutenant. **Abraham Bowman,** 2nd Lieutenant.

COMPANY "A"

Acker, John. (Veteran.) Age 24. Residence Dubuque, nativity Canada. Enlisted Sept. 24, 1861. Mustered Sept. 24, 1861. Re-enlisted and re-mustered Jan. 24, 1864. Mustered out July 18, 1865, Louisville, Ky.

Adams, John. (Veteran.) Age 24. Residence Maquoketa, nativity New York. Enlisted Aug. 15, 1861. Mustered Sept. 24, 1861. Disabled by fall May 19, 1863, Vicksburg, Miss. Promoted Seventh Corporal Dec. 17, 1863. Re-enlisted and re-mustered Jan. 23, 1864. Promoted Sixth Corporal; First Corporal Sept. 23, 1864. Mustered out July 18, 1865, Louisville, Ky.

Alexander, Alpheus. Age 40. Residence Spragueville, nativity Ohio. Appointed Second
Lieutenant Sept. 7, 1861. Mustered Sept. 7, 1861. Resigned Feb. 11, 1862.

Alexander, Austin. (Veteran.) Age 21. Residence Spragueville, nativity Ohio. Enlisted Sept.
15, 1862. Mustered Sept. 15, 1862. Promoted Musician Oct. 10, 1863. Re-enlisted and remustered
Jan. 24, 1864. Mustered out July 18, 1865, Louisville, Ky.

Alexander, John W. Age 29. Residence Spragueville, nativity Ohio. Enlisted as Eighth
Corporal. Mustered Sept. 7, 1861. Killed March 7, 1862, Pea Ridge, Ark. Buried in National
Cemetery, Fayetteville, Ark. Section 2, grave 13.

COMPANY "B"

Ailer, George F. Age 22. Residence Fairview, nativity Virginia. Enlisted Aug. 12, 1861.
Mustered Sept. 24, 1861. Wounded slightly in hip May 22,1863. Mustered out Sept. 24, 1864,
East Point, Ga., expiration of term of service.

Arnold, Riley. Age 18. Residence Madison, nativity New York. Enlisted Sept. 26, 1861.
Discharged for disability Jan. 18, 1862, hospital, Pacific, Mo.

COMPANY "C"

Abbott, George M. Age 21. Residence Barclay, nativity

Connecticut. Enlisted Aug. 13, 1861. Mustered Sept. 24, 1861. Wounded slightly in thigh March 7, 1862, Pea Ridge, Ark. Died of wounds April 21, 1862, Cassville, Mo. Buried in National Cemetery, Springfield, Mo. Section 10, grave 58.

Adams, Horace N. Age 18. Residence Black Hawk County, nativity Illinois. Enlisted March 10, 1864. Mustered March 10, 1864. Mustered out July 18, 1864, Louisville, Ky.

Adams, William. Age 27. Residence Polo, nativity Ohio. Enlisted Aug. 20, 1861. Mustered Sept. 24, 1861. Wounded slightly March 7, 1862, Pea Ridge, Ark. Wounded slightly June 18, 1863, Vicksburg, Miss. Discharged for disability June 14, 1864, Mound City, Ill.

Allen, Edwin J. Age 21. Residence Brandon, nativity New York. Enlisted Aug. 6, 1861. Mustered Sept. 24, 1861. Taken prisoner Oct. 25, 1863, Tuscumbia, Ala. Died in prison of diarrhea March 20, 1864, Danville, Va. Buried in cemetery near Danville, Va.

Allen, Marsena. Age 22. Residence Independence, nativity New York. Enlisted Aug. 23, 1861.
Mustered Sept. 24, 1861. Died May 6, 1862, Cassville, Mo. Buried in National Cemetery,
Springfield, Mo. Section 10, grave 64.

Allison, William. Age 23. Residence Buffalo, nativity Pennsylvania. Enlisted Aug. 10, 1861.
Mustered Sept. 24, 1861. Wounded slightly March 7, 1862, Pea Ridge, Ark. Died of fever June
8, 1862, Forsyth, Mo.

Allspraugh, Perry. Age 20. Residence Center Point, nativity Ohio. Enlisted Aug. 6, 1861.
Mustered Sept. 24, 1861. Mustered out Sept. 24, 1864, East Point, Ga.

Armstrong, Isaac. Age 35. Residence Independence, nativity New York. Enlisted Aug. 29,
1862. Mustered Aug. 29, 1862. Died of chronic diarrhea March 24, 1863, St. Louis, Mo. Buried
in Jefferson Barracks National Cemetery, St. Louis, Mo. Section 5, grave 16.

Iowa 9th Infantry Regiment 49

Arwine, Isaac. Age 26. Residence Independence, nativity Tennessee. Enlisted Aug. 23, 1861.
Mustered Sept. 24, 1861. Wounded severely in shoulder March 7, 1862, Pea Ridge, Ark. Died of
wounds March 15, 1862, Pea Ridge, Ark. Buried in cemetery, Pea Ridge, Ark.
COMPANY "D"
Albright, Benjamin. Age 28. Residence Davenport, nativity Pennsylvania. Enlisted March 31,
1864. Mustered Nov. 31, 1864. Mustered out July 18, 1865, Louisville, Ky.
COMPANY "E"
Allen, Charles A. Age 18. Residence Clayton County, nativity New York. Enlisted Sept. 25,
1861. Wounded in left thigh severely March 7, 1862, Pea Ridge, Ark. Died of chronic diarrhea
Aug. 14, 1863, Vicksburg, Miss.
COMPANY "F"
Abernethy, Alonzo. Age 25. Residence Leo, nativity Ohio. Enlisted Sept. 5, 1861, as First
Sergeant. Mustered Sept. 12, 1861. Wounded slightly March 7, 1862, Pea Ridge, Ark. Promoted
Second Lieutenant March 11, 1862; First Lieutenant Feb. 6, 1863; Captain July 24, 1863; Major
Jan. 1, 1865; Lieutenant Colonel June 19, 1865. Mustered out July 18, 1865, Louisville, Ky.
14
Andress, William. Age 21. Residence Taylorville, nativity Ohio. Enlisted Sept. 9, 1861.
Mustered Sept. 14, 1861. Killed in battle March 7, 1862, Pea Ridge, Ark.
Andrus, Daniel P. Age 27. Residence Lima, nativity New York. Enlisted Feb. 29, 1864.
Mustered March 18, 1864. Wounded in right hand severely May 27, 1864, Dallas, Ga.
Discharged March 10, 1865,

Davenport, Iowa.
Andrus, Horace J. (Veteran.) Age 22. Residence Lima, nativity New York. Enlisted Aug. 27,
1861. Mustered Sept. 12, 1861. Promoted Sixth Corporal March 12, 1863; Fourth Corporal Oct.
6, 1863. Re-enlisted and re-mustered Jan. 23, 1864. Taken prisoner May 27, 1864, Dallas, Ga.
Promoted Second Corporal April 1, 1865; First Corporal May 12, 1865. Mustered out June 17,
1865, Davenport, Iowa.
Avery, John T. (Veteran.) Age 25. Residence Taylorville, nativity Michigan. Enlisted Sept. 4,
1861. Mustered Sept. 14, 1861. Wounded slightly in right hand March 7, 1862, Pea Ridge, Ark.
Wounded slightly in right hand June 5, 1863, Vicksburg, Miss. Re-enlisted and re-mustered Jan.
25, 1864. Wounded slightly in right hand Aug. 18, 1864, Atlanta, Ga. Mustered out March 23,
1865, Davenport, Iowa.
COMPANY "G"
Alexander, Martin. Age 18. Residence Clayton County, nativity Ohio. Enlisted Feb. 28, 1864.
Mustered March 17, 1864. Mustered out July 18, 1865, Louisville, Ky.
Allman, James B. Age 20. Residence Waterloo, nativity Ohio. Enlisted July 28, 1861. Mustered
Sept. 24, 1861. Wounded severely in arm; right arm amputated, March 7, 1862, Pea Ridge, Ark.
Died of wounds at Waterloo, Iowa.
COMPANY "H"
Able, Joseph. Age 33. Residence Keokuk County, nativity Tennessee. Enlisted Nov. 2, 1864.
Mustered Nov. 2, 1864. Mustered out July 18, 1865, Louisville, Ky.
Ackerman, John A. Age 22. Residence Decorah, nativity Indiana. Enlisted Aug. 21, 1861.

Mustered Sept. 24, 1861. Wounded slightly in right hand May 20, 1863, Vicksburg, Miss. Died
of wounds July 6, 1863, Vicksburg, Miss. Buried in National Cemetery, Vicksburg, Miss.
Section G, grave 1249.
Adam, George Gordon. Age 33. Residence Decorah, nativity Calcutta. Enlisted Aug. 21,1861.
Mustered Sept. 24, 1861. Wounded slightly in thigh March 7, 1862, Pea Ridge, Ark. Mustered
out Sept. 24, 1864, expiration of term of service.
Aiken, Eslie. Age 18. Residence Decorah, nativity Wisconsin. Enlisted Aug. 16, 1864.
Mustered Aug. 16, 1864. Mustered out May 4, 1865, Washington, D. C.
Andrew, Hanson. Age 26. Residence Decorah, nativity Norway. Enlisted Dec. 20, 1861.
Promoted Seventh Corporal; Sixth Corporal April 2, 1863. Wounded in left hand severely May 2, 1863, Vicksburg, Miss. Promoted Fifth Corporal Jan. 23, 1864. Died July 11, 1864. Buried in National Cemetery, Vicksburg, Miss. Section B. grave 85.
Anway, Charles. Age 20. Residence Decorah, nativity Illinois. Enlisted Oct. 25, 1861. Promoted Corporal April 2, 1863. Wounded in left side May 23, 1863, Vicksburg, Miss. Died of wounds May 24, 1863.
Atchinson, John. Age 33. Residence Decorah, nativity Scotland. Enlisted Nov. 21, 1861.
Discharged for disability March 28, 1862, Keetsville, Mo.
COMPANY "I"
Allen, Nathan B. Age 41. Residence Springfield, nativity Ohio. Enlisted Aug. 23, 1861.
Mustered Sept. 18, 1861. Mustered out Sept. 24, 1864, East Point, Ga., expiration of term of
service.
Ashley, Charles B. (Veteran.) Age 20. Residence New Oregon, nativity New York. Enlisted
Dec. 22, 1861. Promoted Fourth Corporal July 24, 1862; Fifth

Sergeant May 24, 1863; Fourth
Sergeant July 6, 1863; Third Sergeant Oct. 6, 1863. Re-enlisted and re-mustered Jan. 25, 1864.
Promoted Second Sergeant Jan. 1, 1866; First Lieutenant June 19, 1865. Mustered out July 18,
1865, Louisville, Ky.
Averill, Lariston. Age 18. Residence New Oregon, nativity New York. Enlisted Aug. 18, 1861.
Mustered Sept. 18, 1861. Died of chronic diarrhea Aug. 26, 1863, New Oregon, Iowa.
Axtell, Francis M. Age 19. Residence Janesville, nativity Illinois. Enlisted Feb. 28, 1864.
Mustered March 17, 1864. Promoted Fifer May 1, 1865. Mustered out July 18, 1865, Louisville, Ky.
Ayres, Harvey L. Age 25. Residence New Oregon, nativity New York. Enlisted Sept. 12, 1861. Mustered Sept. 18, 1861.
Transferred to Invalid Corps April 10, 1864. No further record.
COMPANY "K"
Abbe, Augustus W. Age 20. Residence Marion, nativity Iowa. Enlisted Sept. 14, 1861. Mustered Sept. 24, 1861. Wounded severely in leg, side and arm March 7, 1862, Pea Ridge, Ark. Wounded in arm; arm amputated May 22, 1863, Vicksburg, Miss. Discharged July 16, 1863, St. Louis, Mo.
Abbe, William. Age 18. Residence Marion, nativity Iowa. Enlisted Sept. 14, 1861, as Sixth
Corporal. Mustered Sept. 24, 1861. Promoted First Corporal March 3, 1864. Discharged Sept.
23, 1864, East Point, Ga., expiration of term of service.
Alexander, Samuel M. Age 24. Residence Linn County, nativity Indiana. Mustered Sept. 24,
1861. Died of chronic diarrhea Jan. 12, 1864, St. Louis, Mo. Buried in Jefferson Barracks
National Cemetery, St. Louis, Mo. Section 6, grave 191.
Anderson, James C. Age 25. Residence Marion, nativity Indiana. Mustered Sept. 24, 1861.
Discharged Sept. 23, 1864, East Point, Ga.

Austin, William A. Age 25. Residence Marion, nativity Ohio. Enlisted Sept. 14, 1861, as Fourth
Corporal. Mustered Sept. 24, 1861. Wounded severely in elbow March 7, 1862, Pea Ridge, Ark.
Discharged Oct. 12, 1862, St. Louis, Mo.
Axtel, William C. Age 20. Residence Marion, nativity Pennsylvania. Enlisted Sept. 14, 1861.
Mustered Sept. 24, 1861. Killed in battle March 7, 1862, Pea Ridge, Ark.

COMPANY "A"

Bancroft, Ormus D. Age 20. Residence Maquoketa, nativity New York. Enlisted Aug. 8, 1861,
as Sixth Corporal. Mustered Sept. 7, 1861. Killed in battle March 7, 1862, Pea Ridge, Ark. Buried in National Cemetery, Fayetteville, Ark. Section 2, grave 15.
Barns, Addison W. Age 18. Residence Maquoketa, nativity New York. Enlisted Aug. 10, 1861.
Mustered Sept. 24, 1861. Died of typhoid fever Dec. 4, 1861, Calod, Mo.
Beckwith, Emanuel. Age 18. Residence Johnson County, nativity Ohio. Enlisted Feb. 17, 1864.
Mustered March 17, 1864. Promoted Fourth Corporal May 27, 1865. Mustered out July 18,
1866, Louisville, Ky.
Beckwith, Oliver. (Veteran.) Age 21. Residence Maquoketa, nativity Ohio. Enlisted July 29,
1861. Mustered Sept. 24, 1861. Promoted Eighth Corporal Dec. 17, 1863. Re-enlisted and remustered
Jan. 23, 1864. Promoted Second Corporal Sept. 23, 1864; Fifth Sergeant Nov. 1, 1864;
Fourth Sergeant May 1, 1865. Mustered out July 18, 1865, Louisville, Ky.
Beckwith, Samuel. Age 27. Residence Canton, nativity Ohio. Enlisted Aug. 15, 1861. Mustered
Sept. 24, 1861. Died of chronic diarrhea Sept. 4, 1863, Fuller's Mills, Iowa.

Bennett, Lucius. (Veteran) Age 21. Residence Spragueville, nativity Illinois. Enlisted Aug. 8,
1861. Mustered Sept. 24, 1861. Re-enlisted and re-mustered Jan. 23, 1864. Promoted Forth Corporal Nov. 1, 1864; Second Corporal May 27, 1865. Mustered out July 18, 1865, Louisville, Ky.

Billups, John S. (Veteran.) Age 24. Residence Maquoketa, nativity Iowa. Enlisted Aug. 2,
1861. Mustered Sept. 24, 1861. Promoted Fifth Corporal March 10, 1862; Third Corporal June 7,
1863; Second Corporal; First Corporal Dec. 17, 1863. Re-enlisted and re-mustered Jan. 23, 1864.
Promoted Fifth Sergeant Sept. 23, 1864; Fourth Sergeant Oct. 1, 1864; Third Sergeant May 1,
1865. Mustered out July 18, 1865, Louisville, Ky.

Bishop, John R. Age 18. Residence Des Moines, nativity Iowa. Enlisted March 7, 1864.
Mustered March 7, 1864. Mustered out July 18, 1865, Louisville, Ky. See company K, Twentyfifth Infantry.

Brock, William. Age 21. Residence Maquoketa, nativity Canada. Enlisted Aug. 12, 1861.
Mustered Sept. 24, 1861. Died of chronic diarrhea May 16, 1863, Duckport, La.

Brown, Andrew H. Age 32. Residence Brookfield, nativity New York. Enlisted July 29, 1861.
Mustered Sept. 24, 1861. Promoted Wagoner. Discharged Sept. 24, 1864, East Point, Ga.

Brown, Henry. Age 22. Residence Maquoketa, nativity Ohio. Enlisted Aug. 10, 1861. Mustered
Sept. 24, 1861. Discharged for disability Oct. 14, 1862, St. Louis, Mo.

Brown, Josiah. Age 20. Residence Maquoketa, nativity Ohio. Enlisted Aug. 10, 1861. Mustered
Sept. 24, 1861. Died Feb. 12, 1862, Mansfield, Mo.

Brown, Sylvester D. (Veteran.) Age 23. Residence Maquoketa,

nativity Pennsylvania. Enlisted
Aug. 15, 1861. Mustered Sept. 24, 1861. Re-enlisted and re-mustered Jan. 23, 1864. Promoted
Third Corporal May 27, 1865. Mustered out July 18, 1865, Louisville, Ky.
Bump, George M. (Veteran.) Age 25. Residence Maquoketa, nativity New York. Enlisted. Aug.
12, 1861. Mustered Sept. 24, 1861. Re-enlisted and re-mustered Jan. 23, 1864. Wounded in side
May 27, 1864, Dallas, Ga. Died of wounds June 28, 1864, Atlanta, Ga. Buried in National
Cemetery, Marietta, Ga. Section H, grave 238.
COMPANY "B"
Baldwin, Marcellus O. Age 21. Residence Wyoming, nativity Ohio. Enlisted Sept. 18, 1861.
Mustered Sept. 24, 1861. Wounded in thumb June 30, 1862, Vicksburg, Miss. Mustered out
Sept. 24, 1864, East Point, Ga., expiration of term of service.
Barker, Usual. Age 38. Residence Hale, nativity New York. Enlisted Aug. 12, 1861. Mustered
Sept. 24, 1861. Mustered out Sept. 24, 1864, East Point, Ga., expiration of term of service.
Bates, Charles. Age 21. Residence Wayne, nativity New York. Enlisted Aug. 17, 1861.
Mustered Sept. 24, 1861. Wounded slightly in foot and ankle March 7, 1862, Pea Ridge, Ark.
Discharged for wounds Dec. 19, 1862, St. Louis, Mo.
Beaman, Daniel. Age 19. Residence Walnut Fork, nativity Canada. Enlisted Nov. 25, 1861.
Wounded slightly in thigh May 22, 1863, Vicksburg, Miss. Died March 17, 1864, Nashville,
Tenn. Buried in National Cemetery, Nashville, Tenn. Section E, grave 1064.
Blakely, Nelson D. (Veteran.) Age 18. Residence Madison, nativity Pennsylvania. Enlisted Aug.
15, 1861. Mustered Sept. 24, 1861. Reenlisted and re-mustered

Jan. 23, 1864. Wounded slightly
in hand Aug. 31, 1864, Jonesboro, Ga. Mustered out July 18, 1865, Louisville, Ky.
Blizzard, Thomas W. Age 23. Residence Fairview, nativity Ohio. Enlisted Aug. 12, 1861, as
Fourth Corporal. Mustered Sept. 24, 1861. Promoted Third Sergeant Aug. 1, 1862; Second
Sergeant Nov. 1, 1862. Killed in battle May 22, 1863, Vicksburg, Miss.
18
Bowers, George H. Age 28. Residence Hall, nativity England. Enlisted Aug. 12, 1861. Mustered
Sept. 24, 1861. Promoted Eighth Corporal Dec. 11, 1862; Seventh Corporal; Sixth Corporal
March 20, 1863. Killed in battle May 19, 1863, Vicksburg, Miss.
Brickley, James T. Age 30. Residence Jackson, nativity
Maryland. Enlisted Aug. 12, 1861.
Mustered Sept. 24, 1861. Discharged for disability Oct. 9, 1862, Memphis, Tenn.
Brown, James J. Age 18. Residence Fairview, nativity Iowa. Enlisted Aug. 12, 1861. Mustered
Sept. 24, 1861. Discharged for disability Dec. 11, 1862, Helena, Ark.
Brown, James M. Age 18. Residence Louisa County, nativity Iowa. Enlisted March 18, 1864.
Mustered April 16, 1864. Mustered out July 18, 1865, Louisville, Ky. See company I, Twentyfifth
Infantry.
Bryan, William J. Age 18. Residence Walnut Forks, nativity New York. Enlisted Feb. 29, 1864.
Mustered Feb. 29, 1864. Mustered out July 18, 1865, Louisville, Ky.
Bugh, Alexander. (Veteran.) Age 18. Residence Madison, nativity Pennsylvania. Enlisted Aug.
12, 1861. Mustered Sept. 24, 1861. Re-enlisted and re-mustered Jan. 23, 1864. Mustered out July

18, 1865, Louisville, Ky.
Bumgardner, Morgan. Age 20. Residence Rome, nativity Ohio. Enlisted Aug. 12 1861.
Mustered Sept. 24, 1861. Wounded slightly in thigh March 7, 1862, Pea Ridge, Ark. Promoted
Eighth Corporal Nov. 1, 1862; Seventh Corporal Dec. 11, 1862; Sixth Corporal Dec. 8, 1862;
Fifth Corporal March 20, 1863. Wounded in battle; right arm shot off May 22, 1863, Vicksburg,
Miss. Promoted First Sergeant May 23, 1863. Discharged for wounds Dec. 30, 1863, St. Louis,
Mo.
Bunce, Theodore L. Age 19. Residence Rome, nativity Iowa. Enlisted Aug. 12, 1861. Mustered
Sept. 24, 1861. Promoted Drummer. Died of typhoid fever Feb. 1, 1863, Jefferson Barracks, St.
Louis, Mo. Buried in National Cemetery, Jefferson Barracks, Mo. Section 38, grave 270.
COMPANY "C"
Bain, Robert Y. Age 20. Residence Independence, nativity Indiana. Enlisted Sept. 5, 1861, as
Fifth Sergeant. Mustered Sept. 24, 1861. Died of smallpox March 31, 1863, Young's Point, La.
Barber, Thomas J. Age 30. Residence Dubuque, nativity England. Enlisted Sept., 12, 1861.
Mustered Sept. 24, 1861. Promoted Principal Musician Sept. l, 1863. Reduced to ranks June 14,
1864. Taken prisoner Nov. 22, 1864, Sherman's Campaign, Georgia. Discharged July 7, 1865,
Clinton, Iowa.
Barnett, Jesse. Age 25. Residence Chatham, nativity Ohio. Enlisted Aug. 10, 1861. Mustered
Sept. 24, 1861. Wounded slightly in arm March 7, 1862, Pea Ridge, Ark. Wounded slightly June
18, 1863, Vicksburg, Miss. Transferred to Invalid Corps Sept. 1, 1863. Died Oct. 22, 1863, St.

Louis, Mo. Buried in Jefferson Barracks National Cemetery, St. Louis, Mo. Section 7, grave 151.
19
Bellus, Adelbert C. (Veteran.) Age 22. Residence Center Point, nativity Ohio. Enlisted Aug. 12,
1861. Mustered Sept. 24, 1861. Promoted Third Corporal Sept. 3, 1862. Re-enlisted and remustered
Jan. 23, 1864. Promoted Fourth Sergeant April 9, 1865. Mustered out July 18, 1865,
Louisville, Ky.
Bennett, Charles N. (Veteran.) Age 21. Residence Bluff Grove, nativity New York. Enlisted
Aug. 12, 1861, as Third Corporal. Mustered Sept. 24, 1861. Promoted Second Corporal March 8,
1862; First Corporal; Fifth Sergeant April 14, 1863; Fourth Sergeant March 23, 1863. Reenlisted
and re-mustered Jan. 23, 1864. Promoted Second Sergeant April 9, 1865; First Sergeant
June 10, 1865. Mustered out July 18, 1865, Louisville, Ky.
Bower, John H. Age 29. Residence Brandon, nativity Ohio. Enlisted Aug. 10, 1861. Mustered
Sept. 24, 1861. Died of chronic diarrhea Aug. 25, 1863, Black River, Miss. Buried in National
Cemetery, Vicksburg, Miss. Section 1, grave 997.
Brammer, Jahill. (Veteran.) Age 18. Residence Linn County, nativity Iowa. Enlisted Feb. 25,
1864. Mustered March 3, 1864. Mustered out July 18, 1865, Louisville, Ky.
Brown, John C. Age 22. Residence Independence, nativity Illinois. Enlisted Aug. 23, 1861.
Mustered Sept. 24, 1861. Mustered out Sept. 25, 1864, East Point, Ga., expiration of term of
service.
Buckingham, Frederick S. Age 18. Residence Buchanan County, nativity Illinois. Enlisted Feb.
29, 1864. Mustered March 23, 1864. Mustered out July 18, 1865,

Louisville, Ky.
Bull, Hiram C. Age 40. Residence St. Louis, Mo., nativity New York Appointed First
Lieutenant Sept. 2, 1861. Mustered Sept. 2, 1861. Promoted Captain Jan. 29, 1862. Wounded
slightly in leg March 7 1862, Pea Ridge, Ark. Appointed Additional Paymaster June 30, 1862.
Mustered out July 17, 1862, Batesville, Ark.
COMPANY "D"
Beatty, Alexander. Age 18. Residence Monticello, nativity Pennsylvania. Enlisted Aug. 19,
1861. Mustered Sept. 2, 1861. Wounded severely in shoulder and arm March 7, 1862, Pea Ridge,
Ark. Discharged for wounds Aug. 23, 1862, St. Louis, Mo.
Blaisdell, Bogardus A. Age 39. Residence Delaware County, nativity New York. Enlisted Feb.
25, 1864. Mustered March 17, 1864. Mustered out July 18, 1865, Louisville, Ky.
Bledsoe, William J. Age 18. Residence Henry County, nativity Indiana. Enlisted Jan. 4, 1864.
Mustered Jan. 5, 1864. Mustered out July 18, 1865, Louisville, Ky. See company H, Twentyfifth
Infantry
Blue, Calvin C. (Veteran.) Age 29. Residence Cascade, nativity Indiana. Enlisted Aug. 24, 1861.
Mustered Sept. 2, 1861. Re-enlisted and re-mustered Jan. 23, 1864. Mustered out July 18, 1865,
Louisville, Ky.
20
Boyer, Isaiah C. Age 22. Residence Monticello, nativity Pennsylvania. Enlisted Aug. 29, 1861.
Mustered Sept. 2, 1861. Wounded severely in head March 7, 1862, Pea Ridge, Ark. Died of
wounds March 14, 1862, Pea Ridge, Ark.
Boyles, Luther. Age 26. Residence Fremont County, nativity Indiana. Enlisted Nov. 5, 1864.

Mustered Nov. 5, 1864. Mustered out July 18, 1865, Louisville, Ky.

Breen, Michael. (Veteran.) Age 19. Residence Monticello, nativity Ireland. Enlisted Aug. 16,
1861. Mustered Sept. 2, 1861. Wounded slightly in left arm March 7, 1862, Pea Ridge, Ark. Reenlisted
and re-mustered Jan. 23, 1864. Mustered out July 18, 1865, Louisville, Ky.

Brown, Milton. Age 20. Residence Davenport, nativity New York. Enlisted Nov. 19, 1864.
Mustered Nov. 19, 1864. Mustered out July 18, 1865, Louisville, Ky.

Bucher, Eli. (Veteran.) Age 18. Residence Wyoming, nativity Ohio. Enlisted Sept. 2, 186L
Mustered Sept. 2, 1861. Promoted Fourth Corporal Sept. 2, 1861. Wounded slightly in leg March
7, 1862, Pea Ridge, Ark. Re-enlisted and re-mustered Jan. 23, 1864. Promoted Second Corporal
Oct. 1, 1864; First Corporal June 20, 1865. Mustered out July 18, 1865, Louisville, Ky.

Burdick, Joseph A. Age 18. Residence Monticello, nativity Wisconsin. Enlisted Sept. 2, 1861.
Mustered Sept. 2, 1861. Wounded slightly in right arm March 7, 1862, Pea Ridge, Ark.
Promoted First Corporal March 17, 1862; Fourth Sergeant April 28, 1863. Wounded in neck
severely May 22, 1863, Vicksburg, Miss. Promoted Third Sergeant Aug. 4, 1863. Re-enlisted
and re-mustered Jan. 23, 1864. Promoted Sergeant Major May 1, 1864; Captain of company D
Jan. 1, 1865. Mustered out July 18, 1865, Louisville, Ky.

Button, William. Age 30. Residence Monticello, nativity New York. Enlisted Feb. 29, 1864.
Mustered March 17, 1864. Mustered out July 18, 1865, Louisville, Ky.

Byres, Jacob L. Age 26. Residence Monticello, nativity

Pennsylvania. Enlisted April 16, 1861.
Mustered Sept. 2, 1861. Wounded severely in thigh May 22, 1863, Vicksburg, Miss. Mustered
out Sept. 26, 1864, East Point, Ga.
COMPANY "E"
Bachtell, John A. Age 19. Residence Clayton, nativity
Pennsylvania. Enlisted Feb. 27, 1864.
Mustered March 10, 1864. Mustered out July 18, 1865, Louisville, Ky.
Baker, DeWitt C. Age 33. Residence Volga City, nativity New York. Enlisted Sept. 9, 1861.
Appointed First Lieutenant Sept. 24, 1861. Mustered Sept. 24, 1861. Promoted Captain March
8, 1862. Resigned April 2, 1863.
Bakerman, Lewis. Age 30. Residence Guttenburg, nativity Pennsylvania. Enlisted Sept. 9,
1861. Mustered Sept. 24, 1861. Wounded severely in leg March 7, 1862, Pea Ridge, Ark.
Discharged Feb. 5, 1863, Hospital, Pacific City, Mo.
21
Baldwin, George W. Age 18. Residence West Union, nativity Michigan. Enlisted Feb. 24, 1865.
Mustered March 1, 1865. Mustered out July 18, 1865, Louisville, Ky.
Ballou, Almon C. Age 24. Residence Farmersburg, nativity New York. Enlisted Sept. 14, 1861.
Mustered Sept. 24, 1861. Promoted Fourth Sergeant June 18, 1862; Third Sergeant Jan. 23,
1864. Mustered out July 18, 1865, Louisville,
Barnes, Hilon M. Age 20. Residence Volga City, nativity Ohio. Enlisted Sept. 9, 1861.
Mustered Sept. 24, 1861. Died of smallpox March 27, 1863, Younger Point, La.
Barnhouse, James M. (Veteran.) Age 18. Residence Elkader, nativity Ohio. Enlisted Sept. 26,
1861. Mustered Sept. 27, 1861. Promoted Sixth Corporal. Re-

enlisted and re-mustered Jan. 23,
1864. Promoted Second Corporal Jan. 23, 1864. Killed in action May 27, 1864, Dallas, Ga.

Barnhouse, John M. Age 20. Residence Highland, nativity Ohio. Enlisted Sept. 26, 1861.
Mustered Sept. 26, 1861. Killed in battle May 22 1863, Vicksburg, Miss.

Bartholomew, Andrew J. (Veteran.) Age 18. Residence Sperry, nativity Ohio. Enlisted Sept.
24, 1861. Mustered Sept. 24, 1861. Re-enlisted and re-mustered Jan. 23, 1864. Died of fever Feb.
29, 1864, Sperry, Iowa.

Bartholomew, William. Age 42. Residence Volga City, nativity New York. Enlisted Nov. 19,
1861. Mustered Nov. 19, 1861. Died June 4, 1862, Volga City, Iowa.

Bevins, Alva. Age 54. Residence Volga City, nativity Vermont. Appointed Captain Sept. 24,
1861. Mustered Sept. 24, 1861. Killed in battle March 7, 1862, Pea Ridge, Ark. Buried in
National Cemetery, Fayetteville, Ark. Section 1, grave 3.

Bishop, Thompson. Age 20. Residence Highland, nativity Ohio. Enlisted Sept. 24, 1861.
Mustered Sept. 24, 1861. Discharged for disability March 17, 1862, Rolla, Mo.

Bishop, William. Age 21. Residence Highland, nativity Pennsylvania. Enlisted Sept. 12, 1861,
as Seventh Corporal. Mustered Sept. 24, 1861. Promoted Fourth Sergeant; Third Sergeant June
18, 1862. Killed in battle Nov. 27, 1863, Ringgold, Ga.

Bouck, William. (Veteran.) Age 18. Residence Dubuque, nativity Germany. Enlisted Sept. 24,
1861. Mustered Sept. 24, 1861. Re-enlisted and re-mustered March 16, 1864. Mustered out July
18, 1865, Louisville, Ky.

Boyd, Alexander. Age 40. Residence Cox Creek, nativity

Virginia. Enlisted Sept. 9, 1861.
Mustered Sept. 24, 1861. Mustered out Sept. 24, 1864, East Point, Ga., expiration of term of
service.
Bradshaw, Joseph. Age 37. Residence Volga City, nativity Indiana. Mustered Sept. 24, 1861.
Discharged Aug. 30, 1862, Helena, Ark.
22
Brooks, Franklin. Age 21. Residence Yankee Settlement, nativity Ohio. Enlisted Nov. 15, 1864.
Mustered Nov. 15, 1864. Died of fever Feb. 21, 1865, while on march in South Carolina.
Brooks, John. (Veteran.) Age 20. Residence Winneshiek County, nativity Germany. Enlisted
Sept. 24, 1864. Mustered Sept. 24, 1864. Re-enlisted and re-mustered Jan. 23, 1864. Missing in
action May 27, 1864, Dallas, Ga. Mustered out July 18, 1865, Louisville, Ky.
Burdick, Lavern W. Age 19. Residence Elkader, nativity New York. Enlisted Sept. â€", 1861, as
Wagoner. Mustered Sept. 24, 1861. Discharged for disability May 17, 1862, Rolla, Mo. See
company I, Eighth Cavalry.
Burdine, Thomas B. Age 21. Residence Cox Creek, nativity Ohio. Enlisted Sept. 9 1861.
Mustered Sept. 24, 1861. Killed in battle May 22, 1863, Vicksburg, Miss.
COMPANY "F"
Barber, Alanson. Age 27. Residence Windsor, nativity New York. Enlisted as Eighth Corporal.
Mustered Sept. 12, 1861. Promoted Chaplain April 15, 1862. Resigned Feb. 27, 1863.
Barlow. Edwin. (Veteran.) Age 20. Residence Fayette, nativity Pennsylvania. Enlisted Aug. 27,
1861. Mustered Sept. 12, 1861. Re-enlisted and re-mustered Jan. 21, 1864. Promoted Seventh

Corporal April 1, 1865; Fifth Corporal May 12, 1865. Mustered out July 18, 1865, Louisville, Ky.

Barnhouse, Henry Milton. Age 18. Residence West Union, nativity Ohio. Enlisted Sept. 27, 1861. Mustered Sept. 27, 1861. Discharged for disability May 13, 1862. See company E, Ninth Infantry.

Barnhouse, John. (Veteran.) Age 19 Residence West Union, nativity Ohio. Enlisted Aug. 27, 1861. Mustered Sept. 12, 1861. Re-enlisted and re-mustered Jan. 23, 1864. Mustered out July 18, 1865, Louisville, Ky.

Barr, William. Age 19. Residence Otsego, nativity Scotland. Enlisted Feb. 29, 1864. Mustered March 18, 1864. Wounded in neck slightly May 27, 1864, Dallas, Ga. Mustered out July 18, 1865, Louisville, Ky.

Bartlett, John W. Age 18. Residence Elgin, nativity Illinois. Enlisted Feb. 23, 1864. Mustered March 18, 1864. Wounded in right hand slightly Sept. 2, 1864, Lovejoy Station, Ga. Mustered out July 18, 1865, Louisville, Ky.

Benedict, David L. Age 24. Residence Fredericksburg, nativity New York. Enlisted Aug. 27, 1861. Mustered Sept. 12, 1861 Died of chronic diarrhea Feb. 23, 1863, Young's Point, La.

Benedict, George M. Age 20. Residence Fredericksburg, nativity New York. Enlisted Feb. 27, 1864. Mustered March 18, 1864. Mustered out July 18, 1865, Louisville, Ky.

23

Benedict, Myron R. (Veteran.) Age 26. Residence Fredericksburg, nativity New York. Enlisted Sept. 19, 1861. Mustered Sept. 24, 1861. Wounded In arm slightly March 7, 1862, Pea Ridge,

Ark. Re-enlisted and re-mustered Jan. 1, 1864. Promoted Seventh Corporal April 1, 1864; Sixth
Corporal Aug. 1, 1864; Fifth Corporal April 1, 1865; Fifth Sergeant May 12, 1865; Fourth
Sergeant June 6, 1865. Mustered out July 18, 1865, Louisville, Ky.
Bradley, John. Age 22. Residence West Union, nativity Ohio. Enlisted Aug. 27, 1861. Mustered
Sept. 12, 1861. Wounded severely in head March 7, 1862, Pea Ridge, Ark. Died of wounds
March 22, 1862, Springfield, Mo.
Brewer, William W. Age 20. Residence West Union, nativity New York. Enlisted Sept. 8, 1861.
Mustered Sept. 12, 1861. Wounded slightly in leg March 7, 1862, Pea Ridge, Ark. Mustered out
Sept. 24, 1864, East Point, Ga., expiration of term of service.
Briggs, George S. Age 29. Residence Leo, nativity Ohio. Enlisted Feb. 29, 1864. Mustered
March 18, 1864. Promoted Eighth Corporal Jan. 1, 1865; Sixth Corporal April 1, 1865; Fourth
Corporal May 12, 1865. Discharged for disability June 26, 1865, Louisville, Ky.
Briggs, Orion. Age 19. Residence Illyria, nativity Wisconsin. Enlisted Feb. 29, 1864. Mustered
March 18, 1864. Mustered out July 18, 1865, Louisville, Ky.
Broadbent, George M. (Veteran.) Age 25. Residence Eden, nativity England. Enlisted Sept. 8,
1861. Mustered Sept. 12, 1861. Re-enlisted and re-mustered Jan. 24, 1864. Mustered out July 18,
1865, Louisville, Ky.
Broadbent, Robert A. Age 19. Residence Eden, nativity Illinois. Enlisted Feb. 26, 1864.
Mustered March 18, 1864. Mustered out July 18, 1865, Louisville, Ky.
Brown, John A. (Veteran.) Age 20. Residence Taylorville, nativity Ohio. Enlisted Sept. 5, 1861.
Mustered Sept. 14, 1861. Re-enlisted and re-mustered Jan. 23,

1864. Mustered out July 18, 1865,
Louisville, Ky.
Brown, Volney N. (Veteran.) Age 34. Residence Auburn, nativity Vermont. Enlisted Aug. 27,
1861. Mustered Sept. 12, 1861. Re-enlisted and re-mustered Jan. 23, 1864. Mustered out July 18,
1865, Louisville, Ky.
COMPANY "G"
Balkcom, Dexter E. Age 18. Residence Waterloo, nativity New York. Enlisted Aug. 20, 1861.
Mustered Sept. 24, 1861. Died of measles Dec. 20, 1861, Pacific, Mo.
Baninger, James M. Age 19. Residence Waterloo, nativity Ohio. Enlisted Sept. 16, 1861.
Mustered Sept. 24, 1861. Died of consumption March 13, 1864, Waterloo, Iowa.
Barrick, John. Age 20. Residence Janesville, nativity Ohio. Enlisted Aug. 10, 1861. Mustered
Sept. 24, 1861. Discharged for disability May 17, 1862, Batesville, Ark.
24
Baskins, Clark J. Age 19. Residence Waverly, nativity Ohio. Enlisted Aug. 22, 1861. Mustered
Sept. 24, 1861. Promoted Seventh Corporal. Wounded severely in head May 27, 1863,
Vicksburg, Miss. Mustered out Sept. 24, 1864, East Point, Ga., expiration of term of service.
Beebe, Hinkly F. Age 28. Residence Waverly, nativity New York. Appointed First Lieutenant
Sept. 16, 1861. Mustered Sept. 16, 1861. Resigned March 10, 1862.
Beebe, Organ A. Age 21. Residence Waverly, nativity New York. Enlisted July 28, 1861.
Mustered Sept. 24, 1861. Promoted Sixth Corporal Oct. 20, 1861; Fifth Sergeant May 11, 1862.
Discharged for disability July 23, 1862, Helena, Ark.
Benson Augustus H. Age 30. Residence Fayette, nativity New

York. Enlisted Feb. 20, 1861.
Mustered Sept. 24, 1861. Died April 21, 1862, Cassville, Mo. Buried in National Cemetery,
Springfield, Mo. Section 10, grave 65.
Bird, John. Age 28. Residence Waverly, nativity England. Enlisted Sept. 6, 1861. Mustered
Sept. 24, 1861. Died of dropsy Jan. 14, 1864, Nashville, Tenn. Buried in National Cemetery,
Nashville, Tenn. Section D, grave 178.
Bloodsworth, John H. Age 18. Residence Fayette County, nativity Iowa. Enlisted Feb. 28,
1864. Mustered March 17, 1864. Mustered out July 18, 1865, Louisville, Ky.
Bowman, John P. Age 22. Residence Waterloo, nativity Pennsylvania. Enlisted as Fourth
Sergeant. Mustered Sept. 24, 1861. Promoted First Lieutenant May 29, 1863; Captain June 17,
1863. Mustered out Oct. 26, 1864, expiration of term of service.
Braninger, Henry L. (Veteran.) Age 20. Residence Waterloo, nativity Ohio. Enlisted Aug. 26,
1861. Mustered Sept. 24, 1861. Promoted Second Corporal June 7, 1863. Re-enlisted and remustered
Jan. 23, 1864. Promoted Third Sergeant Oct. 1, 1864. Mustered out July 18, 1865,
Louisville, Ky.
Brewster, James P. (Veteran.) Age 18. Residence Black Hawk County, nativity Kentucky.
Enlisted Sept. 24, 1861. Mustered Sept. 24, 1861. Re-enlisted and re-mustered Jan. 23, 1864.
Mustered out July 18, 1865, Louisville, Ky. See company H.
Brown, James. Age 22. Residence Black Hawk County, nativity Illinois. Enlisted Feb. 23, 1864.
Mustered Feb. 23, 1864. Died Sept. 25, 1864, East Point, Ga.
Brown, Thomas W. Age 19. Residence Waverly, nativity New York. Enlisted Aug. 10, 1861.
Mustered Sept. 24, 1861. Wounded slightly In leg March 7, 1862,

Pea Ridge, Ark. Wounded in
both thighs severely May 22, 1863, Vicksburg, Miss. Died of wounds June 25, 1863, Memphis,
Tenn.

Buchman, Amos. Age 32. Residence Waverly, nativity Pennsylvania. Enlisted Aug. 10, 1861.
Mustered Sept. 24, 1861. Wounded severely in head March 7, 1862, Pea Ridge, Ark. Mustered
out Sept. 24, 1864, East Point, Ga., expiration of term of service. 25

Buckmaster, James F. Age 18. Residence Waverly, nativity Ohio. Enlisted Aug. 10, 1861.
Mustered Sept. 24, 1861. Discharged March 12, 1863, St. Louis, Mo.

Burns, John. Age 18. Residence Clayton County, nativity Ireland. Enlisted Feb. 28, 1864.
Mustered March 17, 1864. Died of consumption Aug. 21, 1864, Rome, Ga. Buried in National
Cemetery, Marietta, Ga. Section C, grave 375.

COMPANY "H"

Bailey, Simeon. (Veteran.) Age 18. Residence Waukon, nativity Pennsylvania. Enlisted Sept.
22, 1861. Mustered Sept. 24, 1861. Wounded severely in back Feb. 17, 1865, Columbia, S. C.
Mustered out July 18, 1865, Louisville, Ky.

Barber, Alfred. Age 18. Residence Independence, nativity Wisconsin. Enlisted Sept. 22, 1861.
Mustered Sept. 24, 1861. Died Dec. 25, 1862, Helena, Ark.

Barnett or Barrett, Daniel W. Age 24. Residence Decorah, nativity New York. Enlisted Sept.
10 1861. Mustered Sept. 24, 1861. Wounded severely in breast March 7, 1862, Pea Ridge, Ark.
Died of wounds March 17, 1862, Cassville, Mo.

Barr, James M. (Veteran.) Age 18. Residence Waukon, nativity Scotland. Enlisted Aug. 26,
1861. Mustered Sept. 24, 1861. Wounded in arm March 7, 1862,

Pea Ridge, Ark. Promoted Fifth
Corporal April 2, 1863. Re-enlisted and re-mustered Jan. 23,
1864. Promoted Fourth Corporal
Jan. 23, 1864. Mustered out July 18, 1865, Louisville, Ky.
Barr, Samuel. Age 18. Residence Allamakee County, nativity
Scotland. Enlisted Feb. 24, 1864.
Mustered March 17, 1864. Mustered out July 18, 1865, Louisville,
Ky.
Bartholomew, Jacob W. Age 22. Residence Burr Oak, nativity
Ohio. Enlisted Aug. 21, 1861, as
Second Sergeant. Mustered Sept. 24, 1861. Promoted Second
Lieutenant March 8, 1863.
Wounded in left arm and right hip severely June 30, 1863,
Vicksburg, Miss. Mustered out Oct.
21, 1864, expiration of term of service.
Bentley, William A. Age 24. Residence Waukon, nativity
Connecticut. Enlisted Nov. 22, 1861.
Mustered Jan. 7, 1862. Discharged for disability Oct. 7, 1862,
Helena, Ark.
Binehart, David. Age 43. Residence Keokuk County, nativity
Germany. Enlisted Nov. 2, 1864.
Mustered Nov. 2, 1864. Mustered Nov. 2, 1864. Mustered out
July 18, 1865, Louisville, Ky.
Blackman, Elmer L. Age 18. Residence Freeport, nativity
Connecticut. Enlisted Sept. 10, 1861.
Mustered Sept. 24, 1861. Mustered out Sept. 24, 1864, East Point,
La., expiration of term of
service.
Blair, James. (Veteran.) Age 27. Residence Rome, nativity Ohio.
Enlisted Sept. 22, 1861.
Mustered Sept. 24, 1861. Killed in action June 16 1864, Kenesaw
Mountain, Georgia. Buried in
National Cemetery, Marietta, Ga. Section A, grave 961.
26
Blake, Edward A. (Veteran.) Age 19. Residence Decorah, nativity
New York. Enlisted Aug. 21,

1861. Mustered Sept. 24, 1861. Wounded slightly in thigh March 7, 1862, Pea Ridge, Ark.
Mustered out July 18, 1865, Louisville, Ky.
Blake, George W. Age 45. Residence Burr Oak, nativity Vermont. Enlisted Nov. 18, 1861.
Mustered Nov. 18, 1861. Discharged for disability July 2, 1862, St. Louis, Mo.
Blass, Benoni H. Age 25. Residence Winneshiek County, nativity Illinois. Enlisted Sept. 22,
1861. Mustered Sept. 24, 1861. Discharged for disability March 31, 1862, Cassville, Mo.
Bliss, Orlando M. Age 38. Residence Decorah, nativity Vermont. Enlisted Sept. 24, 1861.
Mustered Sept. 24, 1861. Promoted Third Corporal Oct. 5, 1861; Fifth Sergeant July 19, 1862;
Quartermaster Sergeant Oct. 31, 1862; First Lieutenant Dec. 22, 1862; Captain March 8, 1863.
Severely injured by falling from horse Oct. 4, 1864. Died of wounds March 25, 1865, hospital,
Chattanooga, Tenn.
Blondin, Samuel. Age 23. Residence Dubuque, nativity New York. Enlisted Aug. 21, 1861.
Mustered Sept. 24, 1861. Transferred to Third Iowa Battery.
Brees, Silas F. (Veteran.) Age 22. Residence Waubeek, nativity Ohio. Enlisted Sept. 24, 1861.
Mustered Sept. 24, 1861. Re-enlisted and re-mustered Jan. 23, 1864. Mustered out July 18, 1865,
Louisville, Ky.
Brewster, James T. Age 18. Residence Black Hawk County, nativity Kentucky. Enlisted Sept.
24, 1861. Mustered Sept. 24, 1861. Transferred to company G Sept. 1, 1862.
Brisco, Hezekiah. Age 18. Residence Decorah, nativity New York. Enlisted Aug. 26, 1861.
Mustered Sept. 24, 1861. Died of typhoid pneumonia Jan. 13, 1862, Pacific, Mo.

Bunt, Eli. Age 21. Residence Decorah, nativity New York. Enlisted Aug. 26, 1861. Mustered
Sept. 24, 1861. Wounded slightly in right leg March 7, 1862, Pea Ridge, Ark. Discharged for
disability March 3, 1863, Keokuk, Iowa.
Bunt, James. (Veteran.) Age 21. Residence Winneshiek County, nativity New York. Enlisted
Sept. 5, 1862. Mustered Sept. 5, 1862. Mustered out May 4, 1865, Washington, D. C.
Burk, William. (Veteran.) Age 30. Residence Dubuque, nativity Ireland. Enlisted Aug. 28,
1861. Mustered Sept. 24, 1861. Wounded severely in left breast Aug. 31, 1864, Jonesboro, Ga.
Died of wounds Sept. 21, 1864, Marietta, Ga. Buried in National Cemetery, Marietta, Ga.
Section G, grave 1206.
Bush, Henry. Age 21. Residence Dubuque, nativity Germany. Enlisted Sept. 22, 1861. Mustered
Sept. 24, 1861. Wounded severely in shoulder May 21, 1863, Vicksburg, Miss. Died of wounds
July 10, 1863, Vicksburg, Miss.
COMPANY "I"
27
Barber Myrtello. (Veteran.) Age 18. Residence New Oregon, nativity Illinois, Enlisted Sept. 26,
1861. Mustered Sept. 26, 1861. Re-enlisted and re-mustered Jan. 1, 1864. Wounded slightly June
28, 18G4, Kenesaw Mountain, Ga. Killed in action April 13, 1865, Raleigh, N. C.
Barnes, Sherman W. Age 20. Residence Castalia, nativity New York. Enlisted Sept. 10, 1861.
Mustered Sept. 18, 1861. Died of chronic diarrhea Oct. 10, 1863, St. Louis, Mo. Buried in
National Cemetery, Jefferson Barracks, St. Louis, Mo. Section 7, grave 166.
Bridges, Thomas J. Age 20. Residence Winneshiek County,

nativity Illinois. Enlisted Sept. 15,
1861. Mustered Sept. 18, 1861. Wounded severely in side and arm March 7, 1862, Pea Ridge,
Ark. Died of wounds March 13, 1862, Pea Ridge, Ark. Buried in National Cemetery,
Fayetteville, Ark. Section 2, grave 17.
Briggs, George S. Age 20. Residence Foreston, nativity Illinois. Enlisted Aug. 19, 1861.
Mustered Sept. 2, 1861. Wounded in battle March 7 1862, Pea Ridge, Ark. Died of wounds
March 8, 1862, Pea Ridge, Ark Buried in National Cemetery, Fayetteville, Ark. Section 2, grave
26.
Briney, Andrew J. Age 19. Residence Mahaska County, nativity Ohio. Enlisted Nov. 18, 1864.
Mustered Nov. 18, 1864. Mustered out July 18, 1865, Louisville, Ky.
Bryan, Isaac. (Veteran.) Age 20. Residence New Oregon, nativity Illinois. Enlisted Sept. 11,
1861. Mustered Sept. 18, 1861. Re-enlisted and re-mustered Jan. 23, 1864. Promoted Eighth
Corporal May 1, 1865. Mustered out July 18, 1865, Louisville, Ky.
Bryan, William C. (Veteran.) Age 18. Residence New Oregon, nativity Illinois. Enlisted Dec.
20, 1861. Mustered Sept. 18, 1861. Wounded in action Sept. 3, 1864, Lovejoy Station, Ga.
Discharged July 22, 1865, Davenport, Iowa.
Bunce, Frank. Age 18. Residence Castalia, nativity Connecticut. Enlisted Sept. 10, 1861.
Mustered Sept. 18, 1861. Discharged February 1862, St. Louis, Mo.
Burch, Hiram. Age 28. Residence Vernon Springs, nativity New York. Enlisted Aug. 17, 1861.
Mustered Sept. 18, 1861. Discharged for disability Jan. 19, 1862, Dubuque, Iowa.
Burke, Daniel B. Age 21. Residence New Oregon, nativity New

Iowa 9th Infantry Regiment 73

York. Enlisted Aug. 19, 1861,
as Drummer. Mustered Sept. 2, 1861. Discharged for disability
May 1, 1863, Memphis, Tenn.
COMPANY "K"
Baker, John S. Age 31. Residence Keokuk, nativity Illinois.
Enlisted Nov. 12, 1864. Mustered
Nov. 12, 1864. Mustered out July 18, 1865, Louisville, Ky.
Barlow, Charles H. Age 17. Residence Marion, nativity Iowa.
Enlisted Sept. 14, 1861.
Mustered Sept. 24, 1861. Discharged for disability Jan. 18, 1862,
Pacific City, Mo.
28
Bean, Rinaldo P. Age 22. Residence Keokuk County, nativity
Maine. Enlisted Nov. 19, 1864.
Mustered Nov. 19, 1864. Mustered out July 18, 1865, Louisville,
Ky.
Benham, Richard. Age 38. Residence Marion, nativity Kentucky.
Enlisted Sept. 14, 1861, as
Fifth Sergeant. Mustered Sept. 24, 1861. Promoted Third
Sergeant; Second Lieutenant March 20,
1863. Mustered out July 18, 1865, Louisville, Ky.
Berg, Peter. Age 23. Residence Burlington, nativity Norway.
Enlisted Nov. 16, 1861. Mustered
Nov. 16, 1864. No record after Feb. 13, 1865.
Beswick, William P. (Veteran.) Age 25. Residence Marion,
nativity Ohio. Enlisted Sept. 4,
1861. Mustered Sept. 24, 1861. Promoted Eighth Corporal Feb. 1,
1863. Re-enlisted and remustered
Jan. 1, 1864. Mustered out July 18, 1865, Louisville, Ky.
Bice, Isaac. Age 22. Residence Paris, nativity New York. Enlisted
Sept. 14, 1861. Mustered
Sept. 24, 1861. Wounded Feb. 13, 1864, Claysville, Ala. Promoted
Fifth Corporal March 3,
1864. Discharged Sept. 23, i864, Davenport, Iowa, expiration of
term of service.
Bigger, Wm. T. Age 19. Residence Marion, nativity Iowa.

Enlisted Sept. 14, 1861. Mustered

Sept. 24, 1861,. Discharged for disability Jan. 1, 1862, Pacific City, Mo.

Bliss, John S. (Veteran.) Age 23. Residence Marion, nativity Pennsylvania. Enlisted Sept. 14,

1861. Mustered Sept. 24, 1861. Promoted Third Corporal Oct. 17, 1862; Third Sergeant June 12,

1863. Re-enlisted and re-mustered Jan. 23, 1864. Mustered out July 24, 1865, Clinton, Iowa.

Blodgett, Austin. Age 21. Residence Linn County, nativity Illinois. Mustered Sept. 24, 1861.

Wounded Feb. 13, 1864, Claysville, Ala. Discharged Sept. 23, 1864, East Point, Ga.

Bowman, Abraham. Age 23. Residence Marion, nativity Pennsylvania. Appointed Second

Lieutenant Sept. 24, 1861. Mustered Sept. 24, 1861. Promoted First Lieutenant March 20, 1863;

Captain Jan. 9, 1864. Mustered out July 18, 1865, Louisville, Ky.

Bowman, David. (Veteran.) Age 27. Residence Marion, nativity Pennsylvania. Enlisted Sept.

14, 1861, as Third Sergeant. Mustered Sept. 24, 1861. Promoted First Sergeant Oct. 17, 1862;

First Lieutenant Jan. 9, 1864. Mustered out July 18, 1865, Louisville, Ky.

Bowsman, Jacob. (Veteran.) Age 18. Residence Marion, nativity Virginia. Enlisted Sept. 24,

1861. Mustered Sept. 24, 1861. Re-enlisted and re-mustered Jan. 24, 1864. Mustered out July 18,

1865, Louisville, Ky.

Bridenthall, Henry N. Age 23. Residence Marion, nativity Pennsylvania. Enlisted Sept. 14,

1861. Mustered Sept. 24, 1861. Wounded slightly in foot May 18, 1862, Vicksburg, Miss.

Promoted Second Corporal Sept. 1, 1862. Killed in battle July 19, 1863, Brandon, Miss.

Bromwell, William H. (Veteran.) Age 18. Residence Marion, nativity Iowa. Mustered Sept. 24, 1861. Mustered out July 17, 1865, Louisville, Ky.

Brown, Charles. Age 18. Residence Nashville, Tenn., nativity Missouri Enlisted April 12, 1864. Mustered April 12, 1864. Died June 21, 1864, Rome, Ga. Buried in National Cemetery, Marietta, Ga. Section C, grave 367.

Brown, William L. (Veteran.) Age 20. Residence Marion, nativity Indiana. Enlisted Sept. 14, 1861. Mustered Sept. 24, 1861. Re-enlisted and re-mustered Jan. 23, 1864. Promoted Principal Musician July 20, 1864. Mustered out July 18, 1865, Louisville, Ky.

Bryan, Benjamin. Age 20. Residence Jones County, nativity Ohio. Enlisted Sept. 18, 1861. Mustered Sept. 24, 1861 Absent; sick in Iowa August, 1862. No further record.

Bumgardner, Samuel V. Age 22. Residence Muscatine, nativity Illinois. Enlisted Feb. 26, 1864. Mustered March 3, 1864. Mustered out July 18, 1865, Louisville, Ky.

Burkhart, John H. (Veteran.) Age 20. Residence Center Point, nativity Indiana. Mustered Sept. 24, 1861. Re-enlisted and re-mustered Jan. 23, 1864. Wounded July 22, 1864, Atlanta, Ga. Discharged Sept. 5, 1864.

Burnett, John R. Age 23. Residence Marion, nativity England. Enlisted Aug. 14 1862. Mustered Aug. 14, 1862. Died Nov. 22, 1863, Paducah, Ky.

Burtis, James S. Age 23. Residence Marion, nativity New Jersey. Enlisted Sept. 14, 1861. Mustered Sept. 24, 1861. Died Sept. 12, 1863, Black River, Miss.

COMPANY "A"

Cady, James D. Age 18. Residence Maquoketa, nativity Illinois. Enlisted Feb. 16, 1864. Mustered March 17, 1864. Died Oct. 4, 1864, Eastport, Ga. Buried in National Cemetery, Marietta, Ga. Section C, grave 710.

Cleveland, Henry C. Rejected Aug. 8, 1861, by Mustering Officer.

Coggswell, Frederick A. (Veteran.) Age 20. Residence Maquoketa, nativity Vermont. Enlisted Aug. 12, 1861. Mustered Sept. 24, 1861. Re-enlisted and re-mustered Jan. 23, 1864. Mustered out July 26, 1865, Louisville, Ky.
Coleman, Hiram. Age 22. Residence Spragueville, nativity Ohio. Enlisted July 29, 1861. Mustered Sept. 24, 1861. Promoted Seventh Corporal March 10, 1862; Fifth Corporal June 7, 1863; Fourth Corporal; Third Corporal Dec. 17, 1863. Mustered out Sept. 24, 1864, East Point, Ga. expiration of term of service.
Cornell, Thomas J. Age 19. Residence Maquoketa, nativity New York. Enlisted Aug. 10, 1861. Mustered Sept. 24, 1861. Died of typhoid fever Oct. 12, 1863, Memphis, Tenn. Buried in Mississippi River National Cemetery, Memphis, Tenn. Section 1, grave 165.
Countryman, Jacob. Age 23. Residence Maquoketa, nativity New York. Enlisted Aug. 10, 1861. Mustered Sept. 24, 1861. Mustered out Sept. 23, 1864, Davenport, Iowa, expiration of term of service.
Crane, John H. Age 18. Residence South Fork, nativity New Hampshire. Enlisted Feb. 18, 1864. Mustered March 1, 1864. Mustered out July 18, 1864, Louisville, Ky.
Crawford, Otis. Age 19. Residence Maquoketa, nativity Illinois. Enlisted Aug. 6, 1861. Mustered Sept. 24, 1861. Promoted Sixth Corporal March 10, 1862. Wounded in both shoulders May 22, 1863, Vicksburg, Miss. Promoted Fourth Corporal June 7, 1863; Third Corporal; Second Corporal Dec. 17, 1863. Discharged Dec. 24, 1864, Davenport, Iowa, expiration of term of service.
Cutter, Edwin G. Age 24. Residence Canton, nativity Massachusetts. Enlisted Aug. 6, 1861, as Third Corporal. Mustered Sept. 2, 1861. Died of typhoid fever Dec. 12, 1861, Pacific, Mo.

COMPANY "B"

Carlton, Lorenzo D. Age 40. Residence Oxford, nativity New York. Enlisted Aug. 12, 1861 as First Sergeant. Mustered Sept. 24,

1861. Discharged for disability Dec. 22, 1862, Keokuk, Iowa.
Carpenter, Don A. Age 31. Residence Hale, nativity Ohio. Appointed Captain Sept. 2, 1861. Mustered Sept. 2, 1861. Promoted Major Aug. 1, 1862. Died of consumption Jan. 8, 1864, Rome, Iowa.
Cleveland, Richard J. Age 40. Residence Rome, nativity New York. Enlisted Oct. 9, 1861. Mustered Oct. 9, 1861. Discharged for disability March 21, 1863, Helena, Ark .
Colby, Charles. Age 22. Residence Madison, nativity Illinois. Enlisted Sept. 25, 1861. Mustered Sept. 25, 1861. Discharged Dec. 23, 1861, hospital, Pacific, Mo.
Colby, David. Age 20. Residence Madison, nativity New York. Enlisted Sept. 26, 1861. Mustered Sept. 25, 1861. Mustered out Sept. 24, 1864, East Point, Ga., expiration of term of service.
Cornwell, John or Jacob L. Age 20. Residence Rome, nativity Iowa. Enlisted Aug. 12, 1861. Mustered Sept. 24, 1861. Died Nov. 30, 1863, St. Louis, Mo. Buried in National Cemetery, Jefferson Barracks. St. Louis, Mo. Section 5, grave 178.
Covert, Alonzo W. Age 18. Residence Louisa County, nativity Ohio Enlisted Feb. 29, 1864. Mustered March 4, 1864. Mustered out July 18, 1865, Louisville, Ky. See company I, Twentyfourth Infantry.
Cox, Albert L. Age 18. Residence Des Moines County, nativity Ohio. Enlisted March 24, 1864. Mustered March 24, 1864. Mustered out July 18, 1865, Louisville, Ky. See company I, Twentyfifth Infantry.
Craig, Thomas. Age 31. Residence Louisa County, nativity Tennessee. Enlisted Feb. 29, 1864. Mustered March 4, 1864. Mustered out July 18 1865, Louisville, Ky. See company I, Twentyfifth Infantry.
Crane, George C. Age 34. Residence Waterford. Mustered Sept. 24, 1861. Transferred to Invalid Corps April 30, 1864. No further record.
Crane, Morgan. Age 28. Residence Waterford, nativity Canada. Enlisted Sept. 25, 1861. Mustered Sept. 25, 1861. Promoted Eighth Corporal April 24, 1863; Seventh Corporal; Fourth

Corporal May 23, 1863; Third Corporal May 23, 1863; Second Corporal Dec. 1, 1863. Discharged for disability Jan. 12, 1864, Davenport, Iowa.

Crook, William C. H. Age 20. Residence Fairview, nativity Iowa. Enlisted Aug. 25, 1861. Mustered Sept. 24, 1861. See company K.

Crow, Aquilla B. (Veteran.) Age 23. Residence Fairview, nativity Indiana. Enlisted Sept. 10, 1861. Mustered Sept. 24, 1861. Wounded in hand slightly May 20, 1863, Vicksburg, Miss. Reenlisted and re-mustered Jan. 23, 1864. Promoted Sixth Corporal April 6, 1865; Fifth Corporal July 5, 1865. Mustered out July 18, 1865, Louisville, Ky.

COMPANY "C"

Carnes, John. Age 18. Residence Winneshiek County, nativity Ohio. Enlisted Feb. 29, 1864. Mustered March 16, 1864. Mustered out July 18, 1865, Louisville, Ky.

Carson, Daniel. Age 18. Residence Winneshiek County, nativity Ohio. Enlisted Feb. 29, 1864. Mustered March 16, 1864. Mustered out July 18, 1865, Louisville, Ky.

Cartwright, John. Age 21. Residence Spring Grove, nativity Indiana. Enlisted Aug. 23, 1861. Mustered Sept. 24, 1861. Wounded slightly in ankle March 7, 1862, Pea Ridge, Ark. Died of wounds April 20, 1862, Dubuque, Iowa.

Cates, Valentine. (Veteran.) Age 29. Residence Independence, nativity New York. Enlisted Aug. 19, 1861. Mustered Sept. 24, 1861. Re-enlisted and re-mustered Jan. 23, 1864. Promoted Fifth Corporal; Third Corporal June 14, 1865. Mustered out July 18, 1865, Louisville Ky.

Chaffee, Daniel. Age 21. Residence Buchanan County, nativity New York. Enlisted Feb. 23, 1864. Mustered March 16, 1864. Mustered out July 18, 1865, Louisville, Ky.

Chase, Harvey. Age 25. Residence Buchanan County, nativity New York. Enlisted Feb. 29, 1864. Mustered March 23, 1864. Mustered out July 18, 1865, Louisville, Ky.

Chase, Isaac. (Veteran.) Age 22. Residence Fairbanks, nativity

New York. Enlisted Aug. 10, 1861. Mustered Sept. 24, 1861. Re-enlisted and re-mustered Jan. 23, 1864. Mustered out July 18, 1865, Louisville, Ky.
Clark, F. L. Rejected Aug. 6, 1861, by Mustering Officer.
Coe, David V. Age 25. Residence Independence, nativity New York. Enlisted as Third Sergeant. Mustered Sept. 24, 1861. Discharged for disability Jan. 21, 1862, Pacific City, Mo.
Corbet, C. Sylvanus. (Veteran.) Age 24. Residence Blakeville, nativity York. Enlisted Aug. 13, 1861. Mustered Sept. 24, 1861. Re-enlisted and re-mustered Jan. 1, 1864. Taken prisoner Feb. 28, 1865, Lynch Creek, S. C. Mustered out June 15, 1865, Clinton, Iowa.
Cress, Thomas. (Veteran.) Age 19. Residence Center Point, nativity Indiana. Enlisted Aug. 3, 1861. Mustered Sept. 24, 1861. Re-enlisted and re-mustered Jan. 23, 1864. Mustered out July 18, 1865, Louisville, Ky.
Curtis, Charles G. Age 22. Residence Independence, nativity Indiana. Enlisted as First Corporal. Mustered Sept. 24, 1861. Promoted Fifth Sergeant March 8, 1862; Second Sergeant April 14, 1863. Wounded slightly July 22, 1864, Atlanta, Ga. Promoted First Lieutenant April 9, 1865. Mustered out July 18, 1865, Louisville, Ky.
Curtis, Lewis D. Age 20. Residence Independence, nativity Indiana. Enlisted Aug. 15, 1861. Mustered Sept. 24, 1861. Wounded slightly in thigh March 7, 1862, Pea Ridge, Ark. Mustered out Sept. 25, 1864, East Point, Ga., expiration of term of service.
Curtis, Orin G. Age 25. Residence Independence, nativity Indiana. Enlisted Sept. 2, 1862. Mustered Sept. 2, 1862. Died of smallpox Dec. 13, 1864, Louisville, Ky. Buried in Cave Hill National Cemetery, Louisville, Ky. Section C, range 3, grave 68.
Curtis, Wesley. Age 26. Residence Independence, nativity Indiana. Enlisted Aug. 26, 1861. Mustered Sept. 24, 1861. Promoted Fifth Sergeant May 23, 1863; Third Sergeant April 9, 1865. Mustered out Sept. 25, 1864, East Point, Ga., expiration of term of service.

COMPANY "D"

Calaway, Jacob. Age 43. Residence Oskaloosa, nativity Ohio. Enlisted Nov. 2, 1864. Mustered
Nov. 2, 1864. Mustered out July 18, 1865, Louisville, Ky.
Callahan John O. Age 18. Residence Scotch Grove, nativity Indiana. Enlisted Feb. 26, 1864.
Mustered March 17, 1861. Mustered out July 18, 1866, Louisville, Ky.
Carter, Andrew J. Age 27. Residence Monticello, nativity New York. Enlisted Aug. 16, 1861,
as Fifth Corporal. Mustered Sept. 2, 1861. Wounded severely in breast March 7, 1862, Pea
Ridge, Ark. Died of wounds April 25, 1862, Cassville, Mo. Buried in National Cemetery,
Springfield Mo. Section 10, grave 66.
Cassady, Jackson E. (Veteran.) Age 23. Residence Scotch Grove nativity Kentucky. Enlisted Aug. 16 1861. Mustered Sept. 2, 1861. Re-enlisted and re-mustered Jan. 1 1864. Mustered out July 18, 1865, Louisville, Ky.
Cassady, James P. Age 20. Residence Johnson, nativity Indiana. Enlisted Aug. 30, 1861. Mustered Sept. 2, 1861. Wounded slightly in leg March 7, 1862, Pea Ridge, Ark. Taken prisoner March 14, 1864, Claysville, Ala. Mustered out April 3, 1865, Davenport, Iowa.
Charles, Isaac N. Age 20. Residence Monticello, nativity Pennsylvania. Enlisted Aug. 16, 1861. Mustered Sept. 2, 1861. Wounded slightly in leg March 7, 1862, Pea Ridge, Ark. Discharged March 21, 1863, St. Louis, Mo.
Clark, Albert. Age 18. Residence Liberty, nativity Pennsylvania. Enlisted March 10, 1864. Mustered March 30, 1864. Mustered out July 18, 1865, Louisville, Ky.
Clark, William. Age 21. Residence Scotch Grove, nativity Pennsylvania. Enlisted Aug. 16, 1861. Mustered Sept. 2, 1861. Died April 16, 1862, Cassville, Mo. Buried in National Cemetery,

Springfield, Mo. Section 10, grave 67.
Collins, John H. Age 19. Residence Washington, nativity Iowa. Enlisted Feb. 29, 1864. Mustered March 16, 1864. Died Oct. 26, 1864, Atlanta, Ga. Buried in National Cemetery, Marietta, Ga. Section G, grave 494.
Colyer, Charles C. Age 33. Residence South Fork, nativity Illinois. Enlisted Feb. 27, 1864. Mustered March 17, 1864. Mustered out May 17, 1865, Davenport, Iowa.
Conklin, James W. Age 18. Residence Scotch Grove, nativity New York. Enlisted Feb. 29, 1864. Mustered March 17, 1864. Mustered out July 18, 1865, Louisville, Ky.
Cook, David F. Age 20. Residence Monticello, nativity Pennsylvania. Enlisted Aug. 16, 1861. Mustered Sept. 20, 1861. Died of typhoid fever April 4, 1863, Young's Point, La.
Cook, Edward C. Age 24. Residence Oskaloosa, nativity Maine. Enlisted Nov. 2, 1864. Mustered Nov. 2, 1864. Mustered out July 18, 1865, Louisville, Ky.
Cox, Joshua S. Age 18. Residence Mahaska County, nativity Ohio. Enlisted Nov. 19, 1864. Mustered Nov. 19, 1864. Mustered out July 18, 1865, Louisville, Ky.
Crane, Carson. Age 24. Residence Jones County, nativity New York. Enlisted Aug. 16, 186. Appointed Second Lieutenant Sept. 7, 1861. Promoted First Lieutenant July 9, 1862. Resigned March 14, 1863.
Crane, Winfield S. Age 18. Residence Scotch Grove, nativity Illinois. Enlisted Feb. 25, 1864. Mustered Feb. 29, 1864. Mustered out July 18, 1865, Louisville, Ky.
Gross, Henry. Age 47. Residence Jones County, nativity Massachusetts. Enlisted Sept. 9, 1861. Mustered Sept. 9, 1861. Wounded slightly in shoulder March 7, 1862, Pea Ridge, Ark. Discharged Sept. 24, 1864, East Point, Ga., expiration of term of service.

COMPANY "E"

Carpenter, George. (Veteran.) Age 18. Residence Clayton

County, nativity Illinois. Enlisted
Nov. 19, 1861. Mustered Nov. 19, 1861. Re-enlisted and re-mustered June 23, 1864. Promoted
Sixth Corporal June 1,1864; Fourth Corporal Jan. 24, 1865; Third Corporal Jan. 24, 1865.
Mustered out July 18, 1865, Louisville, Ky.
Chapman, James M. Age 18. Residence Volga City, nativity Illinois. Mustered Sept. 24 1861.
Discharged March 1, 1862, Pacific, Mo.
Chase, William H. Age 18. Residence Farmersburg, nativity Canada. Enlisted Sept. 14, 1861.
Mustered Sept. 24, 1861. Promoted Sixth Corporal March 6, 1863. Died March 27, 1863,
Young's Point, La.
Cline, William. Age 19. Residence Wandena, nativity Illinois. Enlisted September, 1861.
Mustered Sept. 24, 1861. Died of camp fever July 14, 1862, Big Creek, Ark.
Cline William. Age 19. Residence Fayette County, nativity Illinois. Enlisted Feb. 27, 1864.
Mustered March 9, 1864. Mustered out July 18, 1865, Louisville, Ky.
Crane, Edgar. Age 22. Residence Volga City, nativity Illinois. Mustered Sept. 24, 1861.
Discharged for disability Jan. 8, 1862, Pacific, Mo.
Crary, Elisha A. Age 27. Residence Garnavillo, nativity Connecticut. Enlisted Sept. 9, 1861, as Second Sergeant.
Mustered Sept. 24, 1861. Promoted Second Lieutenant Dec. 27, 1861; Captain April 16, 1863. Mustered out Jan. 23, 1865, expiration of term of service.
Corbin, Levi M. (Veteran.) Age 18. Residence Wandena, nativity Illinois. Enlisted Dec. 2 1861. Mustered Dec. 2, 1861. Re-enlisted and re-mustered Jan. 23, 1864. Killed by gun shot wound July 22,1864, Atlanta, Ga.

COMPANY "F"

Carmichael, William H. Age 18. Residence Illyria, nativity Pennsylvania. Enlisted Sept. 6,
1861. Mustered Sept. 12, 1861. Killed in battle March 7, 1862, Pea Ridge, Ark.

Cook, George G. (Veteran.) Age 19. Residence Eden, nativity Illinois. Enlisted Sept. 8, 1861.
Mustered Sept. 12, 1861. Promoted Second Corporal March 12, 1863; First Corporal Oct. 6,
1863. Re-enlisted and re-mustered Jan. 1, 1864. Died July 20, 1864, Decatur, Ga.

Coon, Isaac H. (Veteran.) Age 18. Residence West Union, nativity New York. Enlisted Aug. 28,
1861. Mustered Sept. 12, 1861. Re-enlisted and re-mustered Jan. 23, 1864. Mustered out July 18,
1865, Louisville, Ky.

Cowden. Winfield. Age 18. Residence Des Moines County, nativity Missouri. Enlisted Jan. 25,
1865. Mustered Jan. 25, 1865. Mustered out July 18, 1865, Louisville, Ky. See company G,
Twenty-fifth Infantry.
35

Crane, Webster J. (Veteran.) Age 19. Residence West Union, nativity Indiana. Enlisted Aug.
27, 1861. Mustered Sept. 12, 1861. Re-enlisted and re-mustered Jan. 1, 1864. Wounded severely
in right groin and right hand June 27, 1864, Kenesaw Mountain, Ga. Discharged for wounds Feb.
29, 1865, Davenport, Iowa.

Curtiss, James R. (Veteran.) Age 24. Residence Elgin, nativity Illinois. Enlisted Sept. 3, 1861.
Mustered Sept. 12, 1861. Promoted Fourth Corporal Aug. 1, 1862; Second Corporal Oct. 6,
1863. Re-enlisted and re-mustered Jan. 1, 1864. Taken prisoner March 27, 1864, Dallas Ga.

Promoted First Corporal Aug. 1, 1864. Mustered out July 18, 1865 Louisville, Ky.
COMPANY "G"
Calhoun, Jasper. Age 28. Residence Linn County, nativity Ohio. Enlisted Nov. 3, 1864.
Mustered Nov. 3, 1864. Mustered out July 18, 1865, Louisville, Ky.
Cave, Philip. (Veteran.) Age 21. Residence Spring Lake, nativity Pennsylvania. Enlisted Sept. 3,
1861. Mustered Sept. 24, 1861. Re-enlisted and re-mustered Jan. 23, 1864. Mustered out July 18,
1865, Louisville, Ky.
Chambers, William. Age 36. Residence Bremer County, nativity Canada. Enlisted Feb. 29,
1864. Mustered March 17, 1864. Mustered out July 18, 1865, Louisville, Ky.
Clark, Francis J. Age 21. Residence Waterloo, nativity Ohio. Enlisted Aug. 20, 1861. Mustered
Sept. 24, 1861. Wounded slightly in elbow March 7, 1862, Pea Ridge, Ark. Killed June 13, 1864,
Kenesaw Mountain, Ga.
Clark, William. Age 44. Residence Delaware County, nativity Massachusetts. Enlisted Feb. 23,
1864. Mustered March 16, 1864. Mustered out July 18, 1865, Louisville, Ky.
Costello, Thomas. (Veteran.) Age 31. Residence Dubuque, nativity Ireland. Enlisted Sept. 3,
1861. Mustered Sept. 24, 1861. Re-enlisted and re-mustered Jan. 23, 1864. Mustered out July 18,
1865, Louisville, Ky.
Crane, Earl. Age 19. Residence Grundy Center, nativity New York. Enlisted Aug. 20, 1861.
Mustered Sept. 24, 1861. Died Dec. 27, 1863, Evansville, Ind. Buried in National Cemetery,
Evansville, Ind.
Cuppet, David L. (Veteran.) Age 19. Residence Colesburg,

Iowa 9th Infantry Regiment 85

nativity Pennsylvania. Enlisted
Sept. 10, 1861. Mustered Sept. 24, 1861. Wounded severely in shoulder March 7, 1862, Pea
Ridge, Ark. Re-enlisted and re-mustered Jan. 5, 1864. Promoted Eighth Corporal May 1, 1864;
First Sergeant Aug. 1, 1864. Mustered out July 18, 1865, Louisville, Ky.
Cutts, Levi. Age 26. Residence Janesville, nativity Iowa. Enlisted Aug. 10, 1861. Mustered
Sept. 24, 1861. Discharged for disability April 18, 1862, Forsyth, Mo.,
COMPANY "H"
36
Calkins, Edward A. Age 20. Residence Colesburg, nativity Connecticut. Enlisted Sept. 23,
1861. Mustered Sept. 24, 1861. Died of dysentery July 5, 1863, Vicksburg, Miss.
Carnes, Robert. (Veteran.) Age 18. Residence Independence, nativity Ohio. Enlisted Sept. 22,
1861. Mustered Sept. 24, 1861. Killed in battle May 15, 1864, Resaca, Ga. Buried in National
Cemetery, Chattanooga, Tenn. Section K, grave 67.
Cass, Wallace. Age 24. Residence Decorah, nativity New York. Enlisted Aug. 26 1861.
Mustered Sept. 24, 1861. Mustered out Sept. 24, 1864, East Point, Ga., expiration of term of
service.
Clark, Hiram. Age 19. Residence Decorah, nativity New York. Enlisted Aug. 26, 1861.
Mustered Sept. 24, 1861. Wounded slightly in foot March 7, 1862, Pea Ridge, Ark. Died of
wounds Oct. 17, 1863, Memphis, Tenn. Buried in National Cemetery, Memphis, Tenn. Section
1, grave 215.
Cook, Arthur J. (Veteran.) Age 19. Residence Decorah, nativity New York. Enlisted Oct. 25,

1861. Re-enlisted and re-mustered Jan. 5, 1864. Promoted Sixth Corporal June 17, 1864; Fifth
Corporal July 22, 1864. Mustered out July 18, 1865, Louisville, Ky.

Cook, Wesley D. Age 21. Residence Decorah, nativity New York. Enlisted Oct. 25, 1861.
Mustered Oct. 25, 1861. Died of smallpox March 18, 1863, Young's Point, La.

Craig, James E. Age 18. Residence Decorah, nativity Wisconsin. Enlisted Aug. 25, 1861.
Mustered Sept. 24, 1861. Died Feb. 12, 1862, Pacific, Mo.

Crawford, Henry D. (Veteran.) Age 19. Residence Dubuque, nativity Iowa. Enlisted Oct. 1,
1861. Mustered Oct. 1, 1861. Re-enlisted and re-mustered Jan. 5, 1864. Promoted Drummer.
Mustered out July 18, 1865, Louisville, Ky.

Culver, Elmer R. Age 27. Residence Mahaska County, nativity Ohio. Enlisted Nov. 2, 1864.
Mustered Nov. 2, 1864. Mustered out July 18, 1865, Louisville, Ky.

COMPANY "I"

Capler, Joseph. (Veteran.) Age 17. Residence New Oregon, nativity Ohio. Enlisted Aug. 17,
1861. Mustered Sept. 18, 1861. Re-enlisted and re-mustered Jan. 5, 1864. Mustered out July 18,
1865, Louisville, Ky.

Chapel, Edwin. (Veteran.) Age 22. Residence New Oregon, nativity New York. Enlisted Aug.
17, 1861. Mustered Sept. 2, 1861. Promoted
Sixth Corporal May 24, 1863; Fourth Corporal July 1, 1863; Third Corporal Oct. 6, 1863.
Wounded slightly Nov. 25, 1863, Missionary Ridge, Tenn. Promoted Second Corporal Sept. 16,
1864. Mustered out July 18, 1865, Louisville, Ky.

Clark, James D. Age 18. Residence Mahaska County, nativity Iowa. Enlisted Nov. 19, 1864.

Mustered Nov. 19, 1864. Mustered out July 18, 1865, Louisville, Ky.
37
Colby, Whitman N. Age 23. Residence Vernon Springs, nativity New York. Enlisted Sept. 17,
1861. Mustered Sept. 18, 1861. Wounded severely in shoulder March 7, 1862, Pea Ridge, Ark.
Promoted Seventh Corporal Nov. 19, 1862. Discharged for wounds Sept. 29, 1862, St. Louis,
Mo.
Cole, Ezra M. Age 22. Residence New Oregon, nativity Illinois. Enlisted Aug. 22, 1861.
Mustered Sept. 18, 1861. Discharged Sept. 23, 1864, Davenport, Iowa, expiration of term of
service.
Connable, Edgar W. Age 16. Residence Woodville, nativity Wisconsin. Enlisted April 15,
1864. Mustered. Mustered April 28, 1864. Promoted Drummer May 1, 1865. Mustered out July
18, 1865, Louisville, Ky.
Consadine, Patrick. Age 20. Residence Butler Center, nativity Nova Scotia. Enlisted Aug. 17,
1861. Mustered Sept. 18, 1861. Discharged for disability Aug. 9, 1862, St. Louis, Mo.
Converse, Stillman A. (Veteran) Age 28. Residence Foreston, nativity New Hampshire.
Enlisted Aug. l9, 1861. Mustered Sept. 2, 1861. Wounded slightly in thigh May 22, 1863,
Vicksburg, Miss. Re-enlisted and re-mustered Jan. 5, 1864. Died of wounds Aug. 31, 1864,
Jonesboro, Ga.
Corbin, George W. Age 24. Residence New Oregon, nativity New York. Enlisted Aug. 12,
1861, as First Sergeant. Mustered Sept. 18, 1861. Promoted Second Lieutenant June 14, 1862.
Discharged for ill health Oct. 15, 1862, Helena, Ark.

COMPANY "K"

Carnahan, Christopher. Age 22. Residence Des Moines County, nativity Iowa. Enlisted Feb. 1,
1865. Mustered Feb. 1, 1865. Mustered out July 18, 1865, Louisville, Ky. See company G,
Twenty-fifth Infantry.

Carskaddon, David. Age 37. Residence Marion, nativity Ohio. Enlisted Sept. 14, 1861.
Appointed Captain Sept. 24, 1861. Mustered Sept. 24, 1861. Promoted Colonel March 19, 1863.
Wounded slightly July 29, 1864, Atlanta, Ga. Discharged for disability Dec. 29, 1864.

Channel, Daniel. Age 18. Residence Des Moines County, nativity Virginia. Enlisted Jan. 23,
1865. Mustered Jan. 23, 1865. Mustered out July 18, 1865, Louisville, Ky. See company G,
Twenty-fifth Infantry.

Claflin, Norman W. Age 37. Residence Marion, nativity New York. Enlisted First Lieutenant
Sept. 24, 1861. Mustered Sept. 24, 1861. Resigned Oct. 16, 1862.

Coenen, Joseph. (Veteran.) Age 26. Residence Marion, nativity Prussia. Enlisted Aug. 29, 1862.
Mustered Aug. 29, 1862. Promoted Seventh Corporal Feb. 1, 1863. Re-enlisted and re-mustered
Jan. 23, 1864. Wounded May 13, 1864, Resaca, Ga. Mustered out July 18, 1865, Louisville, Ky.
38

Coenen, William. (Veteran.) Age 19. Residence Marion, nativity Prussia. Enlisted Sept. 2,
1861. Mustered Sept. 24, 1861. Promoted Seventh Corporal Feb. 1, 1863. Re-enlisted and remustered
Jan. 25, 1864. Promoted Third Corporal March 3, 1864; First Corporal Jan. 1, 1865.
Mustered out July 18, 1865, Louisville, Ky.

Cone, John. (Veteran.) Age 19. Residence Marion, nativity Iowa. Enlisted Sept. 14, 1861, as

Fifth Corporal. Mustered Sept. 24, 1861. Wounded slightly March 7, 1862, Pea Ridge, Ark.
Wounded in foot Dec. 29, 1862, Chickasaw Bluffs. Re-enlisted and re-mustered Jan. 23, 1864.
Promoted Fourth Sergeant March 3, 1864; Third Sergeant April 17, 1865. Mustered out July 18,
1865, Louisville, Ky.
Cone, Oliver B. Age 25. Residence Marion, nativity Connecticut. Enlisted Sept. 14, 1861, as
Second Corporal. Mustered Sept. 24, 1861. Severely wounded in back March 7, 1862, Pea
Ridge, Ark. Discharged for disability Aug. 29, 1862, St. Louis, Mo.
Cook, Thomas G. Age 21. Residence Cottage Hill, nativity Iowa. Mustered Sept. 24, 1861.
Wounded in shoulder and hand severely May 27, 1863, Vicksburg, Miss. Mustered out Sept. 23,
1864, East Point, Ga.
Cooper, Benjamin. Deserted June 28, 1865, Louisville, Ky. Joined from company G, Twentyfifth
Infantry.
Cowley, Abraham. Age 22. Nativity England. Mustered Sept. 24, 1861. No further record.
Crook, William C. H. Age 20. Residence Jones County, nativity Iowa. Enlisted Sept. 12, 1861.
Mustered Sept. 24, 1861. Wounded slightly in leg March 7, 1862, Pea Ridge, Ark. Discharged
for disability Feb. 27, 1863, Young's Point, La. See company B. See company K, Ninth Cavalry.
COMPANY "A"
Darling, Benjamin F. Age 25. Residence Maquoketa, nativity Vermont. Enlisted July 29, 1861,
as Second Sergeant. Mustered Sept. 2, 1861. Promoted First Sergeant March 3, 1862. Wounded
in face slightly March 7, 1862, Pea Ridge, Ark. Promoted Second Lieutenant March 8, 1862;

First Lieutenant March 27, 1863; Captain Aug. 8, 1863. Mustered out July 18, 1865, Louisville, Ky.

Darling, Edwin. (Veteran.) Age 23. Residence Maquoketa, nativity Vermont. Enlisted Aug. 12, 1861. Mustered Sept. 24, 1861. Promoted Hospital Steward Aug. 2, 1861. Re-enlisted and remustered Jan. 23, 1864. Transferred to company K. Mustered out July 18, 1865, Louisville, Ky. See company K

Davis, Joseph A. Age 21. Residence Boone Springs, nativity New York. Enlisted Aug. 10, 1861. Mustered Sept. 24, 1861. Wounded severely in leg Nov. 27, 1863, Ringgold, Ga. Wounded severely in leg May 27, 1864, Dallas, Ga. Mustered out Sept. 24, 1864, East Point, Ga., expiration of term of service.

DeGrush, Frederick J. (Veteran.) Age 27. Residence Maquoketa, nativity New York. Enlisted July 29, 1861, as Fourth Sergeant. Mustered Sept. 2, 1861. Promoted Third Sergeant March 3,

39

1862; Second Sergeant March 10, 1862. Re-enlisted and re-mustered Jan. 1, 1864. Mustered out July 26, 1865, Louisville, Ky.

Delano, Smith. (Veteran.) Age 23. Residence Maquoketa, nativity New York. Enlisted Aug. 17, 1861. Mustered Sept. 24, 1861. Wounded in leg May 19, 1863, Vicksburg, Miss. Re-enlisted and re-mustered Jan. 23, 1864. Died of pneumonia April 5, 1864, Nashville, Tenn. Buried in National Cemetery, Nashville, Tenn. Section H, grave 782.

Dickinson, Samuel P. Age 34. Residence Dubuque, nativity Ohio. Enlisted Aug. 31, 1862. Mustered Oct. 14, 1862. Transferred to Invalid Corps Dec. 15, 1863. No further record.

Downey, Ira. (Veteran.) Age 28. Residence Maquoketa, nativity New York. Enlisted Aug. 10,
1861. Mustered Sept. 24, 1861. Re-enlisted and re-mustered Jan. 23, 1864. Mustered out July 23,
1865, Louisville, Ky.
Drips, Andrew W. Age 35. Residence Maquoketa, nativity Pennsylvania. Appointed Captain
Sept. 7, 1861. Mustered Sept. 7, 1861. Killed in battle March 7, 1862, Pea Ridge, Ark.
Drips, John F. Age 22. Residence Maquoketa, nativity Pennsylvania. Enlisted July 29, 1861, as
Second Corporal. Mustered Sept. 2, 1861. Promoted First Corporal March 3, 1862. Died March
27, 1863, Memphis, Tenn.
Dunham, Hazle. Age 21. Residence Sterling, nativity Canada. Enlisted Sept. 7, 1861. Mustered
Sept. 24, 1861. Mustered out Sept. 24, 1864, East Point, Ga., expiration of term of service.
Dupray, William. Age 38. Residence Maquoketa, nativity Pennsylvania. Enlisted Aug. 10,
1861, as Fifth Corporal. Mustered Sept. 2, 1861. Promoted Fourth Corporal Dec. 19, 1861;
Second Corporal March 10, 1862; First Corporal June 2, 1863. Died of congestive chills Oct. 28,
1863, Iuka, Miss.
COMPANY "B"
Dean, John S. Age 37. Residence Jackson, nativity New York. Enlisted Sept. 25, 1861.
Mustered Sept. 25, 1861. Discharged Sept. 26, 1861, Dubuque, Iowa.
Denny, Ebenezer. Age 39. Residence Benton, nativity England. Enlisted Nov. 2, 1864.
Mustered Nov. 2, 1864. Mustered out July 18, 1865, Louisville, Ky.
Dunham, David W. Age 18. Residence Wyoming, nativity Massachusetts. Enlisted Aug. 23,

1861. Mustered Sept. 24, 1861. Transferred to Invalid Corps March 15, 1864. No further record.

COMPANY "C"

Dart, Lyman A. Age 18. Residence Pella, nativity Ohio. Enlisted Oct. 5, 1864. Mustered Oct.
13, 1864. Mustered out July 18, 1865, Louisville, Ky. See Twenty-fifth Infantry.
40

Davis, Billings. Age 23. Residence Independence, nativity Vermont. Enlisted Aug. 24, 1861.
Mustered Sept. 24, 1861. Promoted Fifth Sergeant Sept. 26, 1861; Fourth Sergeant March 8,
1862. Transferred to Invalid Corps Sept. 3, 1863. No further record.

Decker, William. (Veteran.) Age 19. Residence Independence, nativity Ohio. Enlisted Aug. 8,
1861. Mustered Sept. 24, 1861. Re-enlisted and re-mustered Jan. 23, 1864. Mustered out July 18,
1865, Louisville, Ky.

COMPANY "D"

Dale, James J. Age 22. Nativity Pennsylvania. Enlisted Nov. 3, 1864. Mustered Nov. 3, 1864.
Died Jan. 22, 1865, Huntsville, Ala.

Davis, John S. Age 42. Nativity Maryland. Enlisted Nov. 8, 1864. Mustered Nov. 8, 1864. Died
Feb. 20, 1865, Newbern, N.C. Buried in Old Cemetery, Newbern, N. C. No. 33, plot 12, grave
2100.

Dean, William H. Age 20. Residence Scotch Grove, nativity Iowa. Enlisted March 21, 1864.
Mustered March 23, 1864. Drowned Sept. 5, 1864, Marietta, Ga. Buried in National Cemetery,
Marietta, Ga. Section G, grave 1058.

Devore, William. Age 21. Residence Mills County, nativity Ohio. Enlisted Nov. 5, 1864.

Mustered Nov. 5, 1864. Died June 7, 1865, Nashville, Tenn. Buried in National Cemetery,
Nashville, Tenn. Section J, grave 1266.
Dickey, Charles H. Age 19. Residence Hazel Green, nativity New York. Enlisted Feb. 26, 1864.
Mustered March 17, 1864. Mustered out July 18, 1865, Louisville, Ky.
Dickey, Fred N. Age 18. Residence Hazel Green, nativity New York. Enlisted Feb. 20, 1864.
Mustered Feb. 20, 1864. Mustered out July 18, 1865, Louisville, Ky.
Diffendorffer, James. Age 24. Residence Monticello, nativity Pennsylvania. Enlisted Aug. 16,
1861. Mustered Sept. 2, 1861. Transferred to Veteran Reserve Corps Feb. 29, 1864. No further
record.
Dixon, Thomas C. Age 20. Residence Monticello, nativity Illinois. Enlisted Aug. 26, 1861.
Mustered Sept. 2, 1861. Died of pneumonia April 14, 1862, Cassville, Mo. Buried in National
Cemetery, Springfield, Mo. Section 10, grave 57.
Dixon, William H. (Veteran.) Age 24. Residence Wyoming, nativity Ohio. Enlisted Aug. 26,
1861. Mustered Sept. 2, 1861. Wounded slightly in foot May 19, 1863, Vicksburg, Miss. Reenlisted
and re-mustered Jan. 23, 1864. Mustered out July 18, 1865, Louisville, Ky.
Dockstadter, Charles R. Age 18. Residence Wyoming, nativity Pennsylvania. Enlisted Aug. 19
1861. Mustered Sept. 2, 1861. Wounded slightly in hip March 7, 1862, Pea Ridge, Ark. Taken
prisoner March 14, 1864, Claysville, Ala. Mustered out June 19, 1865, Clinton, Iowa.
41
Drakes Abraham. Age 22. Residence Monticello, nativity Ohio. Enlisted Aug. 16, 1861.

Mustered Sept. 2, 1861. Wounded in breast March 6, 1862, Pea Ridge, Ark. Died of wounds
May 7, 1862, Cassville, Mo. Buried in National Cemetery, Springfield, Mo. Section 10, grave
63.
Dreibelbis, John A. Age 21. Residence Monticello, nativity Illinois. Enlisted Aug. 16, 1861, as
Second Corporal. Wounded slightly March 7, 1862, Pea Ridge, Ark. Died Dec. 15, 1862,
Helena, Ark. Buried in National Cemetery, Memphis, Tenn. Section 3, grave 650.
Dubois, Everitt. (Veteran.) Age 19. Residence Scotch Grove, nativity New York. Enlisted
Aug. 26, 1861. Mustered Sept. 2, 1861. Re-enlisted and re-mustered Jan. 23, 1864. Promoted
Third Corporal July 1, 1864; First Corporal Oct. 1, 1864; Fifth Sergeant June 20, 1865.
Mustered out July 18, 1865, Louisville, Ky.
Dunahe, Cyrus. (Veteran.) Age 24. Residence Monticello, nativity Pennsylvania. Enlisted Aug.
29, 1861. Mustered Sept. 2, 1861. Re-enlisted and re-mustered Jan. 23, 1864. Mustered out July
18, 1865, Louisville, Ky.
COMPANY "E"
Davis, Ezra. Age 41. Residence Pottawattamie County, nativity Indiana. Enlisted Nov. 5 1864.
Mustered Nov. 5, 1864. Mustered out July 18, 1865, Louisville, Ky.
Desart, Wesley. Age 21. Residence Elgin, nativity Illinois. Enlisted Sept. 14, 1861. Mustered
Sept. 24, 1861. Mustered out Sept. 24, 1864, Davenport, Iowa, expiration of term of service.
Dockendorf, Nicholas. Age 27. Residence Burlington, nativity Germany. Enlisted Oct. 5, 1864.
Mustered Oct. 5, 1864. Mustered out July 18, 1865, Louisville, Ky. See company G, Twentyfifth

Infantry.
Dorland, Clement. (Veteran.) Age 18. Residence Wandena, nativity Ohio. Enlisted Dec. 2,
1861. Re-enlisted and re-mustered Jan. 23, 1864. Mustered out July 18, 1865, Louisville, Ky.
Dorland, George. (Veteran.) Age 18. Residence Volga City, nativity Ohio. Enlisted Nov. 24,
1861. Mustered Nov. 24, 1861. Re-enlisted and re-mustered Jan. 23, 1864. Promoted Wagoner
Feb. 1, 1864; Sixth Corporal March 27, 1864. Mustered out July 18, 1865, Louisville, Ky.
Dorlond, James. (Veteran.) Age 22. Residence Wandena, nativity Indiana. Enlisted Sept. 24,
1861. Mustered Sept. 24 1861. Re-enlisted and re-mustered Jan. 23, 1864. Wounded in foot
slightly May 15, 1864, Resaca, Ga. Killed March 6, 1865, Cheraw, N. C.
Doty, Thomas. (Veteran.) Age 21. Residence Highland, nativity Pennsylvania. Enlisted Sept.
12, 1861. Mustered Sept. 24, 1861. Promoted Fifth Sergeant June 26, 1863; Fourth Sergeant Jan.
23, 1864. Re-enlisted and re-mustered Jan. 23, 1864. Mustered out July 18, 1865, Louisville, Ky.
42
Doty, William. Age 24. Residence Highland, nativity Pennsylvania. Enlisted Sept. 12, 1861, as
Eighth Corporal. Mustered Sept. 24, 1861. Discharged for disability Oct. 26, 1862, Helena,
Ark.
Dunton, John. Age 40. Residence Clayton County, nativity Vermont. Enlisted Sept. 9. 1861,
as Fourth Corporal. Mustered Sept. 24, 1861. Discharged Dec. 5, 1864, Memphis, Tenn. See
company G.
COMPANY "F"
Dildine, James. Age 31. Residence Eldorado, nativity Ohio.

Enlisted Aug. 27, 1861. Mustered
Sept. 12, 1861. Promoted Wagoner June 9, 1862. Mustered out
Sept. 24, 1864, East Point, Ga.,
expiration of term of service.
Downs, David H. Age 42. Residence Auburn, nativity
Connecticut. Enlisted Aug. 27, 1861.
Mustered Sept. 12, 1861. Died of typhoid fever Dec. 24, 1861,
Pacific, Mo.
COMPANY "G"
Daniel, Andrew L. Age 38. Residence Lee County, nativity
North Carolina. Enlisted Nov. 11,
1864. Mustered Nov. 11, 1864. Mustered out July 18, 1865,
Louisville, Ky.
Day, Otis G. Age 29. Residence LaPorte City, nativity Maine.
Enlisted Aug. 3, 1861, as First
Corporal. Mustered Sept. 24, 1861. Promoted First Sergeant of
Third Battery Oct. 7, 1861.
Debold, Joseph. Age 33. Residence Black Hawk County, nativity
France. Enlisted Feb. 18,
1864. Mustered Feb. 23, 1864. Discharged for disability July 1,
1865, Louisville, Ky.
Dodge Henry L. Age 25. Residence Burlington, nativity
Tennessee. Enlisted Oct. 6 1864.
Mustered Oct. 6, 1864. Mustered out July 31, 1865, Louisville, Ky.
See company G., Twentyfifth
Infantry.
Dunahoo, Andrew J. (Veteran.) Age 26. Residence Waterloo,
nativity Virginia. Enlisted Aug.
20, 1861. Mustered Sept. 24, 1861. Wounded severely in thigh
May 19, 1863, Vicksburg, Miss.
Re-enlisted and re-mustered Jan. 23, 1864. Wounded in left wrist
June 12, 1864, Kingston, Ga.
Mustered out July 18, 1865, Louisville, Ky.
Dunton, John. (Veteran.) Age 43. Residence Clayton County,
nativity Vermont. Enlisted Feb.
12, 1864. Mustered March 2, 1864. Mustered out July 1, 1865,

Louisville, Ky. See company E.
COMPANY "H"
Davis, Clark H. Age 26. Residence Freeport, nativity Connecticut. Enlisted Sept. 10, 1861, as
Eighth Corporal. Mustered Sept. 24, 1861. Wounded in foot and left arm March 7, 1862, Pea
Ridge Ark. Discharged for disability Aug. 16, 1862.
43
Dempsy, Thomas. (Veteran.) Age 32. Residence McGregor, nativity Ireland. Enlisted Sept. 22,
1861. Mustered Sept. 24, 1861. Wounded slightly in thigh March 7, 1862, Pea Ridge, Ark. Reenlisted
and re-mustered Jan. 23, 1864. Mustered out July 18, 1865, Louisville, Ky.
Ditmore, Conrad. (Veteran.) Age 26. Residence Burr Oak, nativity Ohio. Enlisted Aug. 21,
1861, as Third Sergeant. Mustered Sept. 24th 1861. Wounded severely through both thighs
March 19, 1863, Vicksburg, Miss. Promoted First Sergeant April 2, 1863. Re-enlisted and remustered
Jan. 23, 1864. Promoted First Lieutenant April 9, 1865. Mustered out July 18, 1865,
Louisville, Ky.
Drake, Zephaniah, L. Age 39. Residence Freeport, nativity New Jersey. Enlisted Sept. 10,
1861, as First Corporal. Mustered Sept. 24, 1861. Discharged for disability July 16, 1862,
Helena, Ark.
Durham, Levi. Age 18. Residence Independence, nativity New York. Enlisted Sept. 22, 1861.
Mustered Sept. 24, 1861. Discharged for disability June 18, 1862, Pacific, Mo.
COMPANY "I"
Daniels, Charles W. Rejected Aug. 18, 1861, by Mustering Officer.
Daniels, Francis A. Age 23. Residence Foreston, nativity

Michigan. Enlisted Aug. 18, 1861.
Mustered Sept. 18, 1861. Discharged for disability June 3, 1862.
DeMott, Isaac. Age 18. Residence New Hampton, nativity Pennsylvania. Enlisted March 15,
1862. Mustered March 15, 1862. Died of lung fever May 19, 1863, Walnut Hills, Miss.
Douglass, Robert R. Age 19. Residence Mahaska, nativity Kentucky. Enlisted Nov. 14, 1864.
Mustered Nov. 14, 1864. Mustered out July 18, 1865, Louisville, Ky.
COMPANY "K"
Darling, Edwin. (Veteran.) Age 23. Residence Maquoketa, nativity Vermont. Enlisted Aug. 12,
1861. Mustered Sept. 24, 1861. Re-enlisted and re-mustered Jan. 23, 1864. Promoted Hospital
Steward Feb. 1, 1864. Mustered out July 18, 1865, Louisville, Ky. See company A.
Darrow, Daniel L. Age 23. Residence Cottage Hill, nativity New York. Enlisted Sept. 12,
1861. Mustered Sept. 24, 1861. Killed in battle March 7, 1862, Pea Ridge, Ark.
Dingman, Wilson S. Age 23. Residence Marion, nativity Ohio. Enlisted Sept. 24, 1861.
Mustered Sept. 24, 1861. Discharged for disability Jan. 18, 1862, Pacific City, Mo.
Dresser, Ezra. Age 33. Residence Paris, nativity East Canada. Enlisted Sept. 24, 1861. Mustered
Sept. 24, 1861. Wounded severely in side March 7, 1862, Pea Ridge, Ark. Discharged Aug. 10,
1862, St. Louis, Mo.
COMPANY "A"
44
Eby, James B. (Veteran.) Age 24. Residence Maquoketa, nativity Pennsylvania. Enlisted Aug.
8, 1861. Mustered Sept. 24, 1861. Wounded in arm and hip severely May 19, 1863, Walnut

Hills, Miss. Re-enlisted and re-mustered Jan. 23, 1864. Mustered out July 18, 1865, Louisville, Ky.

Esty, I. W. Rejected Aug. 8, 1861, by Mustering Officer. See company L, Second Cavalry.

COMPANY "B"

Eastburn, Charles. Age 36. Residence Rock Island, Ill, nativity Pennsylvania. Enlisted Sept. 2,
1861. Mustered Sept. 24, 1861. Wounded slightly in hand March 7, 1862, Pea Ridge, Ark.
Wounded in ear May 22, 1863, Vicksburg, Miss. Killed June 30, 1863, Vicksburg, Miss.

Easterly, Charles. Age 21. Residence Rome, nativity Ohio. Enlisted Aug. 12, 1861. Mustered
Sept. 24, 1861. Died of typhoid pneumonia Jan. 25, 1862, Hospital, Pacific, Mo.

Ensign, Devolso. Age 21. Residence Wyoming, nativity New York. Enlisted Aug. 23, 1861.
Mustered Sept. 24, 1861. Died April 12, 1862, Forsyth, Mo.

COMPANY "C"

Elson, James M. Age 21. Residence Palo, nativity Ohio. Enlisted Sept. 6, 1861, as Second
Corporal. Mustered Sept. 24, 1861. Promoted First Corporal March 8, 1862; Fourth Sergeant.
Wounded severely in thigh May 22, 1863, Vicksburg, Miss. Promoted Second Lieutenant May
23, 1863. Wounded severely in breast Aug. 17, 1864, Atlanta, Ga. Promoted First Lieutenant
Aug. 25, 1864. Mustered out April 6, 1865, Goldsboro, N. C.

Elson, Jerry E. Age 23. Residence Palo, nativity Ohio. Enlisted Aug. 1, 1861. Mustered Sept.
24, 1861. Slightly wounded in breast March 7, 1862, Pea Ridge, Ark. Promoted First Sergeant
May 29, 1863; Captain April 18, 1864. Mustered out July 18, 1865, Louisville, Ky.

Engle, Alonso K. Age 24. Residence Independence, nativity

Ohio. Enlisted Aug. 20, 1861.
Mustered Sept. 24, 1861. Died May 6, 1862, Cassville, Mo.
Engreman, John. Age 31. Residence Dubuque, nativity New York. Enlisted Sept. 12, 1861.
Mustered Sept. 24, 1861. Promoted Drum Major Sept. 12, 1861. Mustered out Dec. 15, 1862.
COMPANY "D"
East, Wiley H. Age 24. Residence Dubuque, nativity Indiana. Enlisted Aug. 26, 1861. Mustered
Sept. 2, 1861. Died of fever July 3, 1862, Jacksonport, Ark.
Edgington, Thomas J. Age 21. Residence Monticello, nativity Ohio. Enlisted Aug. 16, 1861.
Discharged for disability Jan. 18, 1862, Camp Heron, Mo. See company C, Forty-fourth Infantry.
45
Espy, Robert J. Age 19. Residence Scotch Grove, nativity Pennsylvania. Enlisted Feb. 22,
1864. Mustered Feb. 22, 1864. Wounded in arm severely Aug. 8, 1864, near Atlanta, Ga.
Mustered out July 18, 1865, Louisville, Ky.
Ewing, Milligan. (Veteran.) Age 16. Residence Monticello, nativity Pennsylvania. Enlisted
Aug. 16, 1861. Mustered Aug. 16, 1861. Re-enlisted and re-mustered Jan. 23, 1864. Promoted
Fifth Corporal Jan. 17, 1865; Fourth Corporal June 20, 1865. Mustered out July 18, 1865,
Louisville, Ky.
COMPANY "E"
Eilorck, Joseph. Age 23. Residence Elkader, nativity Hungary. Enlisted Nov. 18, 1861.
Discharged for disability Jan. 8, 1862, Pacific, Mo.
Eller, Daniel. Age 18. Residence Wandena, nativity New York. Enlisted Sept. 9, 1861.
Mustered Sept. 24, 1861. Died of fever Dec. 22, 1861, Pacific, Mo.
Eno, Joseph H. Age 22. Residence McGregor, nativity Canada. Enlisted Sept. 9, 1861, as First

Sergeant. Mustered Sept. 24, 1861. Discharged for disability May 9, 1862, Pacific, Mo.
Ewing, Joseph. Age 18. Residence Volga City, nativity Scotland. Enlisted Sept. 9, 1861.
Mustered Sept. 24, 1861. Mustered out July 18, 1865, Louisville, Ky.
COMPANY "F"
Eaton, Edwin. Age 18. Residence Fayette, nativity Indiana. Enlisted Feb. 29, 1864. Mustered
March 18, 1864. Mustered out July 18, 1865, Louisville, Ky.
Eaton, John C. Age 21. Residence Taylorville, nativity Michigan. Enlisted Sept. 5, 1861, as
Drummer. Mustered Sept. 14, 1861. Discharged for disability March 11, 1862, St. Louis, Mo.
Eggan, Nelson S. Age 26. Residence Eldorado, nativity Norway. Enlisted Sept. 4, 1861.
Mustered Sept. 12, 1861. Died of diarrhea May 14, 1862, Milliken's Bend, La. Buried in
National Cemetery, Vicksburg, Miss. Section E, grave 196,
England, Titus. (Veteran.) Age 21. Residence Arkansas, nativity Tennessee. Enlisted March 1,
1862. Mustered March 1, 1862. Re-enlisted and re-mustered Jan. 23, 1864. Taken prisoner May
27, 1864, Dallas, Ga. Died Oct. 24, 1864, Andersonville, Ga. Buried in National Cemetery,
Andersonville, Ga. Grave 11414.
Eriksen, Edward. Age 22. Residence Clermont, nativity Norway. Enlisted Feb. 25, 1864.
Mustered March 10, 1864. Mustered out July 18, 1865, Louisville, Ky.
COMPANY "G"
46
Eldredge, James R. Age 24. Residence Waverly, nativity New York. Enlisted Aug. 3, 1861, as
Drummer. Mustered Sept. 24, 1861. Transferred as Fifer to company H. See company M, Eighth

Cavalry. See company H.
Ellis, George W. (Veteran.) Age 24. Residence Waverly, nativity New York. Enlisted Aug. 20,
1861. Mustered Sept. 24, 1861. Re-enlisted and re-mustered Jan. 23, 1864. Mustered out July 18,
1865, Louisville, Ky.
Estell, Hiram. Age 19. Residence Waterloo, nativity Canada. Enlisted Aug. 16, 1861. Mustered
Sept. 24, 1861. Wounded mortally in breast and abdomen March 7, 1862, Pea Ridge, Ark. Died
of wounds July 20, 1862, Springfield, Mo.
COMPANY "H"
Eldredge, James R. Age 24. Residence Waverly, nativity New York. Enlisted Aug. 3, 1861.
Promoted Fifer Sept. 1, 1862. Discharged for disability Feb. 9, 1863, St. Louis, Mo. See
company G.
Ellingson, Lois A. Age 20. Residence Decorah, nativity Norway. Enlisted Aug. 21, 1861.
Mustered Sept. 24, 1861. Severely wounded May 22, 1863, Vicksburg, Miss. Died of wounds
May 24, 1863, Walnut Hills, Miss.
COMPANY "I"
Eagan, Michael. Age 38. Residence Des Moines, nativity Ireland. Enlisted Feb. 10, 1865.
Mustered Feb. 10, 1865. Transferred from company G, Twenty-fifth Infantry. Mustered out July
18, 1865, Louisville, Ky.
Eggleston, Orson F. Age 22. Residence Castalia, nativity New York. Enlisted Sept. 19, 1861.
Discharged for disability Sept. 19, 1863, Black River Bridge, Miss.
Elliott, Joel B. (Veteran.) Age 27. Residence Castalia, nativity Ohio. Enlisted Sept. 14, 1861.
Mustered Sept. 18, 1861. Re-enlisted and re-mustered Jan. 23, 1864. Mustered out July 18, 1865,
Louisville, Ky.

Everingham, William. Age 38. Residence Chickasaw, nativity Canada. Enlisted Aug. 13, 1861.
Mustered Sept. 18, 1861. Discharged for disability Oct. 13, 1862, St. Louis, Mo.
COMPANY "K"
Emmitt, George W. Age 21. Residence Lee County, nativity Iowa. Enlisted Oct. 24, 1864.
Mustered Oct. 24, 1864. Mustered out July 18, 1865, Louisville, Ky.
Erwin, George W. Age 29. Residence Johnson County, nativity New York. Enlisted Feb. 29,
1864. Mustered March 14, 1864. Discharged for disability July 1, 1865, Louisville, Ky.
47
Evans, Rufus. Age 23. Residence Marion, nativity Pennsylvania. Enlisted Sept. 14, 1861.
Mustered Sept. 24, 1861. Wounded severely in thigh May 22, 1863, Vicksburg, Miss. Died of
wounds June 8, 1863, Walnut Hills, Miss.
Evans, S. Hamilton. Age 20. Residence Marion, nativity Ohio. Enlisted Sept. 14, 1861.
Mustered Sept. 24, 1861. Wounded slightly in hand May 19, 1863, Vicksburg, Miss. Killed in
battle Nov. 27, 1863, Taylor's Ridge, Ga.
COMPANY "A"
Fisher, Ira. Age 18. Residence Maquoketa, nativity Ohio. Enlisted July 29, 1861. Mustered
Sept. 24, 1861. Wounded in shoulder May 19, 1863, Vicksburg, Miss. Mustered out Sept. 24,
1864, Davenport, Iowa, expiration of term of service.
Foster, Floyd W. Age 22. Residence Sabula, nativity Pennsylvania Enlisted Aug. 8, 1861.
Mustered Sept. 24, 1861. Promoted Sergeant Major Feb. 24, 1862; First Lieutenant of company
G, Aug. 5, 1863. See company G.
Fox, Thomas. Age 18. Residence Henry County, nativity Iowa.

Enlisted Feb. 5, 1864. Mustered
March 5, 1864. Mustered out July 18, 1865, Louisville, Ky. See company K, Twenty-fifth
Infantry.
Fuller, Sidney. Rejected Aug. 8, 1861, by Mustering Officer.
Fulton, Joseph. Age 20. Residence Sterling, nativity Ohio. Enlisted Sept. 7, 1861. Mustered
Sept. 24, 1861. Discharged for disability Sept. 15, 1863, Black River, Miss.

COMPANY "B"

Farley, Owen. Age 22. Residence Rome, nativity New York Enlisted Aug. 12, 1861, as Seventh
Corporal. Mustered Sept. 24, 1861. Promoted Sixth Corporal Aug. 1, 1862; Fifth Corporal Nov.
1, 1862; Fourth Corporal Dec. 8, 1862; Third Corporal March 20, 1863; Second Corporal May
23, 1863; First Corporal Dec. 1, 1863. Mustered out Sept. 24 1864, Davenport, Iowa, expiration
of term of service
Finch, Elkanah D. Age 26. Residence Fairview, nativity New York. Enlisted Aug. 12, 1861.
Mustered Sept. 24, 1861. Discharged March 20, 1862, Hospital, Pacific, Mo.
Finch, Irwin. (Veteran.) Age 19. Residence Fairview, nativity New York. Enlisted Aug. 12,
1861. Mustered Sept. 24, 1861. Re-enlisted and re-mustered Jan. 23, 1864. Promoted Third
Corporal April 6, 1865. Mustered out July 18, 1865, Louisville, Ky.
Fisher, Jonathan C. Age 25. Residence Pottawattamie County, nativity Illinois. Enlisted Nov.
5, 1864. Mustered Nov. 5, 1864. Mustered out July 18, 1865, Louisville, Ky.
Freeman Hanibal. Age 26. Residence Jones County, nativity Ohio. Enlisted Nov. 25, 1861.
Discharged for disability April 18, 1862, Cassville, Mo.

48

Fry, Enoch. (Veteran.) Age 30. Residence Fairview, nativity Ohio. Enlisted Sept. 12, 1861.
Mustered Sept. 24, 1861. Wounded in arm May 22, 1863, Vicksburg, Miss. Re-enlisted and remustered
Jan. 23, 1864. Mustered out July 18, 1865, Louisville, Ky.
Fuller, Oliver N. Age 33. Residence Oxford, nativity New York. Enlisted Aug. 12, 1861.
Mustered Sept. 24, 1861. Died Oct. 15, 1863, Cairo, Ill. Buried in Mound City National
Cemetery, Ill. Section A, grave 471.
COMPANY "C"
Fary, Edwin. Age 22. Residence Brandon, nativity New York. Enlisted Aug. 28, 1861.
Mustered Sept. 24, 1861. Died May 13, 1862, Rolla, Mo.
Fary, Enoch. Age 18. Residence Brandon, nativity Illinois. Enlisted Aug. 10, 1861. Mustered
Sept. 24, 1861. Discharged June 20, 1862, Rolla, Mo.
Fletcher, Thomas J. Age 18. Residence Pella, nativity Indiana. Enlisted Oct. 5, 1864. Mustered
Oct. 13, 1864. Mustered out July 18, 1865, Louisville, Ky. See company H, Twenty-fifth
Infantry.
Ford, John H. Age 30. Residence Fairbank, nativity Pennsylvania. Enlisted Aug. 6, 1861.
Mustered Sept. 24, 1861. Wounded severely in leg and arm March 22, 1863, Vicksburg, Miss.
Died of wounds June 24, 1863, Vicksburg, Miss.
Freeman, Reuben E. Age 18. Residence Independence, nativity New York. Enlisted Aug. 1,
1861. Mustered Sept. 24, 1861. Died Dec. 13, 1861, Pacific, Mo. Buried in National Cemetery,
Franklin, Mo.
Freyberthauser, George. Age 27. Residence Dubuque, nativity Iowa. Enlisted Sept. 21, 1861.
Mustered Sept. 24, 1861. Killed in battle May 22, 1863, Vicksburg,

Miss.
Fuller, Archiphus. Rejected Aug. 31, 1861, by Mustering Officer.
Furcht, Julius. Age 19. Residence Independence, nativity Iowa. Enlisted Aug. 20, 1861.
Mustered Sept. 24, 1861. Killed in battle March 7, 1862, Pea Ridge, Ark.
COMPANY "D"
Fillson, Robert F. Age 18. Residence Scotch Grove, nativity Illinois. Enlisted Feb. 25, 1864.
Mustered March 17, 1864. Died Aug. 13, 1864, Atlanta, Ga. Buried in National Cemetery,
Marietta, Ga. Section H, grave 40.
Fraser, Francis P. (Veteran.) Age 24. Residence Cedar Rapids, nativity Michigan. Enlisted
Aug. 26, 1861. Mustered Sept. 2, 1861. Promoted Third Corporal April 28, 1863; Second
Corporal Aug. 4, 1863. Re-enlisted and re-mustered Jan. 23, 1864. Promoted First Corporal Jan.
49
30, 1864; Fifth Sergeant July 1, 1864; Third Sergeant Oct. 1, 1864; Second Sergeant June 20,
1865. Mustered out July 18, 1865, Louisville, Ky.
Fuller, Charles. Age 18. Residence Monticello, nativity New York. Enlisted Sept. 23, 1861.
Mustered Sept. 23, 1861. Discharged for disability July 24, 1862, St. Louis, Mo.
Fuller, William. Age 18. Residence Monticello, nativity New York. Enlisted Aug. 16, 1861.
Mustered Sept. 2, 1861. Wounded severely in breast March 7, 1862, Pea Ridge, Ark. Discharged
for wounds Aug. 20, 1862, St. Louis, Mo.
COMPANY "E"
Fisher, Thomas. Age 38. Residence Clayton County, nativity Pennsylvania. Enlisted Feb. 1,
1865. Mustered Feb. 1, 1865. Mustered out July 18, 1865, Louisville, Ky.

Flannagan, James. Age 25. Residence Elkader, nativity Ireland. Enlisted Sept. 9, 1861, as
Fourth Sergeant. Mustered Sept. 24, 1861. Slightly wounded March 7, 1862, Pea Ridge, Ark.
Deserted March 6, 1863.
Fobes, Warren S. Age 21. Residence Elkader, nativity Ohio. Enlisted Sept. 10, 1861. Mustered
Sept. 24, 1861. Died Dec. 24, 1861, Pacific, Mo.
Ford, George W. Age 37. Residence Farmersburg, nativity New York. Enlisted Sept. 12, 1861.
Mustered Sept. 24, 1861. Wounded in right hand and thigh May 22, 1863, Vicksburg, Miss.
Transferred to Invalid Corps Feb. 15, 1864. Mustered out Sept. 23, 1864, Rock Island, Ill.
Freeman, Robert E. Age 39. Residence Volga City, nativity New York. Enlisted Sept. 9, 1861,
as Third Sergeant. Mustered Sept. 24, 1861. Discharged for disability June 5, 1862, St. Louis,
Mo.
Fuller, David C. Age 43. Residence Volga City, nativity New York. Enlisted Sept. 2, 1862.
Mustered Sept. 24, 1862. Died Oct. 5, 1863, Corinth, Miss. Buried in Union National Cemetery,
Corinth, Miss. Section A, grave 266.
Fuller, Eleazer. (Veteran.) Age 18. Residence Cox Creek, nativity New York. Enlisted Sept. 24,
1861. Mustered Sept. 24, 1861. Re-enlisted and re-mustered Jan. 23, 1864. Mustered out July 18,
1865, Louisville, Ky.
COMPANY "F"
Farnsworth, James B. Age 21. Residence Decorah, nativity New York. Enlisted Sept. 6, 1861,
as First Corporal. Mustered Sept. 12, 1861. Discharged for disability Aug. 14, 1862, St. Louis,
Mo.
Finch, Laben. Age 25. Residence West Union, nativity

Connecticut. Enlisted Aug. 27, 1861.
Mustered Sept. 12, 1861. Died Feb. 27, 1862, Cross Hollows, Ark. Buried in National Cemetery,
Fayetteville, Ark. Section 2, grave 50.
50
Finney, William H. Age 20. Residence Fayette, nativity Vermont. Enlisted Aug. 27, 1861.
Mustered Sept. 12, 1861. Killed in battle May 27, 1863, Vicksburg, Miss.
Franklin, James L. Age 18. Residence West Union, nativity Iowa. Enlisted Aug. 27, 1861.
Mustered Sept. 12, 1861. Died of typhoid fever Nov. 3, 1861, Pacific, Mo.
COMPANY "G"
Figg, Lewis M. (Veteran.) Age 22. Residence Waverly, nativity New York. Enlisted Aug. 10,
1861. Mustered Sept. 24, 1861. Re-enlisted and re-mustered Jan. 23, 1864. Mustered out July 18,
1865, Louisville, Ky.
Fordney, Francis. Age 27. Residence Burlington, nativity Virginia. Enlisted Oct. 7, 1864.
Mustered Oct. 7, 1864. Mustered out July 18, 1865, Louisville, Ky. See company G, Twentyfifth
Infantry.
Foster, Floyd W. Age 22. Residence Waverly, nativity Pennsylvania. Appointed First
Lieutenant from Sergeant Major Aug. 5, 1863. Mustered Sept. 4, 1863. Wounded in right arm
severely May 13, 1864, Resaca, Ga. Discharged Sept. 17, 1864. See company A.
Fowler, James T. Age 18. Residence Delaware County, nativity Illinois. Enlisted July 28, 1861,
as Wagoner. Mustered Sept. 24, 1861. Mustered out Sept. 24, 1864, East Point, Ga., expiration
of term of service.
Fowler, Milton F. (Veteran.) Age 24. Residence Delaware

County, nativity Illinois. Enlisted
July 28, 1861. Mustered Sept. 24, 1861. Promoted Fourth
Sergeant; Third Sergeant. Re-enlisted
and re-mustered Jan. 23, 1864. Wounded in head severely July
22, 1864, Atlanta, Ga. Promoted
Second Sergeant Oct. 1, 1864. Mustered out July 18, 1865,
Louisville, Ky.
COMPANY "H"
Filley, William. Age 21. Residence Frankville, nativity
Connecticut. Enlisted Sept. 10, 1861.
Mustered Sept. 24, 1861. Promoted Seventh Corporal Jan. 1, 1863.
Wounded slightly in leg
March 22, 1863, Vicksburg, Miss. Promoted Second Corporal
April 2, 1863; Fourth Sergeant;
Third Sergeant April 2, 1863. Mustered out Sept. 24, 1864,
Davenport, Iowa, expiration of term
of service.
Foos, William. Age 24. Residence Anamosa, nativity Indiana.
Enlisted Sept. 23, 1861. Mustered
Sept. 24, 1861. Discharged Nov. 26, 1862, St. Louis, Mo.
Franey, William. Age 40. Residence Dubuque, nativity Ireland.
Enlisted Aug. 28, 1861.
Mustered Sept. 24, 1861. Discharged for disability March 15,
1862, St. Louis, Mo.
COMPANY I
51
Fellows, Samuel. Age 32. Residence New Oregon, nativity New
York. Appointed First
Lieutenant Sept. 2, 1861. Mustered Sept. 2, 1861. Resigned June
13,1862, Red River, Ark.
Fenton, Joseph H. Age 26. Residence New Oregon, nativity New
York. Enlisted Aug. 19, 1861.
Mustered Sept. 18, 1861. Discharged July 19,1862, St. Louis, Mo.
Fontz, Asbury. Age 19. Residence Taylor County, nativity Iowa.
Enlisted Oct. 19, 1864.
Mustered Oct. 19, 1864. Mustered out July 18, 1865, Louisville,

Ky.
Francis, Daniel A. Age 23. Residence Foreston, nativity Michigan. Enlisted Aug. 18, 1861.
Mustered Sept. 18, 1861. Discharged for disability July 13, 1862, St. Louis, Mo.
Freeburn, John P. Age 19. Residence Maysville, nativity Illinois. Enlisted Sept. 20, 1861.
Mustered Sept. 20, 1861. Wounded in right ankle May 22, 1863, Vicksburg, Miss. Discharged
Sept. 24, 1864, Davenport, Iowa, expiration of term of service.
Fultz, Thomas E. Age 28. Residence Castalia, nativity Pennsylvania. Enlisted Sept. 23,1861.
Transferred to Invalid Corps Dec. 15, 1863. Mustered out Sept. 19, 1864, Detroit, Mich.
COMPANY K
Farrington, Thomas A. (Veteran.) Age 33. Residence Manchester, nativity Iowa. Enlisted July
31, 1861, as Fourth Sergeant. Mustered Sept. 24, 1861. Re-enlisted and re-mustered Jan. 24,
1864. Promoted Second Sergeant May 3, 1864. Mustered out July 18, 1865, Louisville, Ky.
COMPANY A
Gordon, Stephen. Rejected Aug. 8, 1861, by Mustering Officer
Gray, Thomas. Age 18. Residence Sabula, nativity Alabama. Enlisted Aug. 8, 1861. Mustered
Sept. 24, 1861. Mustered out Sept. 24, 1864, East Point, Ga., expiration of term of service.
Green, John H. Age 21. Residence Wyoming, nativity Iowa. Enlisted Aug. 3, 1861, as Fifth
Sergeant. Mustered Sept. 2, 1861. Promoted Fourth Sergeant March 3, 1862; Third Sergeant
March 10, 1862; Second Sergeant June 7, 1863; First Lieutenant Aug. 8, 1863. Mustered out July
18,1865, Louisville, Ky.
Grindrod, Joshua. (Veteran.) Age 28. Residence Wyoming, nativity England. Enlisted Aug. 14,

1861. Mustered Sept. 24, 1861. Re-enlisted and re-mustered Jan. 23, 1864. Mustered out July 18,
1865, Louisville, Ky.
Groat, Thomas P. (Veteran.) Age 25. Residence Maquoketa, nativity New York. Enlisted Aug.
14, 1861. Mustered Sept. 24, 1861. Re-enlisted and re-mustered Jan. 23, 1864. Promoted Fifth
Corporal May 27, 1865. Mustered out July 18, 1865, Louisville, Ky.
52
Grote, Henry A. Age 30. Residence Maquoketa, nativity Hanover. Enlisted Aug. 14, 1861.
Mustered Sept. 24, 1861. Wounded severely in head March 7, 1862, Pea Ridge, Ark. Discharged
for wounds July 3, 1862, St. Louis, Mo.
Guenther, Jacob H. Age 20. Residence Sabula, nativity Pennsylvania. Enlisted Aug. 10, 1861.
Mustered Sept. 24, 1861. Promoted Eighth Corporal March 10, 1862; Sixth Corporal June 7,
1863; Fifth Corporal; Fourth Corporal Dec. 17, 1863. Mustered out Sept. 24, 1864, East Point,
Ga., expiration of term of service.
Guist, William H. H. (Veteran.) Age 20. Residence Sabula, nativity Pennsylvania. Enlisted
Aug. 8,1861. Mustered Sept. 24,1861. Re-enlisted and re-mustered Jan. 23, 1864. Mustered out
July 18, 1865, Louisville, Ky.
COMPANY B
Gault, Moses. Age 28. Residence Rome, nativity Pennsylvania. Enlisted Aug. 21, 1861.
Mustered Sept. 24, 1861. Died March 11, 1863, Young's Point, La.
Gilmore, Charles. Age 3 0. Residence Pottawattamie County, nativity Ireland. Enlisted Nov. 5,
1864. Mustered Nov. 5, 1864. Mustered out July 18, 1865, Louisville, Ky.
Gipert, Jacob. Age 21. Residence Pottawattamie County, nativity

Germany. Enlisted Nov. 5,
1864. Mustered Nov. 5, 1864. Mustered out July 18, 1865, Louisville, Ky.

Flick, William H. Age 20. Residence Hale, nativity Indiana. Enlisted Aug. 12, 1861. Mustered
Sept. 24, 1861. Promoted Eighth Corporal April 24, 1863; Fifth Corporal May 23, 1863.
Wounded in left shoulder severely Nov. 25, 1863, Missionary Ridge, Tenn. Promoted Fourth
Corporal; Third Corporal Dec. 1, 1863. Mustered out Sept. 24, 1864, Nashville, Tenn.

Gorsuch, Andrew F. Age 18. Residence Louisa County, nativity Tennessee. Enlisted Feb. 29,
1864. Mustered March 4, 1864. Discharged for disability July 1, 1865, Louisville, Ky. See
company I, Twenty-fifth Infantry.

Graham, William J. (Veteran.) Age 18. Residence Fairview, nativity Iowa. Enlisted Aug. 12,
1861. Mustered Sept. 24, 1861. Wounded slightly in thumb May 22, 1863, Vicksburg, Miss.
Wounded slightly in shoulder Nov. 27, 1863, Ringgold, Ga. Re-enlisted and re-mustered Jan. 23,
1864. Promoted Fifth Sergeant Jan. 20, 1864; First Sergeant April 6, 1865. Mustered out July 18,
1865, Louisville, Ky.

Green, Albert. Age 19. Residence Canton, nativity Ohio. Enlisted 17, 1864. Mustered March
17, 1861. Wounded in action severely March 21, 1865, Bentonville, N. C. Discharged March 30,
1865, Troy, N.Y.

Green, Benton. Age 27. Residence Oxford, nativity Indiana. Enlisted Aug. 25, 1861. Mustered
Sept. 24, 1861. Discharged for disability Jan. 27, 1862, Pacific Hospital, Mo.

53

Green, Jasper. Age 19. Residence Wyoming, nativity Ohio.

Enlisted Sept. 24, 1861. Mustered
Sept. 24, 1861. Discharged for disability April 23,1863, Memphis, Tenn.
COMPANY "C"
Gard, Isaac. Age 18. Residence Buchanan County, nativity Iowa. Enlisted Feb. 28, 1864.
Mustered March 16, 1864. Wounded severely June 14, 1864, Big Shanty, Ga. Discharged June
19, 1865, Indianapolis, Ind.
Gillum, William C. Age 21. Residence Brandon, nativity Indiana. Enlisted Aug. 22, 1861.
Mustered Sept. 24, 1861. Died of chronic diarrhea Jan. 15, 1864, Memphis, Tenn. Buried in
Mississippi River National Cemetery, Memphis, Tenn. Section I, grave 166.
Godfrey, Door E. Age 18. Residence Buffalo Grove, nativity Illinois. Enlisted Aug. 27, 1862.
Mustered Aug. 27, 1862. Mustered out June 4, 1865, Washington, D. C.
Greek, David. Age 19. Residence Brandon, nativity Germany. Enlisted Aug. 10, 1861, as
Drummer. Mustered Sept. 24, 1861. Wounded slightly in ankle March 7, 1862, Pea Ridge, Ark.
Mustered out Sept. 26, 1864, East Point, Ga., expiration of term of service.
Green, Nimrod A. (Veteran.) Age 23. Residence Union, nativity Ohio. Enlisted Aug. 3, 1861.
Mustered Sept. 24, 1861. Promoted Eighth Corporal; Second Corporal. Re-enlisted and remustered
Jan. 23, 1864. Discharged for disability June 14, 1865, Louisville, Ky.
COMPANY "D"
Gale, William L. Age 19. Residence Monticello, nativity New York. Enlisted Aug. 29, 1861.
Discharged for disability Jan. 18, 1862, Camp Heron, Mo.
Gibson, Hiram H. Age 21. Residence Monticello, nativity

Pennsylvania. Enlisted Sept. 22,
1861. Mustered Sept. 22, 1861. Wounded slightly in hand March 7, 1862, Pea Ridge, Ark.
Discharged Sept. 10, 1863, Black River Bridge, Miss.
Gilbert, Amos D. Age 19. Residence Wyoming, nativity New York. Enlisted Aug. 16, 1861.
Mustered Sept. 2, 1861. Taken prisoner March 14, 1864, Claysville, Ala. Died Dec. 9, 1864.
Buried in National Cemetery, Annapolis, Md.
Gilbert, Fred D. Age 22. Residence Wyoming, nativity New York. Enlisted Aug. 29, 1861.
Mustered Sept. 2, 1861. Promoted Fourth Corporal March 7, 1863; Third Corporal Jan. 24, 1863;
First Sergeant April 28, 1863. Killed in battle May 22, 1863, Vicksburg, Miss.
Gillaspie, Henry. Age 20. Residence Plattville, nativity Kentucky. Enlisted Nov. 5, 1864.
Mustered Nov. 5, 1864. Died Jan. 29, 1865, Savannah, Ga. Buried in National Cemetery,
Beaufort, S. C.
Glenn, William C. M. Age 25. Residence Scotch Grove, nativity Pennsylvania. Enlisted as
Third Corporal. Mustered Sept. 2, 1861. Wounded slightly in shoulder March 7, 1862, Pea
54
Ridge, Ark. Promoted Fourth Sergeant April 4, 1862. Died Aug. 2, 1862, camp near Helena,
Ark.
Green, Joseph E. Age 19. Residence Monticello, nativity Iowa. Enlisted Aug. 26, 1861.
Mustered Sept. 2, 1861. Died of measles Nov. 28, 1861, General Hospital, St. Louis, Mo. Buried
in National Cemetery, St. Louis, Mo.
Gridley, Charles. (Veteran.) Age 19. Residence Wyoming, nativity Indiana. Enlisted Aug. 19,
1861. Mustered Sept. 2, 1861. Promoted Fifth Corporal April 29,

1863; Fourth Corporal Aug. 4,
1863. Re-enlisted and re-mustered Jan. 25, 1864. Promoted Second Corporal Jan. 30, 1864; First
Corporal July 1, 1864; Fourth Sergeant Oct. 1, 1864; Third Sergeant June 20, 1865. Mustered out
July 18, 1865, Louisville, Ky.
Groves, James. Age 18. Residence Mount Pleasant, nativity Virginia. Enlisted June 29, 1864.
Mustered July 8, 1864. Mustered out July 18, 1865, Louisville, Ky. See company H, Twentyfifth
Infantry.
COMPANY "E"
Gager, Edward L. Age 26. Residence Clayton County, nativity New York. Mustered Sept. 24,
1861. Discharged for disability Sept. 7, 1862, Black River, Miss.
Gannon, Thomas. (Veteran.) Age 30. Residence Franklin, Mo., nativity Ireland. Enlisted Nov.
17, 1861. Re-enlisted and re-mustered Jan. 23, 1864. Mustered out July 18, 1865, Louisville, Ky.
Gardner, Ralph B. (Veteran.) Age 27. Residence Fredericksburg, nativity Pennsylvania.
Enlisted Aug. 14, 1862. Mustered Sept. 11, 1862. Promoted Fourth Corporal Jan. 23, 1864. Reenlisted
and re-mustered Jan. 23, 1864. Promoted Third Corporal May 27, 1864; Second
Corporal Jan. 4, 1865. Mustered out July 18, 1865, Louisville, Ky.
Garretson, John H. (Veteran.) Age 20. Residence Volga City, nativity Pennsylvania. Enlisted
Sept. 9, 1861. Mustered Sept. 24, 1861. Promoted Fourth Corporal June 18, 1862; Third
Corporal; Second Corporal June 18, 1862; First Corporal. Wounded in side severely May 22,
1863, near Vicksburg, Miss. Re-enlisted and re-mustered Jan. 23, 1864. Promoted Fifth Sergeant
Jan. 23, 1864; First Lieutenant Jan. 1, 1865; Captain Jan. 24, 1865. Mustered out July 18, 1865,

Louisville, Ky.
Garretson, Joseph. (Veteran.) Age 24. Residence Volga City, nativity Pennsylvania. Enlisted
Sept. 9, 1861, as Sixth Corporal. Mustered Sept. 24, 1861. Promoted First Sergeant March 10,
1862. Re-enlisted and re-mustered Jan. 23, 1864. Mustered out July 18, 1865, Louisville, Ky.
Gragg, Thomas J. (Veteran.) Age 18. Residence Wandena, nativity Ohio. Enlisted Nov. 20,
1861. Mustered Nov. 20, 1861. Wounded slightly in head March 7, 1862, Pea Ridge, Ark. Reenlisted
and re-mustered Jan. 23, 1864. Mustered out July 18, 1865, Louisville, Ky.
Greeley, Albert. Age 30. Residence Cox Creek, nativity Vermont. Enlisted Sept. 25, 1861.
Mustered Sept. 25, 1861. Discharged March 15, 1862, Clayton, Iowa.
55
Green, George. Age 18. Residence Elkader, nativity Ohio. Enlisted Sept. 10, 1861. Mustered
Sept. 24, 1861. Died in Marine Hospital Nov. 17, 1862, St. Louis, Mo. Buried in National
Cemetery, Jefferson Barracks, Mo. Section 50, grave 22.
Grupe, Durbin. Age 18. Residence Burlington, nativity Germany. Enlisted Dec. 31, 1863.
Mustered Dec. 31, 1863. Mustered out July 18, 1865, Louisville, Ky. See company G, Twentyfifth
Infantry.
Gulford, Richard. Age 25. Residence Clayton County, nativity England. Enlisted Feb. 29, 1864.
Mustered March 10, 1864. Promoted Seventh Corporal Jan. 5, 1865; Fifth Corporal Jan. 25,
1865. Mustered out July 18, 1865, Louisville, Ky.
COMPANY "F"
Gale, Luther H. Age 18. Residence West Union, nativity Ohio. Enlisted Sept. 8, 1861. Mustered

Sept. 12, 1861. Mustered out Sept. 24, 1864, East Point, Ga., expiration of term of service.
Gardner, Andrew J. Age 30. Residence Fayette, nativity New York. Enlisted Sept. 5, 1861.
Mustered Sept. 12, 1861. Died of chronic diarrhea March 16, 1863, Young's Point, La.
Gardner, Joseph J. (Veteran.) Age 18. Residence Fayette, nativity Wisconsin. Enlisted Sept. 5,
1861. Mustered Sept. 12, 1861. Wounded slightly in leg March 7, 1862, Pea Ridge, Ark.
Wounded slightly in knee May 22, 1863, Vicksburg, Miss. Re-enlisted and re-mustered Jan. 23,
1864. Mustered out July 18, 1865, Louisville, Ky.
Gardner, William G. Age 24. Residence Fayette, nativity Indiana. Enlisted Sept. 5, 1861.
Mustered Sept. 12, 1861. Discharged for disability Feb. 17, 1863, St. Louis, Mo.
Gee, George W. (Veteran.) Age 19. Residence Dubuque, nativity New York. Enlisted Sept. 5,
1861. Mustered Sept. 12, 1861. Re-enlisted and re-mustered Jan. 23, 1864. Mustered out July 18,
1865, Louisville, Ky.
German, David. Age 21. Residence Taylorville, nativity Iowa. Enlisted Sept. 5, 1861. Mustered
Sept. 14, 1861. Killed in battle March 7, 1862, Pea Ridge, Ark.
Glass, Ole. Age 23. Residence Burr Oak, nativity Norway. Enlisted Nov. 21, 1861. Mustered
Jan. 7, 1862. Died of chronic diarrhea Aug. 9, 1862, Vicksburg, Miss.
Goesen, Lars. Age 20. Residence Clermont, nativity Norway. Enlisted Feb. 25, 1864. Mustered
March 10, 1864. Mustered out July 18, 1865, Louisville, Ky.
Guin, James W. (Veteran.) Age 22. Residence Taylorville, nativity Ohio. Enlisted Sept. 5, 1861.
Mustered Sept. 18, 1861. Promoted Third Sergeant. Wounded slightly in knee March 7, 1862,

Pea Ridge, Ark. Promoted First Sergeant Oct. 6, 1863. Re-enlisted and re-mustered Jan. 23,
1864. Promoted First Lieutenant Jan. 1, 1865; Captain March 30, 1865. Mustered out July 18,
1865, Louisville, Ky.
56
Gunsaulus, Alfred C. (Veteran.) Age 20. Residence Fayette County, nativity Pennsylvania.
Enlisted Sept. 8, 1861. Mustered Sept. 12, 1861. Promoted Eighth Corporal July 1, 1862; Third
Corporal March 12, 1863; Fifth Sergeant Oct. 6, 1863. Re-enlisted and re-mustered Jan. 23,
1864. Promoted Commissary Sergeant April 5, 1865; Quartermaster Sergeant April 28, 1865.
Mustered out July 18, 1865, Louisville, Ky.
COMPANY "G"
Gibson, James M. Age 18. Residence Garnavillo, nativity Illinois. Enlisted Dec. 13, 1862.
Mustered Jan. 18, 1863. Died of pneumonia Feb. 7, 1864, Woodville, Ala.
Gieger, Arthur O. Age 20. Residence Des Moines, nativity Germany. Enlisted Jan. 16, 1864.
Mustered Jan. 16, 1864. Mustered out July 18, 1865, Louisville, Ky. See company G, Twentyfifth
Infantry.
Gilham, Jordan. (Veteran.) Age 20. Residence Delaware County, nativity Illinois. Enlisted
Aug. 20, 1861. Mustered Sept. 24, 1861. Re-enlisted and re-mustered March 17, 1864. Promoted
Seventh Corporal Jan. 5, 1865; Sixth Corporal May 1, 1865. Mustered out July 18, 1865,
Louisville, Ky.
Gilham, William. Age 22. Residence Delaware County, nativity Illinois. Enlisted Aug. 10,
1861. Mustered Sept. 24, 1861. Transferred to Invalid Corps March 15, 1864.

Gipe, James H. Age 21. Residence Spring Creek, nativity Pennsylvania. Enlisted Aug. 12, 1861.
Mustered Sept. 24, 1861. Promoted First Corporal March 28, 1862. Wounded severely in thigh,
head and hand May 22, 1863, Vicksburg, Miss. Mustered out Sept. 24, 1864, East Point, Ga.,
expiration of term of service.
Green, Abijah B. (Veteran.) Age 24. Residence Janesville, nativity Illinois. Enlisted Aug. 10,
1861. Mustered Sept. 24, 1861. Re-enlisted and re-mustered Jan. 1, 1864. Discharged June 30,
1865, Louisville, Ky.
COMPANY "H"
Gates, Ambrose H. (Veteran.) Age 20. Residence Hesper, nativity Canada. Enlisted Aug. 21,
1861. Mustered Sept. 24, 1861. Wounded slightly in side March 7, 1862, Pea Ridge, Ark.
Promoted Fifth Sergeant Jan. 1, 1863; Second Sergeant March 14, 1863. Re-enlisted and remustered
Jan. 23, 1864. Mustered out July 18, 1865, Louisville, Ky.
Gay, Kingsbury. Age 37. Residence Mahaska County, nativity Indiana. Enlisted Nov. 2, 1864.
Mustered Nov. 2, 1864. Mustered out July 18, 1865, Louisville, Ky.
Gibbs, Cyrus C. Age 18. Residence Decorah, nativity Ohio. Enlisted Sept. 10, 1861. Mustered
Sept. 24, 1861. Discharged for disability Jan. 11 1862, Pacific, Mo. See company G, First
Cavalry.
57
Gillan, Zachariah. Age 19. Residence Burr Oak, nativity Indiana. Enlisted March 17, 1864.
Mustered March 17, 1864. Wounded mortally in right knee June 16, 1864, Big Shanty, Ga. Died
June 30, 1864, Chattanooga, Tenn. Buried in National Cemetery, Chattanooga, Tenn. Section E,

grave 335.
Graham, Henry R. Age 18. Residence Decorah, nativity Ohio. Enlisted Aug. 21, 1861.
Mustered Sept. 24, 1861. Discharged for disability Jan. 11, 1862, Pacific, Mo.
Green, Levi A. (Veteran.) Age 18. Residence Allamakee County, nativity Pennsylvania.
Enlisted Sept. 10, 1861. Mustered Sept. 24, 1861. Re-enlisted and re-mustered Jan. 23, 1864.
Promoted Sixth Corporal June 1, 1865. Mustered out July 18, 1865, Louisville, Ky.
Gregory, Nathan. Age 33. Residence Hopeville, nativity Indiana. Enlisted Nov. 2, 1864.
Mustered Nov. 2, 1864. Mustered out July 18, 1865, Louisville, Ky.
Grundy, Henry. Age 33. Residence Decorah, nativity Pennsylvania. Enlisted Sept. 10, 1861.
Mustered Sept. 24, 1861. Discharged for disability July 16, 1862, Helena, Ark.
COMPANY "I"
Garver, David. (Veteran.) Age 20. Residence Foreston, nativity Pennsylvania. Enlisted Aug. 19,
1861. Mustered Sept. 18, 1861. Promoted Sixth Corporal Dec. 20, 1862; Fifth Corporal; Third
Corporal July 1, 1863; Second Corporal Oct. 6, 1863. Re-enlisted and re-mustered Jan. 23, 1864.
Promoted First Corporal Sept. 16, 1864. Mustered out July 18, 1865, Louisville, Ky.
Gates, Martin. Age 24. Residence Utica, nativity New York. Enlisted Aug. 16, 1861, as Fifth
Sergeant. Mustered Sept. 2, 1861. Wounded severely in shoulder March 7, 1862, Pea Ridge, Ark.
Died of wounds March 23, 1862, Springfield, Mo.
Gemmill, John. Age 18. Residence McGregor, nativity Scotland. Enlisted Aug. 24, 1861.
Mustered Sept. 2, 1861. Promoted Eighth Corporal April 6, 1863.

Died of sun stroke May 13, 1863, Raymond, Miss.

Goodenough, John. Age 25. Residence Winneshiek County, nativity New York. Enlisted Sept. 4, 1861. Mustered Sept. 18, 1861. Killed in battle March 7, 1862, Pea Ridge, Ark. Buried in National Cemetery, Fayetteville, Ark. Section 2, grave 28.

Griffin, Daniel P. Age 25. Residence New Oregon, nativity Canada. Enlisted Aug. 22, 1861, as Fifth Corporal. Mustered Sept. 18, 1861. Promoted Second Corporal June 23, 1862; Third Sergeant July 24, 1862. Discharged for chronic diarrhea Dec. 9, 1862, Helena, Ark.

COMPANY "K"

Gardner, Edwin. Age 17. Residence Linn County, nativity New York. Enlisted Feb. 23, 1864. Mustered Feb. 23, 1864. Mustered out July 18, 1865, Louisville, Ky.

58

Gibson, Victor. Age 22. Residence Center Point, nativity Ohio. Enlisted Sept. 14, 1861. Mustered Sept. 24, 1861. Promoted Drummer. Discharged Sept. 1, 1862, St. Louis, Mo.

Gieger, Lewis P. Age 18. Residence Des Moines, nativity Germany. Enlisted Jan. 16, 1865. Mustered Jan. 16, 1865. Mustered out July 18, 1865, Louisville, Ky. See company G, Twentyfifth Infantry.

Granger, Albert E. Age 20. Residence Marion, nativity Vermont. Enlisted Aug. 20, 1862. Mustered Aug. 20, 1862. Died of typhoid fever Nov. 30, 1862, Helena, Ark.

Granger, George. Age 23. Residence Marion, nativity Vermont. Enlisted Sept. 14, 1861, as First Sergeant. Mustered Sept. 24, 1861. Promoted First Lieutenant Oct. 17, 1862; Captain

March 20, 1863; Major Jan. 9, 1864. Died Dec. 6, 1864, Nashville, Tenn. See Vol. VII, Roll of
Honor.
Gray, Henry H. (Veteran.) Age 19. Residence Marion, nativity Iowa. Enlisted Sept. 24, 1861.
Mustered Sept. 24, 1861. Promoted Seventh Corporal Nov. 19, 1861; Quartermaster Sergeant
Feb. 1, 1863. Re-enlisted and re-mustered Jan. 23, 1864. Promoted Quartermaster Jan. 9, 1865.
Mustered out July 18, 1865, Louisville, Ky.
Gray, John W. Age 29. Residence Marion, nativity Kentucky. Enlisted Sept. 24 1861. Mustered
Sept. 24, 1861. Wounded slightly in head March 7, 1862, Pea Ridge, Ark. Discharged for
disability July 17, 1862, Pacific City, Mo.
Greenly, George. Age 22. Residence Cottage Hill, nativity England. Enlisted Sept. 14, 1861.
Mustered Sept. 24, 1861. Promoted Sixth Corporal March 3, 1864; Second Corporal Jan. 1,
1865. Mustered out July 18, 1865, Louisville, Ky.
Greenly, William. Age 22. Residence Cottage Hill, nativity England. Enlisted Aug. 28, 1861.
Mustered Sept. 24, 1861. Wounded severely in wrist and upper part of arm March 7, 1862, Pea
Ridge, Ark. Discharged Oct. 14, 1862, Keokuk, Iowa.
Gunn, John A. (Veteran.) Age 18. Residence Marion, nativity Illinois. Mustered Sept. 24, 1861.
Re-enlisted and re-mustered Jan. 23, 1864. Mustered out July 18, 1865, Louisville, Ky.
COMPANY "A"
Hamilton, James S. Age 20. Residence Andrew, nativity Pennsylvania. Enlisted Aug. 10, 1861.
Mustered Sept. 24, 1861. Mustered out Sept. 24, 1864, East Point, Ga., expiration of term of
service.
Harcourt, Silas. Rejected Aug. 8, 1861, by Mustering Officer.

Harvey, James T. Age 18. Residence Jackson County, nativity Illinois. Enlisted Feb. 13, 1864.
Mustered March 1, 1864. Wounded in arm slightly Aug. 31, 1864, Jonesboro, Ga. Mustered out
July 18, 1865, Louisville, Ky.
59
Hodge, Jonathan D. Age 23. Residence Maquoketa, nativity Pennsylvania. Enlisted Aug. 13,
1861. Mustered Sept. 24, 1861. Mustered out Sept. 24, 1864, East Point, Ga., expiration of term
of service.
Holloway, Daniel. Age 37. Residence Boone County, nativity North Carolina. Enlisted Nov. 13,
1864. Mustered Nov. 13, 1864. Mustered out July 18, 1865, Louisville, Ky.
Hopkins, William H. Age 21. Residence Spragueville, nativity New York. Enlisted July 29,
1861. Mustered Sept. 24, 1861. Wounded slightly in arm Nov. 25, 1863, Missionary Ridge,
Tenn. Mustered out Sept. 24, 1864, East Point, Ga., expiration of term of service.
COMPANY "B"
Hager, Horace. Age 18. Residence Oxford, nativity Pennsylvania. Enlisted Aug. 12, 1861.
Mustered Sept. 24, 1861. Discharged for disability July 4, 1862, St. Louis, Mo.
Hall, Andrew H. (Veteran.) Age 23. Residence Wayne, nativity Virginia. Enlisted Aug. 12,
1861. Mustered Sept. 24, 1861. Promoted Seventh Corporal May 22, 1863; Sixth Corporal; Fifth
Corporal Dec. 1, 1863; Third Corporal; Second Corporal May 1, 1863. Re-enlisted and remustered
Jan. 23, 1864. Promoted Third Sergeant April 6, 1865; Second Sergeant Aug. 1, 1865.
Mustered out July 18, 1865, Louisville, Ky.
Hammond, George. Age 37. Residence Jackson, nativity New

York. Enlisted Sept. 25 1861.
Mustered Sept. 25, 1861. Discharged Dec. 31, 1861, Hospital, Pacific, Mo.
Handy, Edward H. Age 42. Residence Rome, nativity New York. Enlisted Aug. 12, 1861, as
Fourth Sergeant. Mustered Sept. 24, 1861. Discharged for disability July 29, 1862, St. Louis,
Mo. See company G, Thirty-first Infantry.
Harrison, Albertus U. (Veteran.) Age 18. Residence Jamestown Wis., nativity Wisconsin.
Enlisted Aug. 28, 1861. Mustered Sept. 24 1861. Wounded slightly in chin May 22, 1863,
Vicksburg, Miss. Re-enlisted and re-mustered Jan. 23, 1864. Promoted Fourth Corporal April 6,
1865. Mustered out July 18, 1865, Louisville, Ky.
Harrison, Benjamin F. Age 21. Residence Rome, nativity Ohio. Enlisted Aug. 12, 1861, as
Drummer. Mustered Sept. 24, 1861. Died of typhoid fever April 30, 1862, Forsythe, Mo.
Hart, James T. Age 22. Residence Keokuk County, nativity Maryland. Enlisted Nov. 12, 1864.
Mustered Nov. 12, 1864. Mustered out July 18, 1865, Louisville, Ky.
Hitchcock. Thomas N. (Veteran.) Age 18. Residence Hale, nativity England. Enlisted Aug. 12,
1861. Mustered Sept. 24, 1861. Re-enlisted and re-mustered Jan. 23, 1864. Taken prisoner May
27, 1864, Dallas, Ga. Died, date not given. Buried in National Cemetery, Chattanooga, Tenn.
Section L, grave 395.
60
Holmes, Austin C. Residence Washington, nativity Ohio. Enlisted March 17, 1865. Mustered
March 17, 1865. Mustered out July 18, 1865, Louisville, Ky. See company I, Twenty-fifth
Infantry.

Hornsby, Marion. Age 28. Residence Pottawattamie County, nativity Missouri. Enlisted Nov. 5,
1864. Mustered Nov. 5, 1864. Mustered out July 18, 1865, Louisville, Ky.
Hull, Benjamin E. Age 25. Residence Hale, nativity Indiana. Enlisted Aug. 12, 1861, as Second
Corporal. Mustered Sept. 24, 1861. Wounded slightly in face March 7, 1862, Pea Ridge, Ark.
Mustered out Sept. 24, 1864, East Point, Ga., expiration of term of service.
COMPANY "C"
Harter, Matthias. (Veteran.) Age 36. Residence Independence, nativity Ohio. Enlisted Aug. 27,
1862. Mustered Oct. 14, 1862. Re-enlisted and re-mustered Jan. 23, 1864. Mustered out July 26,
1865, Louisville, Ky.
Herrington, George. Age 29. Residence Independence, nativity Canada. Enlisted Aug. 27,
1862. Mustered Oct. 14, 1862. Died Aug. 31, 1863, Independence, Iowa.
Hightman, Charles H. Age 18. Residence Buchanan County, nativity New York. Enlisted
March 8, 1864. Mustered March S. 1864. Died April 14, 1864, Chattanooga, Tenn. Buried
National Cemetery, Nashville, Tenn. Section J, grave 506.
Hill, William O. Age 18. Residence Buchanan, nativity Illinois. Enlisted Feb. 29, 1864.
Mustered Feb. 29, 1864. Died Oct. 14, 1864, Chattanooga, Tenn. Buried in National Cemetery,
Chattanooga, Tenn. Section G, grave 81.
Hobert, Charles A. (Veteran.) Age 18. Residence Fairbanks, nativity Ohio. Enlisted Aug. 13,
1861. Mustered Sept. 24, 1861. Wounded in side slightly March 7, 1862, Pea Ridge, Ark. Reenlisted
and re-mustered Feb. 15, 1864. Mustered out July 18, 1865, Louisville, Ky.

Holland, Eli. (Veteran.) Age 18. Residence Quasqueton, nativity Indiana. Enlisted Aug. 27,
1861. Mustered Sept. 24, 1861. Re-enlisted and re-mustered Jan. 23, 1864. Promoted Seventh
Corporal June 14, 1864. Mustered out July 18, 1865, Louisville, Ky.
Hollridge, Hira. Age 20. Residence Independence, nativity New York. Enlisted Aug. 8, 1861, as
Fourth Sergeant. Mustered Sept. 24, 1861. Promoted Third Sergeant March 8, 1862. Died of
chronic diarrhea Feb. 11, 1864, Independence, Iowa.
Holman, Isaac N. Age 22. Residence Spring Grove, nativity Indiana. Enlisted Aug. 23, 1861.
Mustered Sept. 24, 1861. Discharged for disability May 21, 1862, St. Louis, Mo.
Holman, Stephen. Age 22. Residence Spring Grove, nativity Indiana. Enlisted Aug. 23, 1861.
Mustered Sept. 24, 1861. Wounded slightly in thigh March 7, 1862, Pea Ridge, Ark. Mustered
out Sept. 25, 1864, East Point, Ga.
61
Holman, Vinson. Age 19. Residence Buchanan County, nativity Indiana. Enlisted Aug. 23,
1861. Mustered Sept. 24, 1861. Died of jaundice Dec. 7, 1863, Memphis, Tenn. Buried in
Mississippi River National Cemetery, Memphis, Tenn. Section 1, grave 218.
Hord, Jared M. Age 32. Residence Independence, nativity Virginia. Appointed Captain Sept. 2,
1861. Mustered Sept. 2, 1861. Resigned Jan. 28, 1862. See company G, Twenty-fourth Infantry.
Hovey, Nelson. (Veteran.) Age 18. Residence Chatham, nativity Vermont. Enlisted Aug. 12,
1861. Mustered Sept. 24, 1861. Re-enlisted and re-mustered Jan. 23, 1864. Taken prisoner Feb.
28, 1865, Lynch Creek, S. C. Mustered out July 18, 1865,

Louisville, Ky.
Howe, Warrington P. Age 29. Residence Mount Pleasant, nativity Ohio. Enlisted Nov. 4, 1864.
Mustered Nov. 4, 1864. Mustered out July 18, 1865, Louisville, Ky. See Twenty-fifth Infantry.
Hyde, Theodore W. Age 18. Residence Quasqueton, nativity New York. Enlisted Sept. 25,
1861. Mustered Sept. 25, 1861. Killed in action Nov. 25, 1863, Missionary Ridge, Tenn.
COMPANY "D"
Hall, Garret N. Age 19. Residence Marshall County, nativity Netherlands. Enlisted Nov. 18,
1864. Mustered Nov. 18, 1864. Mustered out July 7, 1865, Davenport, Iowa.
Hansen, Hans. Age 36. Nativity Germany. Enlisted Nov. 3, 1864. Mustered Nov. 3, 1864.
Wounded in abdomen, Kingston, N. C. Died of wounds March 21, 1865, Newbern, N. C. Buried
in Old Cemetery, Newbern, N. C. No. 8, plot 12, grave 2154.
Harper, David. Age 31. Residence Jones County, nativity Scotland. Appointed Captain Sept. 7,
1861. Mustered Sept. 7, 1861. Resigned Feb. 14, 1863.
Havens, Romanzo. Age 28. Residence Hazel Green, nativity New York. Enlisted Feb. 26, 1864.
Mustered March 17, 1864. Mustered out July 18, 1865, Louisville, Ky.
Hays, John. Age 20. Residence Dubuque, nativity New York. Enlisted Sept. 26, 1861. Deserted
June 29, 1862, Jacksonport, Ark
Hidinger, William A. Age 18. Residence Allamakee County, nativity Atlantic Ocean. Enlisted
Jan. 14, 1865. Mustered Jan. 14, 1865. Mustered out July 18, 1865, Louisville, Ky.
Himebaugh, George. Age 20. Residence Monticello, nativity Pennsylvania. Enlisted Aug. 16,
1861. Mustered Sept. 2, 1861. Discharged for disability July 13,

1862, St. Louis, Mo.

Hines, Alfred C. Age 21. Residence Monticello, nativity New York. Enlisted Aug. 16, 1861, as
Second Sergeant. Mustered Sept. 2, 1861. Died of wounds March 7, 1862, Pea Ridge, Ark.
Buried in National Cemetery, Fayetteville, Ark. Section 2, grave 33.

Hogeboom, William. (Veteran.) Age 19. Residence Scotch Grove, nativity New York. Enlisted
Aug. 16, 1861. Promoted Fifth Corporal. Re-enlisted and re-mustered Jan. 23, 1864. Promoted
Third Corporal Oct. 1, 1864; Second Corporal June 20, 1865. Mustered out July 18, 1865,
Louisville, Ky.

Holman, Sylvester F. Age 19. Residence Monticello, nativity Virginia. Enlisted Aug. 16, 1861.
Mustered Sept. 2, 1861. Promoted Drummer. Discharged for disability Dec. 17, 1862, Memphis,
Tenn.

Howard, George. Age 24. Residence Scotch Grove, nativity New York. Enlisted Nov. 20, 1861.
Mustered Nov. 20, 1861. Wounded severely in breast March 7, 1862, Pea Ridge, Ark. Died of
wounds March 10, 1862, Pea Ridge, Ark. Buried in Cemetery, Pea Ridge, Ark.

Hunter, William H. (Veteran.) Age 30. Residence Wyoming, nativity New York. Enlisted Aug.
16, 1861. Mustered Sept. 2, 1861. Promoted Fourth Corporal April 29, 1863; Third Corporal
Aug. 4, 1863. Re-enlisted and re-mustered Jan. 23, 1864. Died April 19, 1864, Canton, Iowa.

Hutton, Philander. Age 18. Residence Scotch Grove, nativity Iowa. Enlisted Feb. 26, 1864.
Mustered March 17, 1864. Mustered out July 18, 1865, Louisville, Ky.

COMPANY "E"

Hageman, Isaac A. Age 34. Residence Wandena, nativity New York. Enlisted Sept. 5, 1861.
Mustered Sept. 24, 1861. Died Aug. 21, 1864, Atlanta, Ga. Buried in National Cemetery,
Marietta, Ga. Section H, grave 45.

Hanstet or Hemstead, Herman. Age 24. Residence Butler County, nativity Germany. Enlisted
Nov. 13, 1864. Mustered Nov. 13, 1864. Mustered out July 18, 1865, Louisville, Ky.

Hathaway, Lewis Henry. Age 18. Residence Volga City, nativity New York. Mustered Sept.
24, 1861. Discharged for disability Jan. 8, 1862, Pacific, Mo. See company M, Second Cavalry.

Hendricks, Levi. Age 18. Residence Elkport, nativity Pennsylvania. Mustered Sept. 24, 1861.
Discharged for disability May 7, 1862, Rolla, Mo.

Herrick, Emerson E. Age 32. Residence Pottawattamie County, nativity Massachusetts.
Enlisted Nov. 14, 1864. Mustered Nov. 14, 1864. Mustered out July 18, 1865, Louisville, Ky.

Herriman, Charles. (Veteran.) Age 21. Residence Wandena, nativity Indiana. Enlisted Sept. 4,
1861, as Fifth Corporal. Mustered Sept. 24, 1861. Promoted Second Sergeant Jan. 1, 1862.
Wounded March 7, 1862, Pea Ridge, Ark. Re-enlisted and re-mustered Jan. 23, 1864. Mustered
out July 18, 1865, Louisville, Ky.

Herriman, Samuel K. Age 19. Residence West Union, nativity Indiana. Enlisted Feb. 22, 1864.
Mustered March 9, 1864. Mustered out May 10, 1865, Prairie Du Chein, Wis.

Hill, Darwin. Age 17. Residence Clayton County, nativity New York. Enlisted Feb. 1, 1865.
Mustered Feb. 1, 1865. Mustered out July 18, 1865, Louisville, Ky.

Hofer, Andrew F. Age 39. Residence Elkport, nativity Germany. Appointed Second Lieutenant
Sept. 24, 1861. Mustered Sept. 24, 1861. Resigned Dec. 27, 1861.
Hoousky, Albert. (Veteran.) Age 21. Residence Volga City, nativity Austria. Enlisted Sept. 9,
1861. Mustered Sept. 24, 1861. Wounded slightly in leg May 22, 1863, Vicksburg, Miss. Reenlisted
and re-mustered Jan. 23, 1864. Promoted Third Corporal Jan. 23, 1864; Second Corporal
May 27, 1864. Wounded slightly in left wrist July 2, 1864, Kenesaw Mountain, Georgia.
Promoted First Corporal Jan. 4, 1865. Mustered out July 18, 1865, Louisville, Ky.
Howard, John L. (Veteran.) Age 21. Residence Volga City, nativity Illinois. Enlisted Nov. 24,
1861. Mustered Dec. 12, 1861. Re-enlisted and re-mustered Jan. 23, 1864. Missing in action
Nov. 27, 1864, Ringgold, Ga. Mustered out July 18, 1865, Louisville, Ky.
Huffnie, John. Age 24. Residence Van Buren County, nativity Ohio. Enlisted Nov. 15, 1864.
Mustered Nov. 15, 1864. Mustered out July 18, 1865, Louisville, Ky.
Hughes, Francis M. Age 22. Residence Volga City, nativity Alabama. Enlisted Sept. 9, 1861.
Mustered Sept. 24, 1861. Killed in battle May 19, 1863, Vicksburg, Miss .
Hughes, Hezekiah R. Age 24. Residence Volga City, nativity Alabama. Mustered Sept. 24,
1861. Wounded slightly in face March 7, 1862, Pea Ridge, Ark. Discharged for disability May
17, 1862, Rolla, Mo.
Hull, Perry. Age 25. Residence Volga City, nativity Illinois. Enlisted Sept. 9, 1861 Mustered
Sept. 24, 1861. Killed in battle March 7, 1862, Pea Ridge, Ark.
Hurd, William H. (Veteran.) Age 18. Residence Fairfield,

nativity New York. Mustered Sept.
24, 1861. Re-enlisted and re-mustered Jan. 23, 1864. Mustered out July 18, 1865, Louisville, Ky.
COMPANY "F"
Hall, Eugene G. Age 18. Residence Taylorville, nativity New York. Enlisted Sept. 5, 1861.
Mustered Sept. 14, 1861. Wounded severely in left thigh Oct. 29, 1863, Cherokee, Ala.
Discharged for disability June 29, 1864, Jefferson Barracks, Mo.
Hancock Adelbert J. Age 20. Residence Brush Creek, nativity Michigan. Enlisted Sept. 3,
1861. Mustered Sept. 14, 1861. Died April 23, 1862, Forsythe Mo.
Hancock Samuel M. Age 34. Residence Brush Creek, nativity New York. Enlisted Sept. 5, 1861
as Second Corporal. Mustered Sept. 14, 1861. Died of smallpox April 4, 1863, Helena, Ark.
Harper, George W. (Veteran.) Age 19. Residence West Union, nativity Pennsylvania. Enlisted
Sept. 12, 1861. Mustered Sept. 14, 1861. Re-enlisted and re-mustered Jan. 23, 1864. Wounded in
head severely June 28, 1864, Kenesaw Mountain, Georgia. Mustered out July 18, 1865,
Louisville, Ky.
64
Harper, James L. Age 20. Residence Taylorville, nativity Pennsylvania. Enlisted Sept. 12,
1861. Mustered Sept. 14, 1861. Mustered out Sept. 24, 1864, East Point, Ga.
Hartwell, Franklin G. Age 26. Residence Manchester, nativity New York. Enlisted Sept. 5,
1861. Mustered Sept. 14, 1861. Mustered out July 18, 1865, Louisville, Ky.
Hawthorn, John. Age 43. Residence Fayette, nativity Maine. Enlisted Sept. 5, 1861, as Second
Sergeant. Mustered Sept. 12, 1861. Promoted First Sergeant March 11, 1862; Second Lieutenant

Feb. 6, 1863. Mustered out Dec. 31, 1864, Savannah, Ga. expiration of term of service.
Herriman, Cal C. (Veteran.) Age 26. Residence West Union, nativity Maine. Enlisted Sept. 8,
1861. Mustered Sept. 12, 1861. Re-enlisted and re-mustered Jan. 23, 1864. Mustered out July 18,
1865, Louisville, Ky.
Hill, George. (Veteran.) Age 21. Residence Brush Creek, nativity Michigan. Enlisted Sept. 5,
1861. Mustered Sept. 14, 1861. Promoted Seventh Corporal March 12, 1863; Fifth Corporal Oct.
6, 1863. Re-enlisted and re-mustered Jan. 23, 1864. Missing in action May 27, 1864, Dallas, Ga.
Promoted Third Corporal April 1, 1865; Second Corporal May 12, 1865. Mustered out July 15,
1865, Davenport, Iowa.
Hobson, Nicholas J. Age 26. Residence Lima, nativity Ireland. Enlisted July 10, 1862. Mustered
July 26, 1862. Died of lung fever Nov. 8, 1865, Helena, Ark. Buried in Mississippi River
National Cemetery, Memphis, Tenn. Section 3, grave 661.
Holes, George. Age 18. Residence Taylorville, nativity England. Enlisted Aug. 28, 1861.
Mustered Sept. 12, 1861. Wounded severely, leg broken, March 7, 1862, Pea Ridge, Ark.
Discharged for wounds Oct. 13, 1862, Keokuk, Iowa.
Holton, Miles. (Veteran.) Age 31. Residence Leo, nativity New York. Enlisted Sept. 6, 1861, as
Seventh Corporal. Mustered Sept. 12, 1861. Promoted Fifth Sergeant March 12, 1863; Third
Sergeant Oct. 6, 1863. Re-enlisted and re-mustered Jan. 23, 1864. Promoted First Sergeant Jan.
1, 1865; Second Lieutenant Jan. 3, 1865; First Lieutenant March 31, 1865. Mustered out July 18,
1865, Louisville, Ky.
Hough, Edgar G. (Veteran.) Age 18. Residence West Union,

nativity Norway. Enlisted Sept. 3,
1861. Mustered Sept. 12, 1861. Promoted Drummer. Wounded slightly in leg March 7, 1862,
Pea Ridge, Ark. Re-enlisted and re-mustered Jan. 23, 1864. Mustered out July 18, 1865,
Louisville, Ky.
House, Marshall. (Veteran.) Age 18. Residence Auburn, nativity New York. Enlisted Aug. 27,
1861, as Third Corporal. Mustered Sept. 12, 1861. Wounded severely in thigh March 7, 1862,
Pea Ridge, Ark. Promoted Second Sergeant Oct. 6, 1863. Re-enlisted and re-mustered Jan. 23,
1864. Wounded in left thigh severely; leg amputated Feb. 1, 1865, Hickory Hill, N. C.
Discharged June 6, 1865, Central Park Hospital, New York City.
65
Huff, George W. Age 22. Residence Des Moines County, nativity Indiana. Enlisted Jan. 16,
1865. Mustered Jan. 25, 1865. Mustered out July 18, 1865, Louisville, Ky. See company G.,
Twenty-fifth Infantry.
Huntsinger, Joseph B. Age 24. Residence Eldorado, nativity Indiana. Enlisted Sept. 4, 1861.
Mustered Sept. 12, 1861. Wounded severely in breast March 7, 1862, Pea Ridge, Ark. Died of
chronic diarrhea Dec. 14, 1862, Helena, Ark. Buried in Mississippi River National Cemetery,
Memphis, Tenn. Section 3, grave 675.
COMPANY "G"
Harkness, David. Age 22. Residence Cedar Falls, nativity Ohio. Enlisted Sept. 28, 1861.
Mustered Sept. 28, 1861. Mustered out Sept. 28, 1864, East Point, Ga., expiration of term of
service. See Third Iowa Artillery.
Harwood, Nathan S. Age 19. Residence Janesville, nativity Michigan. Enlisted Aug. 10, 1861,

as Fourth Corporal. Mustered Sept. 24, 1861. Discharged for disability May 17, 1862, Batesville, Ark.
Haskett, Eli. Age 18. Residence Lee County, nativity Indiana. Enlisted Nov. 5, 1864. Mustered
Nov. 5, 1864. Mustered out July 18, 1865, Louisville, Ky.
Haven, George R. Age 24. Residence Colesburg, nativity Vermont. Enlisted Sept. 18, 1861.
Mustered Sept. 24, 1861. Promoted Drummer. Mustered out Sept. 29, 1864, Davenport, Iowa,
expiration of term of service.
Haven, James H. (Veteran.) Age 20. Residence Colesburg, nativity Vermont. Enlisted Sept. 18,
1861. Mustered Sept. 24, 1861. Promoted Fifer. Re-enlisted and re-mustered Jan. 23, 1864.
Mustered out July 18, 1865, Louisville, Ky.
Healis, William. Age 23. Residence Waverly, nativity England. Enlisted Sept. 17, 1861.
Mustered Sept. 24, 1861. Died Oct. 7, 1863, Jefferson Barracks, Mo. Buried in Jefferson
Barracks Cemetery, St. Louis, Mo. Section 31, grave 83.
Heath, Franklin H. Age 22. Residence Waterloo, nativity Vermont. Enlisted Aug. 20, 1861.
Mustered Sept. 24, 1861. Wounded in breast March 7, 1862, Pea Ridge, Ark. Died of wounds
March 28, 1862, Cassville, Mo.
Hill, James G. Age 18. Residence Waterloo, nativity Indiana. Enlisted Aug. 20, 1861. Mustered
Sept. 24, 1861. Discharged for disability Sept. 30, 1862, St. Louis, Mo. See company D, Fortyseventh
Infantry, and company E, Seventh Cavalry.
Hurlbut, Samuel B. (Veteran.) Age 21. Residence Cedar Falls, nativity New York. Enlisted
Sept. 28, 1861. Mustered Sept. 28, 1861 Re-enlisted and re-mustered Jan. 23, 1864. Taken
prisoner while foraging Feb. 26, 1865, Lynch Creek, N. C.

Mustered out July 6, 1865,
Davenport, Iowa. See Third Battery.
66
COMPANY "H"
Hall, Henry E. Age 18. Residence Decorah, nativity Vermont. Enlisted Aug. 21, 1861.
Mustered Sept. 24, 1861. Wounded slightly in leg March 7, 1862, Pea Ridge, Ark. Killed in
battle March 19, 1863, Vicksburg, Miss.
Hall, Ralph R. Age 19. Residence Decorah, nativity Vermont. Enlisted Aug. 21, 1861. Mustered
Sept. 24, 1861. Died of consumption April 4, 1863, Memphis, Tenn.
Hamilton, Andrew. Age 39. Residence Dubuque, nativity Ireland. Enlisted Aug. 28, 1861, as
Third Corporal. Mustered Sept. 24, 1861. Wounded March 7, 1862, Pea Ridge, Ark. Died of
wounds July 16, 1862, Springfield, Mo.
Hanson, Andrew. See Andrew, Hanson.
Hinkley, Albert. (Veteran.) Age 18. Residence Cedar Falls, nativity Iowa. Enlisted Sept. 22,
1861. Mustered Sept. 24, 1861. Wounded slightly in breast May 22, 1863, Vicksburg, Miss. Reenlisted
and re-mustered Jan. 23, 1864. Mustered out July 18, 1865, Louisville, Ky.
Hogan, Thomas J. Age 19. Residence Keokuk County, nativity Ireland. Enlisted Nov. 19, 1864.
Mustered Nov. 19, 1864. Mustered out July 18, 1866, Louisville, Ky.
Hollman, Benjamin. Age 45. Residence Burr Oak, nativity Pennsylvania. Enlisted Dec. 22,
1861. Mustered Jan. 7, 1862. Transferred to Invalid Corps Oct. 17, 1863. Died of pneumonia
April 24, 1864, Washington, D. C.
Huff, Abel M. Age 18. Residence Burr Oak, nativity Michigan. Enlisted Aug. 26, 1861.

Mustered Sept. 24, 1861. Discharged for disability Oct. 10, 1861, St. Louis, Mo.

Huff, Abram C. Age 23. Residence Burr Oak, nativity Michigan. Enlisted Aug. 26, 1861.
Mustered Sept. 24, 1861. Discharged for disability March 31, 1862, Pacific, Mo.

Humphrey, Oscar L. Age 18. Residence Decorah, nativity New York. Enlisted Oct. 15, 1861.
Mustered Nov. 10, 1861. Deserted Jan. 27 1863, Vicksburg, Miss.

COMPANY "I"

Harris, George H. Age 19. Residence Castalia, nativity Vermont. Enlisted Sept. 13, 1861.
Mustered Sept. 18, 1861. Died of lung trouble Dec. 16, 1861, Pacific City, Mo. Buried in
National Cemetery, Jefferson Barracks, St. Louis, Mo. Section 37 1/2, grave 20.

Holsted, Amos S. Age 22. Residence Maysville, nativity Ohio. Enlisted Aug. 22, 1861.
Mustered Sept. 2, 1861. Promoted Seventh Corporal Oct. 16, 1862; Second Corporal; First
Corporal July 1, 1863; Fifth Sergeant Oct. 6, 1863; Fourth Sergeant Sept. 16, 1864; Third
Sergeant Jan. 1, 1865. Mustered out July 18, 1865, Louisville, Ky. 67

Horning, David C. (Veteran.) Age 18. Residence Vernon Springs, nativity Iowa. Enlisted Aug.
17, 1861. Mustered Sept. 18, 1861. Wounded in right arm Dec. 29, 1862, Vicksburg, Miss. Reenlisted
and re-mustered Jan. 23, 1864. Mustered out July 18, 1865, Louisville, Ky.

Hughes, Simon. Age 20. Residence New Oregon, nativity Illinois. Enlisted Aug. 17, 1861.
Mustered Sept. 18, 1861. Discharged for disability Oct. 3, 1862, Memphis, Tenn.

Humphrey, John. Age 38. Residence Decorah, nativity New Hampshire. Enlisted Sept. 5, 1861.

Mustered Sept. 18, 1861. Discharged Aug. 27, 1862, Dubuque, Iowa.

Hurley, Lewellin. Age 18. Residence Foreston, nativity Indiana. Enlisted Sept. 12, 1861.
Mustered Sept. 18, 1861. Mustered out Sept. 24, 1864, East Point, Ga., expiration of term of
service.

Hurley, Robert. Age 21. Residence Foreston, nativity Indiana. Enlisted Sept. 12, 1861.
Mustered Sept. 18, 1861. Killed in battle May 22, 1863, Vicksburg, Miss.

COMPANY "K"

Hagaman, William E. Age 18. Residence Dubuque, nativity Ohio. Enlisted Sept. 19, 1861.
Mustered Sept. 24, 1861. Died Dec. 5, 1861, Pacific, Mo. Buried in National Cemetery,
Jefferson Barracks, St. Louis, Mo. Section 371/2, grave 23.

Hall, George W. (Veteran.) Age 19. Residence Cedar Rapids, nativity Illinois. Enlisted Sept. 14,
1861. Mustered Sept. 24, 1861. Re-enlisted and re-mustered Jan. 23, 1864. Promoted Fifth
Corporal March 7, 1865. Mustered out July 18, 1865, Louisville, Ky.

Hallsted, James. Age 42. Residence Dubuque, nativity Pennsylvania. Enlisted Aug. 22, 1861.
Mustered Sept. 24, 1861. Discharged Aug. 9, 1862, St. Louis, Mo. See company B, Thirty-eighth
Infantry, and company I, Thirty-fourth and Thirty-eighth Consolidated.

Harris, William R. (Veteran.) Age 25. Residence Marion, nativity Canada. Enlisted Sept. 14,
1861, as Third Corporal. Mustered Sept. 24, 1861. Promoted Third Sergeant Oct. 17, 1862;
Second Sergeant. Wounded slightly in hand May 22, 1863, Vicksburg, Miss. Re-enlisted and remustered
Jan. 23, 1864. Promoted First Sergeant March 3, 1864. Mustered

out July 18, 1865,
Louisville, Ky.
Haylan, Isaiah. Age 20. Residence Jefferson County, nativity Indiana. Enlisted Nov. 9, 1864.
Mustered Nov. 11, 1864. Mustered out July 18, 1865, Louisville, Ky.
Hooker, Adam. Age 19. Residence Center Point, nativity Indiana. Enlisted Feb. 24, 1864.
Mustered March 3, 1864. Mustered out July 18, 1865, Louisville, Ky.
Horn, Daniel. Age 32. Residence Marion, nativity Pennsylvania. Enlisted Sept. 14, 1861, as
Eighth Corporal. Mustered Sept. 24, 1861. Wounded severely in foot March 7, 1862, Pea Ridge,
Ark. Discharged for rheumatism Dec. 1, 1862, St. Louis, Mo.
68
Hughes, Aaron. Age 27. Residence Marion, nativity New York. Enlisted Oct. 1, 1861.
Wounded severely in thigh March 7, 1862, Pea Ridge, Ark. Discharged Aug. 27, 1862, Cairo, Ill.
COMPANY "A"
Ingraham. Joseph. Age 32. Residence Monmouth, nativity Connecticut. Enlisted Sept. 10,
1861, as Wagoner. Mustered Sept. 24, 1861. Died of typhoid fever Dec. 3, 1861, Pacific, Mo.
Buried in National Cemetery, Franklin, Mo.
COMPANY "B"
Irwin, Isaac. Age 27. Residence Wyoming, nativity Pennsylvania. Enlisted Aug. 12, 1861.
Mustered Sept. 24, 1861. Killed in battle May 20, 1863, Vicksburg, Miss.
Isabel, Jones. Age 24. Residence North Fork, nativity New York. Enlisted Aug. 15, 1861.
Mustered Sept. 24, 1861. Discharged for disability July 29, 1862, St. Louis, Mo.
COMPANY "C"

Irwin, James A. Age 18. Residence Pella, nativity Ohio. Enlisted Oct. 9, 1864. Mustered Oct.
13, 1864. Mustered out July 18, 1865, Louisville, Ky. See Twenty-fifth Infantry.
COMPANY "D"
Ingels, William B. Age 18. Residence Pella, nativity Wisconsin. Enlisted Oct. 5, 1864. Mustered
Oct. 13, 1864. Mustered out July 18, 1865, Louisville, Ky. See company H, Twenty-fifth
Infantry.
Irwin, John C. Age 23. Residence Monticello, nativity Pennsylvania. Enlisted Aug. 16, 1861, as
Fifth Sergeant. Mustered Sept. 2, 1861. Promoted Third Sergeant Jan. 24, 1863; Second Sergeant
Aug. 4, 1863. Mustered out Sept. 26, 1864, East Point, Ga., expiration of term of service.
Irwin, Thomas. Age 21. Residence Monticello, nativity Pennsylvania. Enlisted Aug. 16, 1861.
Mustered Sept. 2, 1861. Wounded slightly in shoulder March 7, 1862, Pea Ridge, Ark. Died Oct.
21, 1862, Helena, Ark.
COMPANY "F"
Inglebritson, Inglebright. Age 35. Residence Winneshiek County, nativity Norway. Enlisted
Oct. 31, 1864. Mustered Oct. 31, 1864. Mustered out July 18, 1865, Louisville, Ky.
COMPANY "G"
Inglebritson, Hartvig. Age 19. Residence Springfield, nativity Norway. Enlisted Oct. 31, 1864.
Mustered Oct. 31, 1864. Mustered out July 18, 1865, Louisville, Ky.
COMPANY "H"
Irwin, Hugh. Age 29. Residence Hesper, nativity Ireland. Enlisted Sept. 10, 1861. Mustered
Sept. 24, 1861. Killed in battle March 7, 1862, Pea Ridge, Ark.

COMPANY "I"

Inman, Chester W. Age 24. Residence Butler Center, nativity Illinois. Enlisted Aug. 20, 1861.
Mustered Sept. 18, 1861. Promoted Third Corporal June 23, 1862; Second Corporal Dec. 10,
1862; First Corporal; Third Sergeant. Wounded severely May 22, 1863, Vicksburg, Miss.
Promoted Second Sergeant July 6, 1863; Second Lieutenant May 23, 1863; Captain Sept. 12,
1863. Wounded slightly March 21, 1865, Bentonville, N. C. Promoted Major June 19, 1865.
Mustered out July 18,1865, Louisville, Ky.
Inman, Daniel W. Age 29. Residence Butler Center, nativity New York. Enlisted Oct. 10, 1864.
Mustered Oct. 10, 1864. Wounded slightly March 21, 1865, Bentonville, N. C. Mustered out July
18, 1865, Louisville, Ky.
Inman, Franklin E. Age 18. Residence Butler Center, nativity Illinois. Enlisted July 27, 1861.
Discharged for disability April 29, 1862, Pacific City, Mo. See company C, Fourteenth Infantry.
Inman, Joseph G. Age 23. Residence Cedar Falls, nativity Illinois. Enlisted Aug. 17, 1861.
Appointed Second Lieutenant Sept. 18, 1861. Promoted Lieutenant June 14, 1862. Resigned Feb.
15, 1863, Young's Point, La.

COMPANY "B"

James, Walter. (Veteran.) Age 22. Residence Madison, nativity Maryland. Enlisted Aug. 12,
1861, as Sixth Corporal. Mustered Sept. 24, 1861. Promoted Fifth Corporal Aug. 1, 1862; Fourth
Corporal Nov. 1, 1862; Third Corporal Dec. 8, 1862; Second Corporal March 20, 1863; First
Corporal May 23, 1863; First Sergeant Dec. 1, 1863. Re-enlisted and re-mustered Jan. 23, 1864.
Promoted First Lieutenant Jan. 16, 1865. Mustered out July 18,

1865, Louisville, Ky.

Jenkins, John. Age 36. Residence Boone County, nativity Ohio. Enlisted Oct. 27, 1864.
Mustered Oct. 27, 1864. Mustered out May 30, 1865, New York.

Jennings, William L. Age 28. Residence Rome, nativity New York. Enlisted Aug. 12, 1861, as
Third Sergeant. Mustered Sept. 24, 1861. Promoted Second Lieutenant Aug. 1, 1862. Resigned
Sept. 20, 1864.

Johnston. George A. (Veteran.) Age 20. Residence Rome, nativity Ohio. Enlisted Aug. 12,
1861. Mustered Sept. 24, 1861. Re-enlisted and re-mustered Jan. 23, 1864. Promoted Fifth
Corporal April 6, 1865; Fourth Corporal July 5, 1865. Mustered out July 18, 1865, Louisville,
Ky.

Jones, Jacob. Age 38. Residence Rome, nativity Kentucky. Appointed Second Lieutenant Sept.
2, 1861. Mustered Sept. 2, 1861. Promoted First Lieutenant Aug. 1, 1862. Killed in battle May
22, 1863, Vicksburg, Miss.
70

Jones, Jonathan, Jr. Age 22. Residence Platteville, nativity Indiana. Enlisted Nov. 5, 1864.
Mustered Nov. 5, 1864. Mustered out July 18, 1865, Louisville, Ky.

COMPANY "C"

Jones, Henry. Age 22. Residence Springfield, nativity Ohio. Enlisted Aug. 8, 1861. Mustered
Sept. 24, 1861. Died Feb. 15, 1864, Mound City, Ill. Buried in Mound City National Cemetery.
Section A, grave 397.

Jones, William A. Age 18. Residence Spring Creek, nativity Ohio. Enlisted Oct. 1, 1861.
Mustered Oct. 1, 1861. Promoted Eighth Corporal. Wounded slightly March 7, 1862, Pea Ridge,

Ark. Died of fever Oct. 19, 1863, Iuka, Miss. Buried in Union National Cemetery, Corinth, Miss.
Section B, grave 227.
COMPANY "D"
Jenson, Loren P. Age 22. Residence Pottawattamie County, nativity Denmark. Enlisted Nov. 5,
1864. Mustered Nov. 5, 1864. Mustered out July 18, 1865, Louisville, Ky.
Johnson, Calvin. Age 18. Residence Burlington, nativity Ohio. Enlisted Oct. 7, 1864. Mustered
Oct. 7, 1864. Mustered out July 18, 1865, Louisville, Ky. See company H, Twenty-fifth Infantry.
Jones, John. Age 19. Residence Lee County, nativity Illinois. Enlisted Nov. 13, 1864. Mustered
Nov. 13, 1864. Mustered out July 18, 1865, Louisville, Ky.
Jones, Thomas J. Age 18. Residence Washington County, nativity Iowa. Enlisted Nov. 12,
1864. Mustered Nov. 12, 1864. Mustered out July 18, 1865, Louisville, Ky.
COMPANY "E"
Johnson, Samuel. Age 28. Residence Elkader, nativity Norway. Enlisted Sept. 14, 1861.
Mustered Sept. 24, 1861. Discharged May 26, 1863, St. Louis, Mo.
Jones, Aaron B. Age 29. Residence Story County, nativity Ohio. Enlisted Oct. 27, 1864.
Mustered Oct. 27, 1864. Transferred to Veteran Reserve Corps. Discharged July 20, 1865,
Indianapolis, Ind.
COMPANY "G"
Johnson, Joseph. Age 36. Residence Dubuque, nativity New York. Enlisted Aug. 31, 1861.
Mustered Sept. 24, 1861. Wounded slightly in head June 23, 1864, Kenesaw Mountain, Ga.
Mustered out Sept. 24, 1864, East Point, Ga., expiration of term of service.
Jordon, Michael L. (Veteran.) Age 20. Residence Janesville,

nativity New York. Enlisted Aug.
19, 1861. Mustered Sept. 24, 1861. Re-enlisted and re-mustered Jan. 23, 1864. Promoted Third
Corporal May 1, 1865. Mustered out July 18, 1865, Louisville, Ky.
COMPANY "H"
71
Jacoby, Elias. Age 18. Residence Boone, nativity Ohio. Enlisted March 14, 1864. Mustered
March 17, 1864. Died June 5, 1864, Chattanooga, Tenn. Buried in National Cemetery,
Chattanooga, Tenn. Section E, grave 1.
Jacoby, James. Age 16. Residence Jones County, nativity Ohio. Enlisted March 14, 1864.
Mustered March 17, 1864. Mustered out July 18, 1865, Louisville, Ky.
Jones, William H. Age 34. Residence Story County, nativity Pennsylvania. Enlisted Oct. 27,
1864. Mustered Oct. 27, 1864. Mustered out July 18, 1865, Louisville, Ky.
COMPANY "I"
Jacoby, John S. Age 19. Residence Des Moines, nativity Pennsylvania. Enlisted Jan. 23, 1865.
Mustered Jan. 23, 1865. Mustered out July 18, 1865, Louisville, Ky. See company G, Twentyfifth
Infantry.
Johnson, Clark. Age 30. Residence New Oregon, nativity Canada. Enlisted Aug. 17, 1861.
Mustered Sept. 18, 1861. Died July 10, 1863, Vicksburg, Miss.
Johnson, James M. (Veteran.) Age 18. Residence New Oregon, nativity Canada. Enlisted Aug.
17, 1861. Mustered Sept. 18, 1861. Re-enlisted and re-mustered Jan. 23, 1864. No further record.
Johnson, Thomas. Age 39. Residence Mitchell, nativity Norway. Enlisted Sept. 2, 1861.
Mustered Sept. 18, 1861. Wounded severely March 7, 1862, Pea Ridge, Ark. Wounded in head

Oct. 4, 1862, Corinth, Miss. Discharged for wounds Feb. 26, 1863, Keokuk, Iowa.

Johnson, Abram C. (Veteran.) Age 24. Residence Jacksonville, nativity Pennsylvania. Enlisted
Sept. 20, 1861. Re-enlisted and re-mustered Jan. 23, 1864. Mustered out July 18, 1865,
Louisville, Ky.

Johnston George W. Age 21. Residence Utica, nativity Pennsylvania. Enlisted July 2, 1861.
Mustered Sept. 2, 1861. Killed in battle May 22, 1863, Vicksburg, Miss.

Johnston, Noah R. Age 27. Residence Utica, nativity Pennsylvania. Enlisted Aug. 15, 1861, as
Eighth Corporal. Mustered Sept. 18, 1861. Discharged for disability Jan. l9, 1862, Pacific, Mo.

Jones, Edward P. Age 38. Residence Lee County, nativity Ohio. Enlisted Nov. 10, 1864.
Mustered Nov. 10, 1864. Mustered out July 18, 1865, Louisville, Ky.

Jones, Martin B. (Veteran.) Age 19. Residence Maysville, nativity Indiana. Enlisted Aug. 22,
1861. Mustered Sept. 18, 1861. Re-enlisted and re-mustered Jan. 5, 1864. Wounded slightly June
14, 1864, Big Shanty, Ga. Promoted Seventh Corporal May 1, 1865. Mustered out July 18, 1865,
Louisville, Ky.

COMPANY "K"

72

Jacobs, Henry. Age 18. Residence Linn County, nativity Ohio. Enlisted Feb. 22, 1864.
Mustered March 3, 1864. Mustered out July 18, 1865, Louisville, Ky.

Jolly, Beaden B. Age 19. Residence Van Buren County, nativity Pennsylvania. Enlisted Nov.
10, 1864. Mustered Nov. 10, 1864. Mustered out July 6, 1865, Philadelphia, Penn.

Justin, Charles F. Age 21. Residence Paris, nativity New York. Enlisted Oct. 1,1861. Mustered
Oct. 1, 1861. Died April 21, 1862, Linn, Iowa.
Justin, Marion. Age 21. Residence Paris, nativity New York. Mustered Oct. 1, 1861. Died April
21, 1862, Paris, Iowa.
COMPANY "A"
Kelley, Dennis O. Rejected Aug. 8, 1861, by Mustering Officer.
Kelley, James H. (Veteran.) Age 27. Residence Andrew, nativity Pennsylvania. Enlisted Aug.
19, 1861. Mustered Sept. 24, 1862. Re-enlisted and re-mustered Jan. 23, 1864. Mustered out July
18, 1865, Louisville, Ky.
Kelley, Samuel P. Age 23. Residence Andrew, nativity Pennsylvania. Enlisted Aug. 29, 1862.
Mustered Oct. 14, 1862. Transferred to invalid Corps Feb. 18, 1864. Mustered out June 24, 1865.
Kelsey, Florilla M. Age 28. Residence Sabula, nativity New York. Appointed First Lieutenant
Sept. 24, 1862. Mustered Sept. 24, 1862. Wounded March 7, 1862, Pea Ridge, Ark. Promoted
Captain March 8, 1862. Wounded severely in leg; leg amputated May 22, 1863, Vicksburg,
Miss. Died of wounds May 26, 1863, Vicksburg, Miss. Buried in National Cemetery, Vicksburg,
Miss. Section O, grave 18.
Kinney, John. Age 44. Residence Third Congressional District, nativity Ireland. Enlisted Oct.
21, 1864. Mustered Oct. 24, 1864. Mustered out July 18, 1865, Louisville, Ky.
Klinger, Henry L. (Veteran.) Age 25. Residence Maquoketa, nativity Hanover. Enlisted Aug.
29, 1861. Mustered Sept. 24, 1861. Re-enlisted and re-mustered Jan. 23, 1864. Mustered out July
18, 1865,
Louisville, Ky.

Kraft, Oscar. Age 23. Residence Bellevue, nativity Bavaria. Enlisted Aug. 9, 1861. Mustered
Sept. 24, 1861. Mustered out Sept. 24, 1864, East Point, Ga.
COMPANY "B"
Kerr, Samuel P. (Veteran.) Age 25. Residence Fairview, nativity Pennsylvania. Enlisted Aug.
12, 1861. Mustered Sept. 24, 1861. Re-enlisted and re-mustered Jan. 23, 1864. Promoted Sixth
Corporal March 27, 1864; Fifth Sergeant April 6, 1865. Mustered out July 18, 1865, Louisville,
Ky.
73
Knudsen, Trow. Age 31. Residence Springfield, nativity Norway. Enlisted Oct. 31, 1864.
Mustered Oct. 31, 1864. Mustered out July 18, 1865, Louisville, Ky.
COMPANY "C "
King, John M. (Veteran.) Age 19. Residence Buffalo Grove, nativity Illinois. Enlisted Aug. 13,
1861. Mustered Sept. 24, 1861. Re-enlisted and re-mustered Jan. 23, 1864. Mustered out July 18,
1865, Louisville, Ky.
King, Silas E. Age 22. Residence Buffalo Grove, nativity New York. Enlisted Aug. 10, 1861.
Mustered Sept. 24, 1861. Discharged for disability Jan. 21, 1862, Pacific City, Mo.
Klopp, Benjamin. (Veteran.) Age 23. Residence Independence, nativity Pennsylvania. Enlisted
Aug. 13, 1861. Mustered Sept. 24, 1861. Wounded slightly June 17, 1864, Big Shanty, Ga. Reenlisted
and re-mustered Feb. 1, 1864. Wounded slightly July 28, 1864, Atlanta, Ga. Mustered
out July 18, 1865, Louisville, Ky.
COMPANY "D"
Kahoe, Edward. (Veteran.) Age 18. Residence Castle Grove, nativity New York. Enlisted Aug.

16, 1861. Mustered Sept. 2, 1861. Re-enlisted and re-mustered Jan. 23, 1864. Missing in action
Feb. 26, 1865, near Lynch Creek, Mo. Mustered out July 18, 1865, Louisville Ky. ,
Karst, George. Age 25. Residence Monticello, nativity Germany. Enlisted Aug. 16, 1861.
Mustered Sept. 2, 1861. Wounded in arm slightly March 7, 1862, Pea Ridge, Ark. Discharged for
disability Aug. 28, 1862, Cairo, Ill.
Keys, Samuel R. Age 33. Residence Fourth Congressional District, nativity Pennsylvania.
Enlisted Nov. 2, 1864. Mustered Nov. 2, 1864. Mustered out July 18, 1865, Louisville, Ky.
King, John S. Age 29. Residence Marcy Township, nativity Kentucky. Enlisted Oct. 27, 1864.
Mustered Oct. 27, 1864. Mustered out July 18, 1865, Louisville, Ky.
King. William H. (Veteran.) Age 36. Residence South Fork, nativity Ohio. Enlisted Aug. 26,
1861. Mustered Sept. 2, 1861. Re-enlisted and re-mustered Jan. 23, 1864. Mustered out July 18,
1865, Louisville, Ky.
Kirkwood, James C. (Veteran.) Age 18. Residence Delaware County, nativity Scotland.
Enlisted Sept. 5, 1861. Wounded slightly in head March 7, 1862, Pea Ridge, Ark. Promoted Fifth
Corporal Jan. 24, 1863; First Corporal April 29, 1863; Fifth Sergeant Aug. 4, 1863. Re-enlisted
and re-mustered Jan. 23, 1864. Promoted Fourth Sergeant May 2, 1864; Second Sergeant Oct. 1,
1864; First Sergeant June 20, 1865. Mustered out July 18, 1865, Louisville, Ky.
COMPANY "E"
Kaiser, Christian. Age 21. Residence Garnavillo, nativity Germany. Mustered Sept. 24, 1861.
Wounded slightly in foot and severely in leg March 7, 1862, Pea

Ridge, Ark. Discharged for wounds Oct. 23, 1862, St. Louis, Mo.
74
Keller, David. Age 19. Residence Burlington, nativity Iowa. Enlisted Jan. 4, 1864. Mustered
Jan. 4, 1864. Mustered out July 18, 1865, Louisville, Ky. See company G, Twenty-fifth Infantry.
Ketsinger, Michael. Age 40. Residence Winneshiek County, nativity Germany. Enlisted Oct.
31, 1864. Mustered Oct. 31, 1864. Mustered out July 18, 1865, Louisville, Ky.
King, Wilder B. (Veteran.) Age 28. Residence Volga City, nativity Ohio. Mustered Sept. 24,
1861. Re-enlisted and re-mustered Jan. 23, 1864. Wounded severely in left side June 23, 1864,
Kenesaw Mountain, Ga. Discharged for wounds Dec. 8, 1864, Davenport, Iowa.
Kirchner, Henry. Age 27. Residence Lee County, nativity Germany. Enlisted Oct. 24, 1864.
Mustered Oct. 24, 1864. Mustered out July 18, 1865, Louisville, Ky.
Knapp, Edward A. Age 41. Residence Pottawattamie County, nativity New York. Enlisted
Nov. 5, 1864. Mustered Nov. 5, 1864. Mustered out July 18, 1865, Louisville, Ky.
COMPANY "F"
Kearney, Isaac. (Veteran.) Age 18. Residence Taylorville, nativity Illinois. Enlisted Sept. 5,
1861. Mustered Sept. 14, 1861. Re-enlisted and re-mustered Jan. 23, 1864. Mustered out July 18,
1865, Louisville, Ky.
Keasey, William B. Age 18. Residence Fayette, nativity Ohio. Enlisted Sept. 5, 1861. Mustered
Sept. 14, 1861. Died of wounds May 26, 1864, Benton Barracks, Mo. Buried in National
Cemetery, Jefferson Barracks, Mo. Section 8, grave 87.

Kinsey, David. Age 20. Residence Fayette, nativity Wales. Enlisted Sept. 5, 1861. Mustered
Sept. 14, 1861. Died of typhoid fever Jan. 6, 1862, Pacific, Mo.
Knight, John S. Age 18. Residence Clayton County, nativity New York. Enlisted Sept. 5, 1861.
Mustered Sept. 14, 1861. Wounded severely in thigh March 7, 1862, Pea Ridge, Ark. Discharged
Aug. 14, 1862, St. Louis, Mo.
COMPANY "G"
Karker, John. Age 18. Residence Waverly, nativity New York. Enlisted Sept. 3, 1861.
Mustered Sept. 24, 1861. Killed in battle March 7, 1862, Pea Ridge, Ark. Buried in National
Cemetery, Fayetteville, Ark. Section 2, grave 23.
Kilbourn, Hiram. Age 35. Residence Waterloo, nativity New York. Enlisted July 28, 1861.
Mustered Sept. 24, 1861. Promoted Third Corporal Dec. 8, 1861. Wounded in foot Nov. 27,
1863, Ringgold, Ga. Discharged Sept. 23, 1864, Davenport, Iowa, expiration of term of service.
Kinsey, Isaac M. Age 37. Residence Bremer County, nativity Kentucky. Enlisted Feb. 29, 1864.
Mustered March 17, 1864. Wounded in left arm severely July 22, 1864, Atlanta, Ga. Mustered
out July 18, 1865, Louisville, Ky.
75
Kirk, William H. Age 24. Residence Delaware County, nativity Illinois. Enlisted Feb. 21, 1864.
Mustered March 16, 1864. Mustered out July 18, 1865, Louisville, Ky.
Klock, George. (Veteran.) Age 18. Residence Waterloo, nativity New York. Enlisted Aug. 30,
1861. Mustered Sept. 24, 1864. Re-enlisted and re-mustered Jan. 23,1864. Promoted Fifth
Corporal Dec. 1, 1864; Fourth Corporal May 1, 1865. Mustered out July 18, 1865, Louisville,

Ky.
COMPANY "H"
Kelly, William. Age 21. Residence Decorah, nativity Pennsylvania. En-listed Aug. 21, 1861.
Mustered Sept. 24, 1861. Died Jan. 10, 1863, Arkansas Post, Ark.
Knowlton, Alfred. (Veteran.) Age 18. Residence Decorah, nativity Wisconsin. Enlisted Oct. 25,
1861. Mustered Oct. 25, 1861. Promoted Fifer. Re-enlisted and re-mustered Jan. 23, 1864.
Mustered out July 18, 1865, Louisville, Ky.
COMPANY "I"
Kemery, Charles. Age 28. Residence Vernon Springs, nativity Pennsylvania. Enlisted Aug. 17,
1861. Mustered Sept. 18, 1861. Promoted Eighth Corporal Jan. 19, 1862; First Sergeant.
Wounded slightly in arm March 7, 1862, Pea Ridge, Ark. Promoted First Lieutenant April 14,
1863. Wounded severely May 27, 1863, Vicksburg, Miss. Mustered out Oct. 26, 1864,
Chattanooga, Tenn.
Kile, Martin. (Veteran.) Age 26. Residence Foreston, nativity Ohio. Enlisted Aug. 18, 1861. Reenlisted
and re-mustered Jan. 23, 1864. Mustered out July 18, 1865, Louisville, Ky.
Knight, Benjamin F. Age 26. Residence Foreston, nativity Ohio. Enlisted Aug. 18, 1861.
Mustered Sept. 18, 1861. Wounded slightly in leg March 7, 1862, Pea Ridge, Ark. Wounded
severely in right leg; leg amputated May 22, 1863, Vicksburg, Miss. Died June 20, 1863,
Vicksburg, Miss.
Knight, John F. Age 27. Residence Castalia, nativity Pennsylvania. Enlisted Sept. 14, 1861.
Mustered Sept. 18, 1861. Promoted Sixth Corporal March 23, 1862; Fourth Corporal Dec. 20,
1862; First Corporal July 6, 1863; Fifth Sergeant July 6, 1863;

Fourth Sergeant Oct. 6, 1863.
Missing in action Oct. 14, 1864, Claysville, Ala. Died Oct. 22, 1864, Andersonville, Ga. Buried
in Andersonville National Cemetery, Ga. Grave 11281.
COMPANY "K"
Kernes, Daniel. Age 21. Residence Fairbanks, nativity Pennsylvania. Enlisted Sept. 14, 1861.
Mustered Sept. 24, 1861. Wounded severely in breast March 7, 1862, Pea Ridge, Ark.
Discharged for disability Feb. 27, 1863, Young's Point, La.
76
Kidder, Ezra. Age 41. Residence Jackson, nativity New Hampshire. Enlisted Dec. 22, 1863.
Mustered Dec. 22, 1863. Died June 8, 1864, New Albany, Ind. Buried in Cemetery, New
Albany, Ind.
Kriger, August. Age 27. Residence Johnson County, nativity Prussia. Enlisted March 14, 1864.
. Mustered March 15, 1864. Mustered out July 18, 1865, Louisville, Ky.
COMPANY "A"
Leebur, Aaron. Rejected Aug. 8, 1861, by Mustering Officer.
Lest, Daniel. Age 36. Residence Boone County, nativity Illinois. Enlisted Oct. 27, 1864.
Mustered Oct. 27, 1864. Mustered out July 18, 1865, Louisville, Ky.
Littell, George W. Age 20. Residence Maquoketa, nativity Canada. Enlisted Aug. 12, 1861.
Mustered Sept. 24, 1861. Discharged for disability Sept. 15, 1862, Davenport, Iowa.
Littell, Hiram B. Age 26. Residence Marion, nativity Canada. Enlisted Sept. 10, 1861. Mustered
Sept. 24, 1861. Mustered out Sept. 24, 1864, East Point, Ga., expiration of term of service.
Livingston, William H. (Veteran.) Age 20. Residence Jackson County, nativity Pennsylvania.

Enlisted Aug. 12, 1861. Mustered Sept. 24, 1861. Re-enlisted and re-mustered Jan. 23, 1864.
Mustered out July 18, 1865, Louisville, Ky.
Lyle, Josiah A. Age 18. Residence South Fork, nativity Pennsylvania. Enlisted Feb. 29, 1864.
Mustered March 9, 1864. Mustered out July 18, 1865, Louisville, Ky.
Lyman, Charles H. (Veteran.) Age 19. Residence Maquoketa, nativity Illinois. Enlisted Aug. 6,
1861, as First Corporal. Mustered Sept. 2, 1861. Promoted Fifth Sergeant March 3, 1862; Fourth
Sergeant May 10, 1862; First Sergeant June 7, 1863; Second Lieutenant July 13, 1863. Wounded
in side slightly Nov. 27, 1863. Re-enlisted and re-mustered Jan. 23, 1864. Promoted Adjutant
Jan. 9, 1865. Mustered out July 18, 1865, Louisville, Ky.
COMPANY "B"
Lane, Clement H. Age 34. Residence Rome, nativity Ohio. Enlisted Aug. 12, 1861, as Third
Corporal. Mustered Sept. 24, 1861. Promoted Fourth Sergeant July 29, 1862; Third Sergeant
March 23, 1863; Second Sergeant Jan. 20, 1864. Mustered out Sept. 24, 1864, East Point, Ga.,
expiration of term of service.
Long, Daniel R. (Veteran.) Age 28. Residence Spring Creek, nativity Ohio. Enlisted Aug. 30,
1861. Mustered Sept. 24, 1861. Re-enlisted and re-mustered Jan. 23, 1864. Missing in action
May 27, 1864, Dallas, Ga. Mustered out July 18, 1865, Louisville, Ky.
Long, George W. Age 21. Residence LaPorte City, nativity Indiana. Enlisted Dec. 12, 1863.
Mustered Dec. 22, 1863. Killed in action May 27, 1864, Dallas, Ga. 77
Long, Joel. Age 30. Residence Rome, nativity Ohio. Enlisted Aug. 12, 1861. Mustered Sept. 24,

1861. Died Dec. 22, 1863, Nashville, Tenn. Buried in National Cemetery, Nashville, Tenn.
Section D, grave 165.
Lukscart, James. Age 44. Residence Washington, nativity Ohio. Enlisted Oct. 27, 1864.
Mustered Oct. 27, 1864. Mustered out July 18, 1865, Louisville, Ky.
Luther, Jonathan. Age 18. Residence Rome, nativity Illinois. Enlisted Aug. 12, 1861. Mustered
Sept. 24, 1861. Wounded severely in abdomen May 19, 1863. Promoted Sixth Corporal May 20,
1863; Fifth Corporal; Fourth Corporal Dec. 1, 1863. Taken prisoner March 14, 1864, Claysville,
Ala. Died Nov. 2, 1864, Andersonville, Ga. Buried in National Cemetery, Andersonville, Ga.
Grave 11752.
COMPANY "C"
Lawson, Frank. (Veteran.) Age 23. Residence Hazelton, nativity England. Enlisted Sept. 7,
1862. Mustered Oct. 14, 1862. Re-enlisted and re-mustered Jan. 23, 1864. Mustered out July 18,
1865, Louisville, Ky.
Leatherman, James or John. Age 20. Residence Spring Grove, nativity Ohio. Enlisted Aug. 24,
1861. Mustered Sept. 24, 1861. Wounded slightly in leg March 7, 1862, Pea Ridge, Ark.
Discharged Oct. 17, 1862, Hospital, Keokuk, Iowa.
Lines, Nelson. Age 33. Residence Buchanan County, nativity New York. Enlisted Feb. 15, 1864.
Mustered Feb. 15, 1864. Wounded severely May 16, 1864, Resaca, Ga. Died of wounds May 18,
1864. Buried in National Cemetery, Chattanooga, Tenn. Section K, grave 65.
Little, Edmund C. Age 18. Residence Independence, nativity Illinois. Enlisted Aug. 5, 1861, as
Eighth Corporal. Mustered Sept. 24, 1861. Promoted Third

Sergeant Jan. 21, 1862; First
Sergeant March 8, 1862; Second Lieutenant July 18, 1862; Captain March 8, 1863. Wounded in
arm May 22, 1863, Vicksburg, Miss. Discharged for wounds Feb. 3, 1864, Woodville, Ala.

Losey, Alpheus. (Veteran.) Age 18. Residence Independence, nativity New York. Enlisted Aug.
26, 1861. Mustered Sept. 24, 1861. Promoted Eighth Corporal March 8, 1862; Third Corporal.
Wounded in arm severely May 22, 1863, Vicksburg, Miss. Re-enlisted. and re-mustered Jan. 23,
1864. Mustered out July 18, 1865, Louisville, Ky.

Lucky, Orlando F. (Veteran.) Age 19. Residence Independence, nativity New York. Enlisted
Aug. 26, 1861. Mustered Sept. 24, 1861. Promoted Seventh Corporal. Wounded slightly in hip
March 7, 1862, Pea Ridge, Ark. Re-enlisted and re-mustered Jan. 23, 1864. Promoted Fifth
Corporal June 14, 1865. Mustered out July 18, 1865, Louisville, Ky.

COMPANY "D"

Langstaff, Enoch. Age 21. Residence Fourth Congressional District, nativity Ohio. Enlisted
Nov. 2, 1864. Mustered Nov. 2, 1864. Mustered out July 18, 1865, Louisville, Ky.

78

Larimore, John. Age 41. Residence Fourth Congressional District, nativity Pennsylvania.
Enlisted Nov. 2, 1864. Mustered Nov. 2, 1864. Mustered out July 18, 1865, Louisville, Ky.

Lee, Israel. Age 26. Residence Boone County, nativity Illinois. Enlisted Oct. 27, 1864. Mustered
Oct. 27, 1864. Mustered out July 18, 1865, Louisville, Ky.

Lichtenheim, Lavine A. (Veteran.) Age 20. Residence Dubuque, nativity New York. Enlisted
Aug. 16, 1861. Mustered Aug. 16, 1861. Wounded slightly in

hand March 7, 1862. Wounded
slightly in knee May 22, 1863. Re-enlisted and re-mustered Jan. 23, 1864. Promoted Fourth
Corporal Oct. 1, 1864; Third Corporal June 20, 1864. Wounded severely March 21, 1865,
Bentonsville, S. C. Mustered out July 18, 1865, Louisville, Ky.
Lowbower, John C. Age 20. Residence Monticello, nativity Switzerland. Enlisted Aug. 16,
1861. Mustered Sept. 2, 1861. Discharged for disability July 27, 1863, St. Louis, Mo.
Lowe, Christian. Age 39. Residence Third Congressional District, nativity Germany. Enlisted
Oct. 5, 1864. Mustered Oct. 5, 1864. Mustered out July 18, 1865, Louisville, Ky.
COMPANY "E"
Lampert, Joseph. Age 25. Residence Guttenburg, nativity Germany. Enlisted Aug. 16, 1861.
Mustered Sept. 24, 1861. Promoted Eighth Corporal Dec. 18, 1862; Fifth Corporal Dec. 18,
1862. Killed May 22, 1863, Vicksburg, Miss.
Lenhart, John. Age 44. Residence Scotch Grove, nativity Germany. Enlisted Feb. 20, 1864.
Mustered Feb. 20, 1864. Missing in action May 27, 1864, Dallas, Ga. Mustered out July 18,
1865, Louisville, Ky.
Lockard, Robert W. Age 19. Residence Volga City, nativity Ohio. Enlisted Nov. 20, 1861.
Wounded severely in groin March 7, 1862, Pea Ridge, Ark. Died of measles Jan. 27, 1863,
Hospital Boat "Tony Bullet."
Logan, Lyman B. Age 18. Residence Elgin, nativity Indiana. Enlisted Sept. 14, 1861. Mustered
Sept. 24, 1861. Promoted Second Corporal. Discharged Dec. 9, 1862, Helena, Ark. See company
F, Second Cavalry.
Long, William. (Veteran.) Age 23. Residence Clayton County,

nativity Ireland. Mustered Sept. 24, 1861. Re-enlisted and re-mustered Jan. 23, 1864. Mustered out July 18, 1865, Louisville, Ky.
Longneckhard, Henry. Age 18. Residence Dubuque, nativity Prussia. Mustered Sept. 24, 1861.
Discharged for disability Jan. 8, 1862, Pacific, Mo.
Lott, Thomas B. Age 18. Residence Elgin, nativity Illinois. Enlisted Sept. 14, 1861. Mustered
Sept. 24, 1861. Mustered out Sept. 24, 1864, expiration of term of service.
Love, Daniel. Age 26. Residence Washington County, nativity Pennsylvania. Enlisted Oct. 24,
1864. Mustered Oct. 24, 1864. Mustered out July 18, 1865, Louisville, Ky.
79
Lovesee, Isaac A. Age 28. Residence Fredericksburg, nativity England. Enlisted Sept. 13, 1862.
Mustered Sept. 13, 1862. Wounded severely May 27, 1863, Vicksburg, Miss. Died of wounds
July 16, 1863. Buried in National Cemetery, Vicksburg, Miss. Section G, grave 1275.
COMPANY "F"
Lackey, Augustus. Age 18. Residence Strawberry Point, nativity Canada. Enlisted Sept. 5,
1861. Mustered Sept. 14, 1861. Died April 22, 1862, Forsyth, Mo.
Larabee, Franklin L. Age 22. Residence Fayette, nativity Pennsylvania. Enlisted Sept. 8, 1861.
Mustered Sept. 12, 1861. Died of wounds March 9, 1862, Pea Ridge, Ark.
Larson, Hans. (Veteran.) Age 20. Residence Clermont, nativity Norway. Enlisted Sept. 9, 1861.
Mustered Sept. 12, 1861. Promoted Sixth Corporal Oct. 6, 1863. Re-enlisted and re-mustered
Jan. 23, 1864. Promoted Fifth Corporal Aug. 1, 1864. Wounded in neck March 21, 1865,
Bentonville, N. C. Promoted Fourth Corporal April 1, 1865;

Third Corporal May 13, 1865.
Mustered out July 18, 1865, Louisville, Ky.
Laumsden, John A. (Veteran.) Age 22. Residence Lima, nativity Ireland. Enlisted July 10,
1862. Mustered July 25, 1862. Promoted Fifth Corporal March 12, 1863; Third Corporal Oct. 6,
1863. Re-enlisted and re-mustered Jan. 23, 1864. Promoted Second Corporal Aug. 1, 1864; Third
Sergeant Jan. 4, 1865; Second Sergeant June 6,1865. Mustered out July 18, 1865, Louisville, Ky.
Lee, Albert. Age 20. Residence Windsor, nativity Ohio. Enlisted Sept. 5, 1861. Mustered Sept.
12, 1861. Mustered out Sept. 24, 1864, East Point, Ga.
Lee, Jasper. Age 21. Residence Auburn, nativity Ohio. Enlisted Dec. 24, 1863. Mustered Dec.
24, 1863. Mustered out July 18, 1865, Louisville, Ky.
Lee, Martin. Age 18. Residence Eldorado, nativity Norway. Enlisted Sept. 5, 1861. Mustered
Sept. 12, 1861. Wounded severely in shoulder March 7, 1862, Pea Ridge, Ark. Discharged for
wounds Aug. 27, 1862, Cairo, Ill. See company H, Thirty-eighth Infantry, and Thirty-fourth and
Thirty-eighth Consolidated.
Lyon, Alfred P. Age 19. Residence Elgin, nativity New York. Enlisted Feb. 22, 1864. Mustered
March 18, 1864. Mustered out July 18, 1865, Louisville, Ky.
COMPANY "G"
Lamson, James H. Age 18. Residence Waverly, nativity New York. Enlisted Aug. 15, 1861.
Mustered Sept. 24, 1861. Mustered out Sept. 23, 1864, Davenport, Iowa, expiration of term of
service.
Larue, Francis. Age 36. Residence Butler County, nativity Ohio. Enlisted Feb. 29, 1864.
Mustered March 11, 1864. Mustered out July 18, 1865, Louisville, KY.

80
Leverich, Asbury. Age 38. Residence Janesville, nativity Ohio. Appointed Second Lieutenant
Sept. 16, 1861. Mustered Sept. 16, 1861. Resigned May 11, 1862.
Leverich, Willard. Age 20. Residence Shell Rock, nativity Iowa. Enlisted Sept. 3, 1861.
Mustered Sept. 24, 1861. Shot in breast and killed March 7, 1862, Pea Ridge, Ark. Buried in
Cemetery, Pea Ridge, Ark.
Lightly, David. Age 19. Residence Clayton County, nativity Ohio. Enlisted Feb. 20, 1864.
Mustered March 17, 1864. Mustered out July 18, 1865, Louisville, Ky.
Linsey, James S. Age 18. Residence Waverly, nativity New York. Enlisted July 28, 1861.
Mustered Sept. 24, 1861. Died of fever June 23, 1862, Springfield, Mo.
Little, Sardis. Age 40. Residence Waterloo, nativity New York. Enlisted Sept. 6, 1861.
Mustered Sept. 16, 1861. Discharged for disability Rolla, Mo.
Lockerly, Nelson. Age 45. Residence Waterloo, nativity New York. Enlisted Aug. 5, 1861.
Mustered Sept. 24, 1861. Discharged for disability June 23, 1862, Batesville, Ark.
Lucas, Alexander J. Age 18. Residence Waverly, nativity Indiana. Enlisted Aug. 23, 1861.
Mustered Sept. 24, 1861. Died of smallpox March 30, 1863, Vicksburg, Miss.
COMPANY "H"
LaMont, Joseph. Age 18. Residence Allamakee County, nativity Illinois. Enlisted March 2,
1864. Mustered March 21, 1864. Mustered out July 18, 1865, Louisville, Ky.
Landers, Jonas W. Age 24. Residence Sigourney, nativity Indiana. Enlisted Nov. 2, 1864.
Mustered Nov. 2, 1864. Mustered out July 18, 1865, Louisville,

Ky.
Little, John. Age 33. Residence Oskaloosa, nativity Connecticut. Enlisted Jan. 1, 1864.
Mustered Jan. 1, 1864. Mustered out July 18, 1865, Louisville, Ky. See company G. Twentyfifth
Infantry.
Long, James P. Age 20. Residence Keokuk County, nativity Iowa. Enlisted Nov. 19, 1864.
Mustered Nov. 19, 1864. Mustered out July 18, 1865, Louisville, Ky.
Lough, John B. Age 38. Residence Mahaska, nativity Ohio. Enlisted Nov. 2, 1864. Mustered
Nov. 2, 1864. Mustered out July 18, 1865, Louisville, Ky.
COMPANY "I"
Lane, William. Age 26. Residence Davenport, nativity Ireland. Enlisted Nov. 16, 1864.
Mustered Nov. 16, 1864. Deserted June 26, 1865, Louisville, Ky.
81
Lawrence, John. (Veteran.) Age 24. Residence Albia, nativity Ireland. Enlisted Aug. 14, 1861.
Mustered Sept. 18, 1861. Re-enlisted and re-mustered Jan. 23, 1864. Discharged for disability
July 1, 1865, Louisville, Ky.
Leggett, Herman C. Age 18. Residence Geneva, nativity Ohio. Enlisted Feb. 29, 1864.
Mustered Feb. 29, 1864. Mustered out July 18, 1865, Louisville, Ky.
Levy, Frederick. Age 18. Residence Burlington, nativity New York. Enlisted Jan. 27, 1865.
Mustered Jan. 27, 1865. Mustered out July 18, 1865, Louisville, Ky. See company G, Twentyfifth
Infantry.
Lockwood, Charles U. Age 18. Residence Castalia, nativity New York. Enlisted Sept. 10, 1861.
Mustered Sept. 18, 1861. Wounded severely in knee March 7, 1862, Pea Ridge, Ark. Discharged

for disability July 1, 1865, Louisville, Ky.
Logue, John. (Veteran.) Age 22. Residence New Oregon, nativity Ireland. Enlisted Aug. 17,
1861. Mustered Sept. 2, 1861. Promoted Sixth Corporal July 1, 1863; Fifth Corporal Oct. 6,
1863. Re-enlisted and re-mustered Jan. 23, 1864. Promoted Fourth Corporal Sept. 16, 1864;
Third Corporal May 1, 1865. Mustered out July 18, 1865, Louisville, Ky.
Long, John. Age 20. Residence Castalia, nativity Illinois. Enlisted Sept. 12, 1861. Mustered
Sept. 18, 1861. Discharged Feb. 29, 1862, Pacific City, Mo.
Lutes, Osborn. (Veteran.) Age 21. Residence Castalia, nativity Ohio. Enlisted Sept. 14, 1861.
Mustered Sept. 18, 1861. Promoted Seventh Corporal May 24, 1863; Fifth Corporal July 1,
1863; Fourth Corporal Oct. 6, 1863. Re-enlisted and re-mustered Jan. 23, 1864. Promoted Third
Sergeant Sept. 16, 1864; Fifth Sergeant May 1, 1865. Mustered out July 18, 1865, Louisville,
Ky.
COMPANY "K"
Lutz, Joseph W. Age 21. Residence Marion, nativity Pennsylvania. Enlisted Sept. 21, 1861.
Mustered Sept. 24, 1861. Discharged for disability Jan. 11, 1862, Pacific City, Mo.
COMPANY "A"
McComb, Samuel. Age 23. Residence Andrew, nativity Pennsylvania. Enlisted Aug. 12, 1861.
Mustered Sept. 24, 1861. Killed in battle March 7, 1862, Pea Ridge, Ark. Buried in National
Cemetery, Fayetteville. Ark. Section 2, grave 16.
McCrea, Charles. Age 43. Residence Fourth Congressional District, nativity Ohio. Enlisted
Nov. 2, 1864. Mustered Nov. 2, 1864. Mustered out July 18, 1865, Louisville, Ky.

McGaffee, John S. Age 21. Residence Maquoketa, nativity Canada. Enlisted Aug. 10, 1861.
Mustered Sept. 24, 1861. Wounded in foot slightly May 19, 1863, Vicksburg, Miss. Received a
sun stroke July 11, 1863. Discharged for disability Feb. 11, 1864, St. Louis, Mo.
82
McManus, John. Age 18. Residence Henry County, nativity Indiana. Enlisted Feb. 29, 1864.
Mustered March 5, 1864. Mustered out July 18, 1865, Louisville, Ky. See company K, Twentyfifth
Infantry.
McMeans, Andrew. Age 26. Residence Andrew, nativity Pennsylvania. Enlisted Sept. 10, 1862.
Mustered Sept. 15, 1862. Killed in battle May 19, 1863, Vicksburg, Miss.
McMeans, John W. Age 22. Residence Andrew, nativity Pennsylvania. Enlisted Aug. 12, 1861.
Mustered Sept. 24, 1861. Wounded slightly in hand March 7, 1862, Pea Ridge, Ark. Wounded in
shoulder severely May 19, 1863, Vicksburg, Miss. Mustered out Sept. 24, 1864, East Point, Ga.,
expiration of term of service.
McNally, James. Age 28. Residence Sabula, nativity Ireland. Enlisted Aug. 10, 1861. Mustered
Sept. 24, 1861. Wounded slightly in hand March 7, 1862, Pea Ridge, Ark. Mustered out Sept. 24,
1864, East Point, Ga., expiration of term of service.
COMPANY "B"
McCardoe, James. Age 21. Residence Black Hawk County, nativity Ireland. Enlisted Oct. 25,
1864. Mustered Oct. 27, 1864. Mustered out July 18, 1865, Louisville, Ky.
McCarty, Charles. Age 22. Residence Fairview, nativity New York. Enlisted Aug. 23, 1861.
Mustered Sept. 24, 1861 Discharged Dec. 11, 1862.

McGowan, Calvin. Age 23. Residence Fairview, nativity Pennsylvania. Enlisted Aug. 12, 1861.
Mustered Sept. 27, 1861. Mustered out Sept. 24, 1864, East Point, Ga., expiration of term of
service.
McGuigan, Thomas. Age 21. Residence Langworthy, nativity Maryland. Enlisted Aug. 12,
1861. Mustered Sept. 24, 1861. Discharged for disability Aug. 27, 1862, St. Louis, Mo.
McKinney, James R. Age 18. Residence Louisa County, nativity Ohio. Enlisted Feb. 29, 1864.
Mustered March 4, 1864. Mustered out July 18, 1865, St. Louis, Mo. See company I, Twentyfifth
Infantry.
McMellen, James. Age 30. Residence Fairview, nativity Ohio. Enlisted Aug. 12, 1861.
Mustered Sept. 24, 1861. Discharged for disability March 11, 1863, Young's Point, La.
McSweeney, Paul. Age 24. Residence Dubuque, nativity Rhode Island. Appointed First
Lieutenant Sept. 2, 1861. Mustered Sept. 2, 1861. Promoted Captain Aug. 1, 1862. Wounded in
hand slightly May 22, 1863, Vicksburg, Miss. Mustered out Jan. 15, 1865, Savannah, Ga.,
expiration of term of service.
COMPANY "C"
McCalla, George. Age 23. Enlisted Aug. 24, 1863. Mustered Nov. 30, 1863. Mustered out May
27, 1865, Davenport, Iowa.
83
McCurniff, Thomas. Age 18. Residence Buchanan County, nativity Michigan. Enlisted Feb. 29,
1864. Mustered March 16, 1864. Mustered out July 18, 1865, Louisville, Ky.
McGuire, Henry O. Age 18. Residence Buchanan County, nativity New York. Enlisted March

1, 1864. Mustered March 16, 1864. Mustered out June 12, 1865, Davenport, Iowa.
McKisson, Martin V. B. Age 26. Residence Buchanan County, nativity Ohio. Enlisted Feb. 29,
1864. Mustered Feb. 29, 1864. Wounded severely Aug. 6, 1864, Atlanta, Ga. Mustered out July
18, 1865, Louisville, Ky.
COMPANY "D"
McCullough, William. Age 35. Residence South Fork, nativity Ireland. Enlisted Aug. 30, 1862.
Mustered March 12, 1863. Promoted Fifth Corporal Aug. 4, 1863; Fourth Corporal Jan. 30,
1864; Second Corporal July 1, 1864; Fifth Sergeant Oct. 1, 1864; Fourth Sergeant June 20, 1865.
Mustered out July 18, 1865, Louisville, Ky.
McDaniel, Orlando. Age 21. Residence Monticello, nativity Ohio. Enlisted Sept. 5, 1861.
Mustered Sept. 5, 1861. Wounded severely in back March 7, 1862, Pea Ridge, Ark. Discharged
for wounds Aug. 28, 1862, Cairo, Ill.
McDavitt, Martin S. Age 19. Residence Marshall County, nativity Ohio. Enlisted Nov. 15,
1864. Mustered Nov. 15, 1864. Discharged for disability Aug. 2, 1865, Jackson, Mich.
McIntosh, James F. Age 28. Residence Pottawattamie County, nativity Illinois. Enlisted Nov. 5,
1864. Mustered Nov. 5, 1864. Mustered out July 18, 1865, Louisville, Ky.
McKean, Francis C. Age 19. Residence Scotch Grove, nativity Ohio. Enlisted Aug. 16, 1861, as
First Sergeant. Mustered Sept. 2, 1861. Promoted Second Lieutenant July 9, 1862; Captain Feb.
15, 1863. Mustered out Dec. 31, 1864.
McVey, William H. Age 20. Residence Bowen's Prairie, nativity Ohio. Enlisted Aug. 16, 1861.
Mustered Aug. 16, 1861. Promoted Fifth Corporal April 4, 1862.

Discharged for disability Oct. 13, 1862, Helena, Ark.
COMPANY "E"
McCabe, William. (Veteran.) Age 40. Residence Volga City, nativity Ohio. Enlisted Sept. 9,
1861, as Third Corporal. Mustered Sept. 24, 1861. Promoted Second Corporal; First Corporal.
Wounded slightly in left foot March 7, 1862, Pea Ridge, Ark. Re-enlisted and re-mustered Jan.
23, 1864. Mustered out July 18, 1865, Louisville, Ky.
McCaffery, John. Age 27. Residence Wandena, nativity Ireland. Enlisted Sept. 4, 1861.
Mustered Sept. 24, 1861. Wounded in arm March 7, 1862, Pea Ridge, Ark. Discharged for
wounds Oct. 22, 1862, St. Louis, Mo.
84
McLavy, Allen. Age 19. Residence Volga City, nativity Pennsylvania. Enlisted Nov. 24, 1861.
Mustered Nov. 24, 1861. Discharged Feb. 21, 1863, St. Louis, Mo.
McLavy, William E. Age 19. Residence West Union, nativity Pennsylvania. Enlisted Feb. 22,
1862. Mustered March 9, i862. Promoted Sixth Corporal Jan. 4, 1863; Fifth Corporal Jan. 4,
1865; Fourth Corporal Jan. 25, 1865. Mustered out July 18, 1865, Louisville, Ky.
McVerts, Lewis C. Age 17. Residence Des Moines County, nativity Pennsylvania. Enlisted
March 28, 1864. Mustered March 28, 1864. Mustered out July 18, 1865, Louisville, Ky.
COMPANY "F"
McAlavay, Charles. Age 29. Residence Taylorville, nativity Pennsylvania. Enlisted Sept. 5,
1861. Mustered Sept. 14, 1861. Died of dropsy Nov. 17, 1862, St. Louis, Mo. Buried in National
Cemetery, Jefferson Barracks, Missouri. Section 50, grave 30.
McQuillan, William H. Age 18. Residence Clermont, nativity

Iowa. Enlisted Sept. 26, 1861.
Mustered Sept. 26, 1861. Died May 21, 1862, Batesville, Miss.
COMPANY "G"
McAlpin, Benjamin F. Age 23. Residence Dubuque, nativity Indiana. Enlisted Aug. 26, 1861.
Mustered Aug. 26, 1861. Died of smallpox March 7, 1863, Vicksburg, Miss. Buried in National
Cemetery, Vicksburg, Miss. Section C, grave 12.
McGuigan, William H. Age 25. Residence Colesburg, nativity Pennsylvania. Enlisted July 28,
1861. Mustered Sept. 24, 1861. Killed in battle May 22, 1863, Vicksburg, Miss.
McKinnis, Robert. Age 19. Residence Dubuque, nativity Ohio. Enlisted Feb. 20, 1864.
Mustered March 17, 1864. Wounded in arm severely July 22, 1864, Atlanta, Ga. Mustered out
July 18, 1865, Louisville, Ky.
McRoberts, Alonzo. Age 19. Residence Janesville, nativity Missouri. Enlisted Sept. 6, 1861.
Mustered Sept. 24, 1861. Died of smallpox April 21, 1863, Vicksburg, Miss.
COMPANY "H"
McCuin, James B. Age 43. Residence Centerville, nativity Ireland. Enlisted Nov. 3, 1864.
Mustered Nov. 3, 1864. Mustered out July 18, 1865, Louisville, Ky.
McQuay, Thomas. Age 44. Residence Winneshiek County, nativity Ireland. Enlisted March 24,
1864. Mustered Nov. 12, 1864. Mustered out July 18, 1865, Louisville, Ky.
COMPANY "I"
McCrea, William. Age 22. Residence Castalia, nativity Canada. Enlisted Sept. 14, 1861.
Mustered Sept. 18, 1861. Wounded slightly in leg March 7, 1862, Pea Ridge, Ark. Promoted

First Corporal May 4, 1862; Fifth Sergeant Dec. 10, 1862. Killed in battle May 22, 1863,
Vicksburg, Miss.
0 NINTH INFANTRY 89
McIntosh, Andrew. (Veteran.) Age 22. Residence Marble Rock, nativity New York. Enlisted
Aug. 22, 1861. Mustered Sept. 18, 1861. Re-enlisted and re-mustered Jan. 23, 1864. Mustered
out July 2, 1865.
McMartin, Daniel A. Age 29. Residence Winneshiek County, nativity Canada. Enlisted Sept.
14, 1861. Mustered Sept. 18, 1861. Promoted Fourth Corporal March 23, 1862. Mustered out
Sept. 24, 1864, East Point, Ga. Expiration of term of service.
McVey, James D. Age 22. Residence Oskaloosa, nativity Maryland. Enlisted Nov. 2, 1864.
Mustered Nov. 2, 1864. Mustered out July 18, 1865, Louisville, Ky.
COMPANY "K"
McCoy, James K. Age 18. Residence Marion, nativity Iowa. Enlisted Sept. 14, 1861. Mustered
Sept. 24, 1861. Killed March 7, 1862, Pea Ridge, Ark.
McFerren, Jacob. (Veteran.) Age 30. Residence Marion, nativity Pennsylvania. Mustered Sept.
24, 1861. Promoted Wagoner. Re-enlisted and re-mustered Jan. 23, 1864. Mustered out July 18,
1865, Louisville, Ky.
McKee, John S. Age 19. Residence Cedar Rapids, nativity Pennsylvania. Enlisted Sept. 21,
1861. Mustered Sept. 24, 1861. Wounded severely in leg March 7, 1862, Pea Ridge, Ark.
Promoted Fifth Sergeant March 3, 1864; Fourth Sergeant April 17, 1865. Mustered out July 18,
1865, Louisville, Ky.
COMPANY "A"
Malony, William H. Age 21. Residence Montgomery County,

nativity Maryland. Enlisted Nov. 5, 1864. Mustered Nov. 5, 1864. Mustered out July 18, 1865, Louisville, Ky.
Markle, John R. Age 18. Residence Maquoketa, nativity Canada. Enlisted Aug. 10, 1861.
Mustered Sept. 24, 1861. Discharged for disability Dec. 1, 1862, St. Louis, Mo.
Markle, Joseph. Age 18. Residence Maquoketa, nativity Canada. Enlisted Nov. 25, 1863.
Mustered Nov. 25, 1863. Mustered out July 18, 1865, Louisville, Ky.
Martin, Leonard L. Age 28. Residence Maquoketa, nativity Vermont. Enlisted Aug. 6, 1861, as
Third Sergeant. Mustered Sept. 2, 1861. Promoted Second Sergeant March 3, 1862; First
Sergeant May 10, 1862. Wounded in left ankle severely May 18, 1863, Vicksburg, Miss.
Promoted Second Lieutenant May 27, 1863. Died of wounds July 11, 1863, Memphis, Tenn.
Martin, Stephen R. Age 18. Residence Maquoketa, nativity Vermont. Enlisted Aug. 8, 1861.
Mustered Sept. 24, 1861. Discharged for disability Oct. 7, 1861, Benton Barracks, St. Louis, Mo.
86
Milhausen, Henry H. P. (Veteran.) Age 31. Residence Maquoketa, nativity Denmark. Enlisted
July 29, 1861, as Seventh Corporal. Mustered Sept. 7, 1861. Promoted Sixth Corporal March 7,
1862; Fourth Corporal March 10, 1862; Third Corporal; Second Corporal June 2, 1863; First
Corporal; Fifth Sergeant Dec. 17, 1863. Re-enlisted and re-mustered Jan. 23, 1864. Killed in
battle May 30, 1864, Dallas, Ga. Buried in National Cemetery, Marietta, Ga. Section A, grave 358.
Miller, Peter J. (Veteran.) Age 23. Residence Maquoketa, nativity

New York. Enlisted Aug. 13,
1861. Mustered Sept. 24, 1861. Re-enlisted and re-mustered Jan. 23, 1864. Mustered out July 18,
1865, Louisville, Ky.
Miller, Philip A. (Veteran.) Age 19. Residence Maquoketa, nativity Massachusetts. Enlisted
Aug. 10,1861. Mustered Sept. 24, 1861. Re-enlisted and re-mustered Jan. 23, 1864. Mustered out
July 18, 1865, Louisville, Ky.
Miller, Samuel. Age 18. Residence Johnston County, nativity New York. Enlisted Feb. 23,
1864. Mustered March 17, 1864. Mustered out July 18, 1865, Louisville, Ky.
Moore, William. Age 17. Residence Henry County, nativity Iowa. Enlisted April 6, 1864.
Mustered April 13, 1864. Mustered out July 18, 1865, Louisville, Ky. See company K, Twentyfifth
Infantry.
COMPANY "B"
Mason, John M. Age 19. Residence Rome, nativity Ohio. Enlisted Aug. 12, 1861, as Fifth
Corporal. Mustered Sept. 24, 1861. Promoted Fourth Corporal Oct. 1, 1862; Third Corporal Nov.
1, 1862; Second Corporal Dec. 8, 1862; First Corporal March 20, 1863; Fifth Sergeant May 23
1863; Fourth Sergeant Jan. 20, 1864. Mustered out Sept. 24, 1864, East Point, Ga., expiration of
term of service.
Matteson, Daniel M. (Veteran.) Age 22. Residence Madison, nativity New York. Enlisted Aug.
20, 1862. Mustered Aug. 29, 1862. Re-enlisted and re-mustered Jan. 23, 1864. Mustered out July
18, 1865, Louisville, Ky.
Matteson, Elisha C. Age 18. Residence Madison, nativity New York. Enlisted Aug. 12, 1861.
Mustered Sept. 2, 1861. Wounded while assisting First Iowa

Battery May 19, 1863, Vicksburg,
Miss. Died of wounds May 22, 1863, Vicksburg, Miss.
Merrett, Horatio M. Age 33. Residence Rome, nativity New York. Enlisted Aug. 12, 1861.
Mustered Sept. 24, 1861. Discharged for disability March 11, 1862, Hospital, Pacific, Mo.
Metcalf, Arthur. (Veteran.) Age 18. Residence Jones County, nativity Indiana. Enlisted Aug.
12, 1861. Mustered Sept. 24, 1861. Re-enlisted and re-mustered Jan. 23, 1864. Wounded
severely in back June 23, 1864, Kenesaw Mountain, Ga. Discharged for wounds Dec. 8, 1864,
Davenport, Iowa.
87
Miller, David E. Age 20. Residence Hale, nativity Ohio. Enlisted Aug. 12, 1861. Mustered Sept.
24, 1861. Discharged for disability March 11, 1863, Young's Point, La.
Miller, Robert H. Age 40. Residence Lee County, nativity New York. Enlisted Oct. 24, 1864.
Mustered Oct. 24, 1864. Mustered out July 18, 1865, Louisville, Ky.
Moore, James. Age 38. Residence Boone County, nativity Illinois. Enlisted Oct. 27, 1864.
Mustered Oct. 27, 1864. Mustered out July 18, 1865, Louisville, Ky.
Moore, John D. Age 36. Residence Boone County, nativity Ohio, Enlisted Oct. 27, 1864.
Mustered Oct. 27, 1864. Mustered out July 18, 1865, Louisville, Ky.
COMPANY "C"
Merrill, James H. Age 27. Residence Independence, nativity New York. Enlisted as Fifth
Corporal. Mustered Sept. 24, 1861. Promoted Fourth Corporal March 8,1862. Died of dysentery
Sept. 3, 1862, Helena, Ark.

Milliken, John. Age 18. Residence Black Hawk County, nativity Pennsylvania. Enlisted Feb.
22, 1864. Mustered Feb. 23, 1864. Mustered out July 18, 1865, Louisville, Ky.
Monroe, Samuel. Age 19. Residence Buchanan County, nativity Iowa. Enlisted Feb. 28, 1864.
Mustered March 16, 1864. Mustered out May 17, 1865, Davenport, Iowa.
COMPANY "D"
Mabin, Harrison. Age 18. Residence Keokuk, nativity Indiana. Enlisted Nov. 19, 1864.
Mustered Nov. 19, 1864. Died Feb. 18, 1865, Evansville, Ind. Buried in National Cemetery,
Evansville, Ind.
Magee, David F. Age 38. Residence Jones County, nativity Pennsylvania. Appointed First
Lieutenant Sept. 2, 1861. Mustered Sept. 2, 1861. Resigned July 8, 1862.
Magee, Francis A. Age 18. Residence Scotch Grove, nativity Pennsylvania. Enlisted Feb. 22,
1864. Mustered Feb. 22, 1864. Mustered out July 18, 1865, Louisville, Ky.
Magee, John C. Age 20. Residence Scotch Grove, nativity Pennsylvania. Enlisted Feb. 22,
1864. Mustered Feb. 22, 1864. Promoted Seventh Corporal June 20, 1865. Mustered out July 18,
1865, Louisville, Ky.
Mahony, Michael. Age 32. Residence Third Congressional District, nativity Ireland. Enlisted
Oct. 14, 1864. Mustered Oct. 14, 1864. Mustered out July 18, 1865, Louisville, Ky.
Manwarin, Emery. Age 26. Residence Butler County, nativity New York. Enlisted Feb. 23,
1864. Mustered March 11, 1864. Mustered out July 18, 1865, Louisville, Ky.

Marcelles, Charles. Age 21. Residence Anamosa, nativity New York. Enlisted Aug. 16, 1861.
Mustered Sept. 2, 1861. Wounded slightly in arm March 7, 1862, Pea Ridge, Ark. Died of
wounds May 16, 1863, Milliken's Bend, La.
Marcelles, John. (Veteran.) Age 30. Residence Anamosa, nativity New York. Enlisted Sept. 12,
1861. Mustered Sept. 12, 1861. Re-enlisted and re-mustered Jan. 23, 1864. Died of chronic
diarrhea March 9, 1864, Anamosa, Iowa.
Marsh, William A. Age 28. Residence Boone County, nativity Indiana. Enlisted Oct. 27, 1864.
Mustered Oct. 27, 1864. Mustered out July 18, 1865, Louisville, Ky.
Matthew, Lewis. (Veteran.) Age 43. Residence South Fork, nativity Ohio. Enlisted Aug. 23,
1861. Mustered Aug. 23, 1861. Re-enlisted and re-mustered Jan. 23, 1864. Mustered out July 18,
1865, Louisville, Ky.
Merwin, Byron W. Age 19. Residence Monticello, nativity Pennsylvania. Enlisted Aug. 19,
1861. Mustered Sept. 12, 1861. Wounded in breast severely March 7, 1862, Pea Ridge, Ark.
Discharged on account of wounds Aug. 28, 1862, Cairo, Ill.
Miller, Isaac A. Age 21. Residence Monticello, nativity Ohio. Enlisted Aug. 16, 1861, as
Seventh Corporal. Mustered Aug. 16, 1861. Wounded slightly in breast March 7, 1862, Pea
Ridge, Ark. Promoted Fifth Sergeant Jan. 24, 1863. Discharged for disability March 10, 1863, St.
Louis, Mo.
Miller, James. Age 33. Residence Boone County, nativity Ohio. Enlisted Oct. 27, 1864.
Mustered Oct. 27, 1864. Discharged May 30, 1865, New York City.
Miller, James J. (Veteran.) Age 20. Residence Scotch Grove,

nativity Indiana. Enlisted Sept. 3,
1861. Wounded severely in arm May 19, 1863, Vicksburg, Miss. Re-enlisted and re-mustered
Jan. 23, 1864. Taken prisoner Feb. 26, 1865, near Lynch Creek, S. C. Mustered out July 18,
1865, Louisville, Ky.
Miller, John. Age 40. Residence Fourth Congressional District, nativity Pennsylvania. Enlisted
Nov. 2, 1864. Mustered Nov. 2, 1864. Mustered out July 18, 1865, Louisville, Ky.
Miller, John B. Age 21. Residence Monticello, nativity New York. Enlisted Sept. 3, 1861.
Mustered Sept. 7, 1861. Promoted Sixth Corporal Feb. 1, 1862; Fourth Sergeant Jan. 24, 1863;
Second Sergeant March 15, 1863. Wounded slightly in abdomen May 16, 1863, Vicksburg,
Miss. Promoted First Sergeant Aug. 4, 1863. Wounded in shoulder severely July 22, 1864, near
Atlanta, Ga. Mustered out Sept. 24, 1864, Davenport, Iowa, expiration of term of service.
Mitts, Jesse B. Age 44. Nativity Kentucky. Enlisted Nov. 2, 1864. Mustered Nov. 2, 1864. Died
Jan. 26, 1865, Bridgeport, Penn. Buried in National Cemetery, Chattanooga, Tenn. Section H,
grave 519.
NINTH INFANTRY 93
89
Moore John J. (Veteran.) Age 22. Residence Jones County, nativity Illinois. Enlisted Aug. 16,
1861. Mustered Aug. 16, 1861. Wounded slightly in arm March 7, 1862, Pea Ridge, Ark. Reenlisted
and re-mustered Jan. 23, 1864. Discharged for disability June 27, 1865, Louisville, Ky.
Moore, Zadoc. (Veteran.) Age 21. Residence Scotch Grove, nativity Illinois. Enlisted Aug. 16,
1861. Mustered Sept. 2, 1861. Promoted Third Corporal April 4,

1862; Second Corporal Jan. 24,
1863; Fifth Sergeant April 29, 1863; Fourth Sergeant Aug. 4, 1863.
Re-enlisted and re-mustered
Jan. 23, 1864. Promoted Third Sergeant May 2, 1864. Wounded in
ankle July 28, 1864, Atlanta,
Ga. Promoted First Sergeant Oct. 1, 1864; First Lieutenant June
20, 1865. Mustered out July 18,
1865, Louisville, Ky.
Morgan, Franklin. Age 18. Residence Allamakee County,
nativity Ohio. Enlisted Oct. 31,
1864. Mustered Oct. 31, 1864. Died Jan. 4, 1865. Buried in
National Cemetery, Nashville, Tenn.
Section H, grave 225.
Mower, Nathan A. Age 26. Residence Boone County, nativity
Pennsylvania. Enlisted Oct. 27,
1864. Mustered Oct. 27, 1864. Mustered out July 18, 1865,
Louisville, Ky.
Murphy, William L. Age 21. Residence Monticello, nativity
Indiana. Enlisted Aug. 16, 1861, as
First Corporal. Mustered Sept. 2, 1861. Wounded severely in left
lung March 7, 1862, Pea Ridge,
Ark. Died of wounds March 10, 1862, Pea Ridge, Ark.
Myers, Cyrus. Age 19. Residence Boone County, nativity
Pennsylvania. Enlisted Nov. 7, 1864.
Mustered Nov. 7, 1864. Mustered out July 18, 1865, Louisville,
Ky.
COMPANY "E"
Manka, Gottleib. Age 21. Residence Guttenburg, nativity
Germany. Enlisted Sept. 9, 1861.
Mustered Sept. 24, 1861. Promoted Fifth Corporal Jan. 23, 1864;
Fourth Corporal May 27, 1864.
Wounded severely in thigh May 27, 1864, Dallas, Ga. Discharged
for wounds Dec. 8, 1864,
Davenport, Iowa.
Masley, Charles. Age 27. Residence Illyria, nativity Switzerland.
Enlisted Feb. 22 1864.

Mustered March 9, 1864. Died of chronic diarrhea July 27 1864, Marietta, Ga. Buried in
National Cemetery, Marietta, Ga. Section G, grave 1515.
Meisner, Fred. (Veteran.) Age 24. Residence Elkader, nativity Germany. Mustered Sept. 24,
1861. Re-enlisted and re-mustered Jan. 23, 1864. Wounded severely in both legs Aug. 31, 1864,
Jonesboro, Ga. Mustered out July 18, 1865, Louisville, Ky.
Metcalf, Michael. Age 19. Residence Winneshiek County, nativity Germany, Enlisted Oct. 31,
1864. Mustered Oct. 31, 1864. Mustered out July 18, 1865, Louisville, KY.
Moats, John S. Age 19. Residence Clayton County, nativity Ohio. Enlisted March 12, 1864.
Mustered July 17, 1864. Mustered out March 18, 1865, Louisville, Ky.
90
Moran, John. Age 19. Residence Winneshiek County, nativity Ireland. Enlisted Oct. 31, 1864.
Mustered Oct. 31, 1864. Mustered out July 18, 1865, Louisville, Ky.
Morrison, John. Age 44. Residence Volga City, nativity Ireland. Mustered Sept. 24, 1861.
Discharged Aug. 30, 1862, Helena, Ark.
Muline, Elmer. Age 19. Residence Clayton County, nativity Iowa. Enlisted March 12, 1864.
Mustered March 17, 1864. Mustered out July 18, 1865, Louisville, Ky.
Myers, George. Age 33. Residence Fourth Congressional District, nativity Germany. Enlisted
Nov. 2, 1864. Mustered Nov. 2, 1864. Mustered out July 18, 1865, Louisville, Ky.
COMPANY "F"
Mead, Charles W. Age 25. Residence Taylorville, nativity New York. Enlisted Sept. 5, 1861.
Mustered Sept. 14, 1861. Died of chronic diarrhea March 3, 1863.

Merry, Ezra H. Age. 18. Residence Strawberry Point, nativity New York. Enlisted Sept. 4,
1861. Mustered Sept. 14, 1861. Wounded severely in shoulder March 19, 1863, Vicksburg, Miss.
Discharged July 27, 1863, St. Louis, Mo.
Merry, Jeremiah. (Veteran.) Age 18. Residence Strawberry Point, nativity New York. Enlisted
Sept. 4, 1861. Mustered Sept. 14, 1861. Re-enlisted and re-mustered Jan. 23, 1864. Mustered out
July 18, 1865, Louisville, Ky.
Millar, Charles H. Age 22. Residence West Union, nativity New York. Enlisted Sept. 19, 1861.
Mustered Sept. 24, 1861. Discharged for promotion as Captain of company G, Thirty-eighth
Infantry Oct. 17, 1862. See company G, Thirty-eighth Infantry.
Morley, William R. Age 18. Residence Taylorville, nativity Massachusetts. Enlisted Feb. 29,
1864. Mustered March 18, 1864. Mustered out July 18, 1865, Louisville, Ky.
Munger, Charles E. Age 19. Residence Taylorville, nativity Michigan. Enlisted Sept. 5, 1861.
Mustered Sept. 14, 1861. Wounded severely in leg March 7, 1862, Pea Ridge, Ark. Deserted
Feb. 5, 1863, Young's Point, La.
Munger, William H. Age 21. Residence Taylorville, nativity Michigan. Enlisted Sept. 4, 1861.
Mustered Sept. 14, 1861. Wounded slightly in wrist March 7, 1862, Pea Ridge, Ark. Discharged
for disability April 5, 1863, Young's Point, La.
Murphy, Michael. Age 26. Residence Des Moines County, nativity Ireland. Enlisted March 16,
1864. Mustered March 21, 1861. Mustered out July 18, 1865, Louisville, Ky. See company G,
Twenty-fifth Infantry.
Myers, George W. Age 24. Residence West Union, nativity Indiana. Enlisted Sept. 4, 1861.

Mustered Sept. 4, 1861. Discharged for disability April 19, 1862, Young's Point, La.
NINTH INFANTRY 95
91
Myers, John C. Age 20. Residence Eldorado, nativity Indiana. Enlisted as Fourth Corporal.
Mustered Sept. 12, 1861. Discharged for disability Dec. 2, 1862, St. Louis, Mo.
COMPANY "G"
Malory, Charles W. (Veteran.) Age 25. Residence Janesville, nativity Illinois. Enlisted Aug. 10,
1861, as Sixth Corporal. Mustered Sept. 24, 1861. Promoted Third Corporal Feb. 15, 1862;
Second Corporal Dec. 6, 1862; Commissary Sergeant June 7, 1863. Re-enlisted and re-mustered
Jan. 23, 1864. Discharged for disability March 7, 1865, Mound City, Ill.
Martin, David I. Age 26. Residence Eldora, nativity Ohio. Enlisted Aug. 19, 1861, as Third
Corporal. Mustered Sept. 24, 1861. Discharged for disability April 18, 1862, Pacific City, Mo.
Means, Jasper. Age 15. Residence Delaware, nativity Iowa. Enlisted Feb. 29, 1864. Mustered
March 17, 1864. Wounded accidentally; lost three fingers July 15, 1864, Chattahoochee River.
Mustered out July 18, 1865, Louisville, Ky.
Meligan, Alfred. Age 18. Residence Dubuque, nativity Iowa. Enlisted Sept. 23, 1861. Mustered
Sept. 24, 1861. Died April 9, 1863, Vicksburg, Miss.
Metz, Silas. Age 20. Residence Mound Prairie, nativity Indiana. Enlisted Oct. 6, 1864. Mustered
Oct. 6, 1864. Mustered out July 18, 1865, Louisville, Ky.
Michaels, Aaron. Age 22. Residence Colesburg, nativity New York. Enlisted Sept. 18, 1861.
Mustered Sept. 24, 1861. Wounded severely in knee March 7, 1862, Pea Ridge, Ark. Died of

wounds March 15, 1862, Pea Ridge, Ark.

Mitchell, Charles A. Age 20. Residence LaPorte City, nativity Maine. Enlisted Aug. 12, 1861. Mustered Sept. 24, 1861. See Third Iowa Artillery.

More, Robert. Age 21. Residence Janesville, nativity Indiana. Enlisted Aug. 10, 1861. Mustered Sept. 24, 1861. Discharged for disability Pacific City, Mo.

Mores Jerome. (Veteran.) Age 18. Residence Bradford, nativity Illinois. Enlisted Sept. 30, 1862. Mustered Jan. 18, 1863. Re-enlisted and re-mustered Jan. 23, 1864. Mustered out July 18, 1865, Louisville, Ky. See Third Iowa Battery.

Morton, Franklin A. Age 27. Residence Janesville, nativity Ohio. Enlisted July 28, 1861. Mustered Sept. 24, 1861. Promoted Commissary Sergeant Sept. 20, 1862; Quartermaster March 16, 1863. Mustered out Jan. 10, 1865, Savannah, Ga.

Musser, James P. (Veteran.) Age 21. Residence Mitchell County, nativity Ohio. Enlisted Sept. 19, 1861. Mustered Sept. 24, 1861. Re-enlisted and re-mustered Jan. 23, 1864. Mustered out July 18, 1865, Louisville, Ky.

92

Myers, John M. Age 18. Residence Shell Rock, nativity New York. Enlisted Aug. 24, 1861. Mustered Sept. 24, 1861. Killed in battle March 7, 1862, Pea Ridge, Ark. Buried in Cemetery, Pea Ridge, Ark.

Myers, Philip B. (Veteran.) Age 20. Residence Waverly, nativity Pennsylvania. Enlisted Aug. 10, 1861. Mustered Sept. 24, 1861. Re-enlisted and re-mustered Jan. 23, 1864. Wounded in head severely July 28, 1864, Atlanta, Ga. Died of wounds Aug. 1, 1864, Marietta, Ga. Buried in National Cemetery, Marietta, Ga. Section G, grave 1383.

COMPANY "H"

Machett, Joseph R. Age 30. Residence Poweshiek County, nativity Pennsylvania. Enlisted
Nov. 2, 1864. Mustered Nov. 2, 1864. Mustered out July 18, 1865, Louisville, Ky.
Mackenzie, Charles. Age 21. Residence Dubuque, nativity New York. Appointed First
Lieutenant Sept. 24, 1861. Mustered Sept. 24, 1861. Promoted Adjutant Oct. 12, 1862. Resigned
March 30, 1863. Re-entered service Aug. 10, 1863. Re-appointed Adjutant Aug. 10, 1863.
Mustered out Jan. 5, 1865.
Mann, Garrison C. Age 19. Residence Iowa Falls, nativity Indiana. Enlisted Sept. 22, 1861.
Mustered Sept. 24, 1861. Wounded slightly in hip March 7, 1862, Pea Ridge, Ark. Wounded
severely in both thighs May 22, 1863, Vicksburg, Miss. Died of wounds June 2, 1863, Walnut
Hills, Miss.
Maricle, Joel G. Age 18. Residence Decorah, nativity New York. Enlisted Sept. 15, 1861.
Mustered Sept. 24, 1861. Wounded slightly March 7, 1862, Pea Ridge, Ark. Transferred to
Invalid Corps Nov. 20, 1863. Mustered out Sept. 23, 1864, Davenport, Iowa.
Maricle, Justus. (Veteran.) Age 19. Residence Winneshiek County, nativity Pennsylvania.
Enlisted Sept. 15, 1861. Mustered Sept. 25, 1861. Wounded slightly in right thigh March 7,
1862, Pea Ridge, Ark. Re-enlisted and re-mustered Jan. 23, 1864. Promoted Corporal July 1,
1865. Mustered out July 18, 1865, Louisville, Ky.
Martinson, Christian. Age 22. Residence Dubuque, nativity Norway. Enlisted Dec. 16, 1861.
Mustered Jan. 5, 1862. Wounded in knee. Leg amputated March 7, 1862, Pea Ridge, Ark. Died
of wounds March 15, 1862, Pea Ridge, Ark.

Matteson, Abel. Age 38. Residence Burr Oak, nativity New York. En- listed Nov. 18, 1861.
Mustered Nov. 18, 1861. Discharged for disability July 16, 1862, Helena, Ark.
Meader, Charles E. Age 22. Residence Hesper, nativity Indiana. Enlisted Aug. 26, 1861, as
Fourth Sergeant. Mustered Sept. 24, 1861. Wounded. slightly in knee March 7, 1862, Pea Ridge,
Ark. Discharged March 7, 1863, Keokuk, Iowa.
Melot, Benjamin. Age 45. Residence Lime Springs, nativity Canada. Enlisted Oct. 25, 1861.
Mustered Oct. 25, 1861. Discharged Jan. 18, 1862, Pacific, Mo.
93
Milliken, Henry. Age 24. Residence Talleyrand, nativity Ohio. Enlisted Nov. 5, 1864. Mustered
Nov. 5, 1864. Mustered out July 18, 1865, Louisville, Ky.
Monroe, Eugene B. Age 23. Residence Burr Oak, nativity Ohio. Enlisted Aug. 26, 1861.
Appointed Second Lieutenant Sept. 24, 1861. Mustered Sept. 24, 1861. Resigned Feb. 14, 1863.
Moore, Martin A. Age 37. Residence Decorah, nativity Connecticut. Appointed Captain Sept.
24, 1861. Mustered Sept. 24, 1861. Resigned March 7, 1863.
Moore, William H. Age 18. Residence Decorah, nativity Wisconsin. Enlisted Nov. 26, 1861.
Mustered Nov. 26, 1861. Wounded in right arm Dec. 7, 1862, Pea Ridge, Ark. Discharged for
wounds Sept. 14, 1862, St. Louis, Mo.
Moulton, Jasper N. (Veteran.) Age 19. Residence Decorah, nativity Illinois. Enlisted Oct. 25,
1861. Mustered Oct. 25, 1861. Promoted Third Corporal; Second Corporal July 19, 1862; Fifth
Sergeant Jan. 23, 1864. Re-enlisted and re-mustered Jan. 23, 1864. Mustered out July 18, 1865,
Louisville, Ky.
Murphy, Albert. Age 18. Residence Burlington, nativity Indiana.

Enlisted Jan. 19 1865.
Mustered Jan. 19, 1865. Mustered out July 18, 1865, Louisville, Ky. See company G, Twentyfifth
Infantry,
COMPANY "I"
Mather, Esquire. Age 22. Residence Postville, nativity Ohio. Enlisted Sept. 9, 1861. Mustered
Sept. 18, 1861. Died Sept. 26, 1863, Lansing, Iowa.
Mather, John S. (Veteran.) Age 18. Residence Postville, nativity Ohio. Enlisted Sept. 9, 1861.
Mustered Sept. 18, 1861. Promoted Fifth Corporal; Third Corporal Dec. 10, 1862; Second
Corporal; Fourth Sergeant May 24, 1863; Third Sergeant July 6, 1863; Second Sergeant Oct. 6,
1863. Re-enlisted and re-mustered Jan. 23, 1864. Promoted First Lieutenant Jan. 1, 1865;
Captain June 19, 1865. Mustered out July 18, 1865, Louisville, Ky.
Mead, Harrison H. Age 19. Residence Maysville, nativity Wisconsin. Enlisted Aug. 22, 1861.
Mustered Sept. 18, 1861. Promoted Sixth Corporal May 1, 1865. Mustered out July 18, 1865,
Louisville, Ky.
Miller, Andrew. Age 21. Residence Foreston, nativity Canada. Enlisted Aug. 17, 1861, as
Second Corporal. Mustered Sept. 18, 1861. Promoted Third Sergeant June 23, 1862; Second
Sergeant. Wounded in left arm May 22, 1863, Vicksburg, Miss. Died of wounds July 5, 1863,
Vicksburg, Miss.
Miller, Edwin A. Age 26. Residence Maysville, nativity Ohio. Enlisted Aug. 22, 1861.
Mustered Sept. 18, 1861. Discharged for disability Jan. 19, 1862, Pacific City, Mo.
Minnard, James. Age 18. Residence Burlington, nativity Illinois. Enlisted Jan. 5, 1864.

Mustered Jan. 5, 1864. Mustered out July 18, 1865, Louisville, Ky. See company G, Twentyfifth
Infantry.
Mintey, Walter. Age 20. Residence New Oregon, nativity England. Enlisted Aug. 17, 1861.
Mustered Sept. 18, 1861. Discharged for disability Jan. 19, 1862, Pacific City, Mo. See company
I, Thirty-eighth Infantry and Thirty-fourth and Thirty-eighth Consolidated.
Mitchell, John G. Age 35. Residence Maysville, nativity New York. Enlisted Aug. 22, 1861, as
Sixth Corporal. Mustered Sept. 2, 1861. Died April 2, 1863, St. Louis, Mo.
Morgan, Edwin. (Veteran.) Age 30. Residence Bloomfield, nativity New York. Enlisted Aug.
29, 1862. Mustered Sept. 30, 1862. Re-enlisted and re-mustered Jan. 23, 1864. Mustered out July
18, 1865, Louisville, Ky.
Mower, James E. Age 24. Residence Burlington, nativity Iowa. Enlisted Oct. 7, 1864. Mustered
Oct. 7, 1864. Mustered out July 18, 1865, Louisville, Ky. See company G, Twenty-fifth Infantry.
Murray, William. Age 19. Residence Winneshiek County, nativity Ireland. Enlisted Oct. 31,
1864. Mustered Oct. 31, 1864. Mustered out July 18, 1865, Louisville, Ky.
COMPANY "K"
Mills, Marvin. Age 24. Residence Central City, nativity Iowa. Enlisted Oct. 1, 1861. Mustered
Oct. 1, 1861. Wounded severely March 7, 1862, Pea Ridge, Ark. Died of wounds March 25,
1862, Springfield, Mo.
Monroe, Jonathan W. (Veteran.) Age 18. Residence Central City, nativity Pennsylvania.
Enlisted Sept. 14, 1861. Mustered Sept. 24, 1861. Wounded in foot slightly May 22, 1863,

Vicksburg, Miss. Re-enlisted and re-mustered Jan. 23, 1864. Promoted Fourth Corporal March 1,
1865. Mustered out July 18, 1865, Louisville, Ky.
Montgomery, Hugh H. Age 22. Residence Marion, nativity Indiana. Enlisted Sept. 14, 1861.
Mustered Sept. 24, 1861. Wounded severely in abdomen May 22, 1863, Vicksburg, Miss.
Promoted Third Corporal June 12, 1863. Died Jan. 2, 1864, Tallahoma, Tenn.
Montgomery, Joseph. Age 18. Residence Dubuque, nativity Iowa. Enlisted Sept. 6, 1861, as
Seventh Corporal. Died Nov. 10, 1863, Memphis, Tenn.
Morehead, James C. Age 25. Residence Cedar Rapids, nativity Pennsylvania. Enlisted Sept. 14,
1861, as First Corporal. Mustered Sept. 24, 1861. Promoted Second Sergeant June 1, 1862. Died
Oct. 3, 1863, Corinth, Miss. Buried in Union National Cemetery, Corinth, Miss. Section D, grave
11.
Moriarty, Miletus E. Age 18. Residence Marion, nativity Iowa. Enlisted Sept. 14, 1861.
Mustered Sept. 24, 1861. Wounded severely Aug. 22, 1864, Atlanta, Ga. Mustered out June 8,
1865, Davenport, Iowa.
95
Morton, Thomas J. Age 33. Residence Fremont County, nativity Pennsylvania. Enlisted Nov. 5,
1864. Mustered Nov. 5, 1864. Mustered out July 18, 1865, Louisville, Ky.
Moyer, Emanuel. Age 18. Residence Boone County, nativity Pennsylvania. Enlisted Nov. 7,
1864. Mustered Nov. 7, 1864. Mustered out July 18, 1865, Louisville, Ky.
COMPANY "A"
Nixon, Herbert E. Age 21. Residence Johnson County, nativity Virginia. Enlisted Feb. 16,

1864. Mustered March 17, 1864. Mustered out July 18, 1865, Louisville, Ky.
Norton, Alfred M. Age 20. Residence Wyoming, nativity Michigan. Enlisted Aug. 3, 1861.
Mustered Sept. 24, 1861. Transferred to Invalid Corps. Died of chronic diarrhea Sept. 15, 1863,
Davenport, Iowa.
Norton Francis P. Age 19. Residence Wyoming, nativity Michigan. Enlisted Aug. 3, 1861.
Mustered Sept. 24, 1861. Wounded severely in shoulder March 7, 1862, Pea Ridge, Ark. Died
April 3, 1862, Cassville, Mo.
COMPANY "B"
Niles, John W. Age 30. Residence Madison, nativity New York. Enlisted Aug. 12, 1861, as
Second Sergeant. Mustered Sept. 24, 1861. Promoted First Sergeant Nov. 1, 1862; First
Lieutenant May 23, 1863; Captain Jan. 16, 1865. Mustered out July 18, 1865, Louisville, Ky.
COMPANY "D"
Nichols, John C. (Veteran.) Age 18. Residence Wyoming, nativity Iowa. Enlisted Aug. 16,
1861. Mustered Aug. 16, 1861. Wounded in arm, back and head May 22, 1863, Vicksburg, Miss.
Re-enlisted and re-mustered Jan. 23, 1864. Promoted Sixth Corporal June 20, 1865. Mustered
out July 18, 1865, Louisville, Ky.
Nichols, Otho D. Age 25. Residence Wyoming, nativity Ohio. Enlisted Sept. 19, 1861. Mustered
Sept. 19, 1861. Discharged for disability May 29, 1862, Little Red River, Ark.
Nuckolls, Ezra. Age 18. Residence Anamosa, nativity Iowa. Enlisted Aug. 16, 1861, as Fourth
Corporal. Mustered Aug. 16, 1861. Promoted Second Sergeant March 17, 1862; Second
Lieutenant March 15, 1863. Mustered out Oct. 21, 1864,

expiration of term of service.
COMPANY "F"
Neff, Abner G. M. Age 32. Residence Auburn, nativity Pennsylvania. Appointed First
Lieutenant Sept. 12, 1861. Mustered Sept. 12, 1861. Wounded through right lung March 7, 1862,
Pea Ridge, Ark. Died of wounds March 12, 1862, in field hospital.
Nichols, George. Age 21. Residence West Union, nativity New York. Enlisted Sept. 3, 1861.
Mustered Sept. 12, 1861. Died Feb. 3, 1863, Young's Point, La. 96
COMPANY "G"
Nackey, Frederick. Age 18. Residence Dubuque, nativity Germany. Enlisted Sept. 18, 1861.
Mustered Sept. 24, 1861. Mustered out Sept. 24, 1864, East Point, Ga., expiration of term of
service.
Neff, Cyrenus D. (Veteran.) Age 20. Residence Waverly, nativity Canada. Enlisted as Second
Corporal. Mustered Sept. 24, 1861. Promoted Fifth Sergeant Sept. 5, 1862; First Lieutenant Sept.
8, 1864; Captain Jan. 1, 1865. Mustered out July 18, 1865, Louisville, Ky.
Newman, James H. Age 32. Residence Lick Creek, nativity Illinois. Enlisted Oct. 25, 1864.
Mustered Oct. 25, 1864. Mustered out July 18, 1865, Louisville, Ky.
COMPANY "H"
Nelson, John G. Age 20. Residence Decorah, nativity Norway. Enlisted Aug. 26, 1861.
Mustered Sept. 24, 1861. Wounded slightly in arm March 7, 1862, Pea Ridge, Ark. Killed in
battle May 23, l863, Vicksburg, Miss.
Newton, James. Age 25. Residence Burlington, nativity New York. Enlisted Jan. 19, 1865.

Mustered Jan. 19, 1865. Died July 6, 1865, Louisville, Ky. Buried in Cave Hill National
Cemetery, Louisville, Ky. Section C, range 7, grave 122.
COMPANY "I"
Niles, Sylvester J. Age 27. Residence Castalia, nativity Ohio. Enlisted Sept. 13, 1861, as Second
Sergeant. Mustered Sept. 18, 1861. Died of pneumonia June 23, 1862, Springfield, Mo.
COMPANY "K"
Nicholson, Thomas P. Age 23. Residence Cottage Hill, nativity England. Enlisted Aug. 28,
1861. Mustered Sept. 24, 1861. Wounded severely in thigh March 7, 1862, Pea Ridge, Ark. Died
of wounds April 10, 1862, Cassville, Mo. Buried in National Cemetery, Springfield, Mo. Section
10, grave 69.
Norton, John W. Age 34. Residence Lee County, nativity Indiana. Enlisted Oct. 24, 1864.
Mustered Oct. 24, 1864. Mustered out July 18, 1865, Louisville, Ky.
Nutt, Cyrus E. Age 24. Residence Marion, nativity Ohio. Enlisted Sept. 24, 1861. Mustered
Sept. 24, 1861. Promoted First Corporal June 1, 1862. Died March 13, 1863, Hospital Boat.
Nutting, Lucien H. C. Age 19. Residence Linn County, nativity New York. Mustered Sept. 24,
1861. Discharged Sept. 23, 1864, East Point, Ga., expiration of term of service.
COMPANY "A"
97
Ogden, Henry T. Age 19. Residence Dubuque, nativity Ohio. Enlisted Sept. 24, 1861. Mustered
Sept. 24, 1861. Wounded in right shoulder May 19, 1863, Vicksburg, Miss. Discharged for
wounds Jan. 2, 1864, Vicksburg, Miss.
O'Morrow, William. (Veteran.) Age 20. Residence Jackson

County, nativity Georgia. Enlisted
July 29, 1861. Mustered Sept. 24, 1861. Re-enlisted and re-mustered Jan. 23, 1864. Mustered out
July 18, 1865, Louisville, Ky.
COMPANY "B"
Osborne, John V. Age 20. Residence Madison, nativity Illinois. Enlisted Aug. 12, 1861.
Mustered Sept. 24, 1861. Killed March 7, 1862, Pea Ridge, Ark.
Overacker, Horace T. Age 18. Residence Jones County, nativity Iowa. Enlisted Aug. 12, 1861,
as Fifer. Mustered Sept. 24, 1861. Discharged for disability Jan. 18, 1862, Pacific City, Mo.
COMPANY "D"
Oats, James A. Age 18. Residence Des Moines County, nativity Indiana. Enlisted Nov. 15,
1864. Mustered Nov. 18, 1864. Transferred to Veteran Reserve Corps, Indianapolis, Ind. No
further record.
Overly, Henry. Age 19. Residence Monticello, nativity Kentucky. Enlisted Aug. 16, 1861.
Mustered Sept. 2, 1861. Wounded slightly in arm March 7, 1862, Pea Ridge, Ark. Died of lung
fever April 7, 1862, Cassville, Mo. Buried in National Cemetery, Springfield, Mo. Section 10,
grave 68.
Overly, James F. Age 24. Residence Scotch Grove, nativity Kentucky, enlisted Aug. 16, 1861.
Mustered Sept. 2, 1861. Died of pneumonia Jan. 31, 1862, Pacific City, Mo.
Owens, James, Jr. Age 28. Residence South Fork, nativity Norway. Enlisted Feb. 26, 1864.
Mustered March 17, 1864. Mustered out July 18, 1865, Louisville, Ky.
COMPANY "E"
Oberholzer, John. Age 30. Residence Elkader, nativity Germany. Enlisted Sept. 9, 1861.

Mustered Sept. 24, 1861. Died of diarrhea April 21, 1863, Granville, Miss.
COMPANY "F"
Oakly, Peter W. Age 25. Residence Rippon, Wis., nativity New York. Enlisted as Sixth
Corporal. Mustered Sept. 14, 1861. Wounded severely in thigh March 7, 1862, Pea Ridge, Ark.
Discharged for wounds Aug. 23, 1862, St. Louis. Mo.
O'Brien, Michael. Age 21. Residence Strawberry Point, nativity Wisconsin. Enlisted Sept. 4,
1861. Mustered. Sept. 14,1861. Wounded severely in leg March 7, 1862, Pea Ridge, Ark.
Discharged Aug. 27, 1862, Cairo, Ill.
98
Ort, John. (Veteran.) Age 27. Residence West Union, nativity Germany. Enlisted Aug. 28,
1861. Mustered Sept. 12, 1861. Wounded slightly in hip March 7, 1862, Pea Ridge, Ark. Reenlisted
and re-mustered Jan. 23, 1864. Mustered out July 18, 1865, Louisville, Ky.
Osgood, Levi A. (Veteran.) Age 18. Residence Eden, nativity New York. Enlisted Sept. 8, 1861.
Mustered Sept. 12, 1861. Re-enlisted and re-mustered Jan. 23, 1864. Promoted Sixth Corporal
May 12, 1865. Mustered out July 18, 1865, Louisville, Ky.
COMPANY "H"
Obert, Lewis. (Veteran.) Age 21. Residence Waterloo, nativity Pennsylvania. Enlisted Sept. 10,
1861. Mustered Sept. 24, 1861. Promoted Sixth Corporal Jan. 1, 1863; Third Corporal April 2,
1863. Wounded slightly in right leg May 22, 1869, Vicksburg, Miss. Re-enlisted and re-mustered
Jan. 23, 1864. Promoted Second Corporal Jan. 23, 1864. Mustered out July 18, 1865, Louisville,
Ky.
Obrihan, Edwin C. (Veteran.) Age 23. Residence Freeport,

nativity New York. Enlisted Sept.
10, 1861, as Seventh Corporal. Mustered Sept. 24, 1861. Promoted Sixth Corporal; First
Corporal May 14, 1863. Re-enlisted and re-mustered Jan. 23, 1864. Wounded severely in right
hand Aug. 19, 1864, Atlanta, Ga. Mustered out July 18, 1865, Louisville, Ky.
Odell, Hiram A. Age 34. Residence Decorah, nativity New York. Enlisted Aug. 26, 1861.
Mustered Sept. 24, 1861. Died Feb. 5, 1863, Young's Point, La.
Older, Augustus H. Age 40. Nativity New York. Enlisted Sept. 22, 1861, as Fourth Corporal.
Mustered Sept. 24, 1861. Discharged Feb. 28, 1862. See company D, Forty-seventh Infantry.
Oleson, Jacob. Age 28. Residence Winneshiek County, nativity Norway. Enlisted March 1,
1864. Mustered March 17, 1864. Died Oct. 7, 1864, Chicago, Ill.
COMPANY "I"
O'Donnell, Joseph D. Age 21. Residence New Oregon, nativity Canada. Enlisted Dec. 1, 1861.
Mustered Dec. 1. 1861. Transferred to Invalid Corps Sept. 1, 1863. No further record.
Oren, John. (Veteran.) Age 23. Residence New Oregon, nativity Pennsylvania. Enlisted Aug.
17, 1861. Mustered Sept. 18, 1861. Re-enlisted and re-mustered Jan. 23, 1864. Mustered out July
18, 1865, Louisville, Ky.
Owen, George A. Age 25. Residence New Oregon, nativity New York. Enlisted Aug. 19, 1861,
as Fourth Sergeant. Mustered Sept. 18, 1861. Promoted Second Sergeant; Second Lieutenant
April 14, 1863. Killed in battle May 22, 1863, Vicksburg, Miss.
COMPANY "K"
99
Oliver, John H. Age 18. Residence Marion, nativity Iowa. Enlisted Sept. 14, 1861. Mustered

Sept. 24, 1861. Died March 23, 1863, Memphis, Tenn.
COMPANY "A"
Parnell, Francis. Rejected Aug. 8, 1861, by Mustering Officer.
Patter, Alphonso. Age 18. Residence Mahaska, nativity Ohio.
Enlisted Nov. 15, 1864. Mustered
Nov. 15, 1864. Discharged Jan. 31, 1865, St. Louis, Mo.
Patterson, David B. Age 18. Residence Fulton, nativity
Pennsylvania. Enlisted Aug. 13, 1861.
Mustered Sept. 24, 1861. Killed in battle March 7, 1862, Pea
Ridge, Ark. Buried in National
Cemetery, Fayetteville, Ark. Section 2, grave 20.
Pearce, George C. Age 22. Residence Maquoketa, nativity Iowa.
Enlisted Aug. 10 1861.
Mustered Sept. 24, 1861. Wounded severely in lungs March 7,
1862, Pea Ridge, Ark. Died of
wounds March 13, 1862, Cassville, Mo. Buried in National
Cemetery, Springfield, Mo. Section
10, grave 7.
Pierce, Levi L. Age 21. Residence Maquoketa, nativity Iowa.
Enlisted Aug. 10, 1861. Mustered
Sept. 24, 1861. Wounded slightly in breast May 19, 1863,
Vicksburg, Miss. Promoted Seventh
Corporal June 7, 1863; Sixth Corporal; Fifth Corporal Dec. 17,
1863. Discharged Sept. 24, 1864,
East Point, Ga.
COMPANY "B"
Palmer, Henry C. Age 29. Residence Pottawattamie County,
nativity New York. Enlisted Nov.
5, 1864. Mustered Nov. 5, 1864. Mustered out July 18, 1865,
Louisville, Ky.
Peet, William T. Age 23. Residence Fairview, nativity New York.
Enlisted Aug. 17, 1861, as
Fifth Sergeant. Mustered Sept. 24, 1861. Promoted Third
Sergeant Nov. 1, 1862; Second
Sergeant May 23, 1863. Transferred to Invalid Corps April 10,
1864. No further record.

Phipp, James T. Age 32. Residence Mahaska County, nativity England. Enlisted Nov. 19, 1864. Mustered Nov. 19, 1864. Mustered out July 18, 1865, Louisville, Ky.

Porter, George. Age 20. Residence Washington County, nativity Pennsylvania. Enlisted Feb. 26, 1864. Mustered March 3, 1864. Promoted Sixth Corporal July 5, 1865. Mustered out July 18, 1865, Louisville, Ky. See company I, Twenty-fifth Infantry.

Price, John N. Age 28. Residence Jackson, nativity Indiana. Enlisted Aug. 12, 1861, as First Corporal. Mustered Sept. 24, 1861. Discharged Dec. 6, 1862, St. Louis, Mo.

COMPANY "C"
100

Pangburn, Daniel D. (Veteran.) Age 47. Residence Center Point, nativity New York. Enlisted Aug. 26, 1861. Mustered Sept. 24, 1861. Re-enlisted and re-mustered Jan. 23, 1864. Mustered out July 18, 1865, Louisville, Ky.

Patchen, Eugene U. Age 21. Residence Chatham, nativity Ohio. Enlisted Aug. 3, 1861. Mustered Sept. 24, 1861. Transferred to Signal Corps Sept. 1, 1863.

Perdue, Isaiah. Age 26. Residence Cedar Falls, nativity Virginia. Enlisted Sept. 12, 1861. Mustered Sept. 24, 1861. Died June 6, 1862, Fairview, Ark.

Persall, Lewis A. Age 18. Residence Independence, nativity Illinois. Enlisted Aug. 26, 1861. Mustered Sept. 24, 1861. Promoted Second Corporal April 14, 1863. Killed in battle May 18, 1863, Vicksburg, Miss. Buried in National Cemetery, Vicksburg, Miss. Section G, grave 68.

Platt, Enoch. Age 23. Residence Fairbanks, nativity Illinois. Enlisted Aug. 12, 1861. Mustered Sept. 24, 1861. Wounded severely July 2, 1864, Kenesaw

Mountain, Ga. Mustered out Sept. 24, 1864, East Point, Ga.
Pope, William. Age 20. Residence Dubuque, nativity Iowa. Enlisted Sept. 26, 1861. Mustered Sept. 26, 1861. Died March 25, 1863, St. Louis, Mo. Buried in National Cemetery, Jefferson Barracks, Mo. Section 38, grave 226.
Powers, Benjamin W. Age 29. Residence Spring Grove, nativity Ohio. Enlisted Aug. 13, 1861. Mustered Sept. 24, 1861. Discharged for disability Aug. 24, 1863, Vicksburg, Miss.
COMPANY "D"
Palmer, Leroy. Age 18. Residence Anamosa, nativity New York. Enlisted Aug. 19, 1861. Mustered Sept. 2, 1861. Taken prisoner March 14, 1864, Claysville, Ala. Died of dropsy July 4, 1864, Andersonville, Ga. Buried in National Cemetery, Andersonville, Ga. Grave 2869.
Phelps, John. Age 31. Residence Anamosa, nativity Massachusetts. Enlisted Oct. 15, 1861. Mustered Oct. 15, 1861. Died April 9, 1862, Cross Timbers, Mo.
Phillips, Alexander. Age 21. Residence Monticello, nativity Delaware. Enlisted Aug. 23, 1861. Mustered Sept. 2, 1861. Discharged Jan. 18, 1862, Camp Heron, Mo.
Pierce, George W. Age 37. Residence Keokuk, nativity Virginia. Enlisted Nov. 19, 1864. Mustered Nov. 19, 1864. Mustered out July 18, 1865, Louisville, Ky.
Powell, Joseph. Age 24. Residence Washington County, nativity Ohio. Enlisted Oct. 24, 1864. Mustered Oct. 24, 1864. Died. Buried in National Cemetery, Chattanooga, Tenn. Section G, grave 456.
Price, Samuel. Age 26. Residence Pottawattamie County, nativity England. Enlisted Nov. 5,

1864. Mustered Nov. 3, 1864. Mustered out July 18, 1865, Louisville, Ky.
101
COMPANY "E"
Partch, Wilbur V. Age 18. Residence Clayton County, nativity New York. Enlisted Feb. 1,
1865. Mustered Feb. 1, 1865. Mustered out July 18, 1865, Louisville, Ky.
Perry, John. Age 25. Residence Clayton County, nativity Wales. Enlisted Feb. 1, 1865.
Mustered Feb. 1, 1865. Mustered out July 18, 1865, Louisville, Ky.
Pieper, Joseph. Age 23. Residence Lee County, nativity Prussia. Enlisted Nov. 16, 1864.
Mustered Nov. 16, 1864. Mustered out July 18, 1865, Louisville, Ky.
Plein, Alexander. Age 20. Residence Keokuk County, nativity Germany. Enlisted Nov. 19,
1864. Mustered Nov. 19, 1864. Mustered out July 18, 1865, Louisville, Ky.
Potts, Samuel K. Age 35. Residence Fourth Congressional District, nativity Virginia. Enlisted
Nov. 3, 1864. Mustered Nov. 3, 1864. Mustered out July 18, 1865, Louisville, Ky.
Proctor, Samuel O. Age 27. Residence Cox Creek, nativity Ohio. Enlisted Sept. 9, 1861.
Mustered Sept. 24, 1861. Mustered out Jan. 18, 1864, Nashville, Tenn.
Putnam, Henry. Age 32. Residence Clayton County, nativity Canada. Enlisted Feb. 1, 1865.
Mustered Feb. 1, 1865. Mustered out July 18, 1865, Louisville, Ky.
COMPANY "F"
Padden, Loron. Age 18. Residence Fredericksburg, nativity Pennsylvania. Enlisted Feb. 27,
1864. Mustered March 18, 1864. Mustered out July 18, 1865, Louisville, Ky.
Parker, William B. Age 30. Residence Fayette, nativity

Pennsylvania. Enlisted Aug. 26, 1861,
as Fourth Sergeant. Mustered Sept. 12, 1861. Wounded severely in groin March 7, 1862, Pea
Ridge, Ark. Promoted First Sergeant March 12, 1863; Second Lieutenant July 24, 1863; First
Lieutenant July 24, 1863. Mustered out Oct. 26, 1864, Chattanooga, Tenn.
Penrod, Franklin. Age 19. Residence Fayette, nativity Wisconsin. Enlisted Sept. 6, 1861.
Mustered Sept. 12, 1861. Died of smallpox July 16, 1863, Vicksburg, Miss.
Peters, John F. Age 21. Residence Illyria, nativity Ohio. Enlisted Feb. 29, 1864. Mustered
March 18, 1864. Mustered out July 18, 1865, Louisville, Ky.
Peters, William R. Age 23. Residence Illyria, nativity Virginia. Enlisted Feb. 29, 1864.
Mustered March 18, 1864. Wounded in right side May 14, 1864, Resaca, Ga. Mustered out July
18, 1865, Louisville, Ky.
Peterson, Thomas. Age 18. Residence Eldorado, nativity Norway. Enlisted Feb. 27, 1864.
Mustered Feb. 27, 1864. Mustered out July 18, 1865, Louisville, Ky.
102
Potter, Benjamin B. Age 18. Residence Fredericksburg, nativity Pennsylvania. Enlisted Feb. 27,
1864. Mustered March 18, 1864. Wounded severely in right arm May 13, 1864, Resaca, Ga.
Mustered out July 18, 1865, Louisville, Ky.
Pratt, Elvin L. Age 18. Residence West Union, nativity New York. Enlisted Aug. 28, 1861.
Mustered Sept. 12, 1861. Discharged for disability Sept. 28, 1862, St. Louis, Mo.
COMPANY "G"
Parker, Joseph. Age 20. Residence Waterloo, nativity Ohio. Enlisted Aug. 10, 1861. Mustered

Sept. 24, 1861. Killed in battle March 7, 1862, Pea Ridge, Ark.
Parker, William H. Age 21. Residence Waterloo, nativity Ohio. Enlisted Aug. 20, 1861.
Mustered Sept. 24, 1861. Died of wounds Nov. 12, 1861, Pacific, Mo.
Peacock, Henry L. Age 22. Residence Waverly, nativity Ohio. Enlisted Aug. 20, 1861, as
Second Sergeant. Mustered Sept. 24, 1861. Promoted First Sergeant March 28, 1862; Second
Lieutenant May 12, 1862. Resigned Aug. 3, 1863.
Pelton, William A. (Veteran.) Age 32. Residence Waverly, nativity New York. Enlisted Aug.
20, 1861, as Eighth Corporal. Mustered Sept. 24, 1861. Promoted Sixth Corporal; Fifth Corporal.
Re-enlisted and: re-mustered Jan. 23, 1864. Promoted Second Corporal Oct. 1, 1864.
Mustered out July 18, 1865, Louisville, Ky.
Piggott, John W. Age 33. Residence Waverly, nativity England. Enlisted July 28, 1861, as
Third Sergeant. Mustered Sept. 24, 1861. Discharged for disability April 26, 1863, Vicksburg,
Miss.
Platt, Jacob. (Veteran.) Age 21. Residence Delaware County, nativity Pennsylvania. Enlisted
July 28, 1861, as Fifth Sergeant. Mustered July 28, 1861. Promoted First Sergeant May 12, 1862;
Second Lieutenant Aug. 4, 1863. Re-enlisted and re-mustered Jan. 23, 1864. Discharged for
disability July 25, 1864.
Pregler, George. (Veteran.) Age 19. Residence Dubuque, nativity Germany. Mustered Sept. 24,
1861. Re-enlisted and re-mustered Jan. 23, 1864. Wounded in right side March 21, 1865,
Bentonville, N. C. Promoted Eighth Corporal May 1, 1865. Mustered out July 22, 1865, New
York City, N. Y.

Price, Anthony. Age 27. Residence Waterloo, nativity New York. Enlisted Aug. 24, 1861.
Mustered, Sept. 24, 1861. Died March 27, 1863, Vicksburg, Miss.
COMPANY "H"
Parr, Philemon. Age 18. Residence Burlington, nativity Iowa. Enlisted Jan. 30, 1865. Mustered
Jan. 30, 1865. Mustered out July 18, 1865, Louisville, Ky. See company G, Twenty-fifth
Infantry.
103
Peddler, Philip. Age 23. Residence Bluffton, nativity Ohio. Enlisted Sept. 22, 1861. Mustered
Sept. 24, 1861. Wounded slightly in leg March 7, 1862, Pea Ridge, Ark. Mustered out July 29,
1862, St. Louis, Mo.
Perkins, George. Age 43. Residence Oskaloosa, nativity Kentucky. Enlisted Nov. 2, 1864.
Mustered Nov. 2, 1864. Mustered out July 18, 1865, Louisville, Ky.
Perry, Alvin M. Age 19. Residence Bluffton, nativity New York. Enlisted Aug. 26, 1861.
Mustered Sept. 24, 1861. Wounded slightly in left side March 7, 1862, Pea Ridge, Ark.
Discharged Oct. 24, 1862, Keokuk, Iowa.
Perry, Wesley D. Age 18. Residence Decorah, nativity New York. Enlisted Aug. 26, 1861.
Mustered Sept. 24, 1861. Died of lung fever April 25, 1862, Forsyth, Mo.
Phillips, Hugh K. Age 44. Residence Allamakee County, nativity Ireland. Enlisted March 14,
1864. Mustered April 12, 1864. Mustered out July 18, 1865, Louisville, Ky.
Phillips, John W. Age 35. Residence Waukon, nativity England. Enlisted Aug. 21, 1861, as
First Sergeant. Mustered Sept. 24, 1861. Promoted First Lieutenant March 8, 1863; Captain April

9, 1865. Mustered out July 18, 1865, Louisville, Ky.
Powers, John M. Age 25. Residence Polk County, nativity Indiana. Enlisted Sept. 26, 1864.
Mustered Sept. 26, 1864. Mustered out June 23, 1865, Louisville, Ky.
Powers, Wilbur F. Age 24. Residence Plymouth Rock, nativity Ohio. Enlisted Sept. 22, 1861.
Mustered Sept. 24, 1861. Died typhoid fever July 15, 1863, Vicksburg, Miss.
Purcell, Garrett. Age 18. Residence Alamakee County, nativity Illinois. Enlisted Feb. 27, 1864.
Mustered March 17, 1864. Mustered out July 18, 1865, Louisville, KY.
COMPANY "I"
Pepin, Francis J. Age 21. Residence New Oregon, nativity Michigan. Enlisted Feb. 29, 1864.
Mustered March 23, 1864. Mustered out July 18, 1865, Louisville, Ky.
Peters, Silas G. W. (Veteran.) Age 18. Residence Maysville, nativity New York. Enlisted Aug.
22, 1861. Mustered Sept. 2, 1861. Re-enlisted and re-mustered Jan. 23, 1864. Mustered out July
18, 1865, Louisville, Ky.
Pierce, Finley D. (Veteran.) Age 18. Residence New Oregon, nativity Ohio. Enlisted Aug. 19,
1861. Mustered Sept. 2, 1861. Wounded in foot May 19, 1863, Vicksburg, Miss. Re-enlisted and
re-mustered Jan. 23, 1864. Promoted Fifth Corporal Sept. 16, 1864; Fourth Corporal May 1,
1865. Mustered out July 18, 1865, Louisville, Ky.
Polley, Charles W. (Veteran.) Age 26. Residence Castalia, nativity New York. Enlisted Sept.
12, 1861. Mustered Sept. 18, 1861. Mustered out July 18, 1865, Louisville, Ky.
104
Polley, David C. Age 32. Residence Cantalia, nativity New York.

Enlisted Sept. 12, 1861.
Mustered Sept. 18, 1861. Promoted Second Corporal July 24, 1862; First Corporal Dec. 10,
1862. Mustered out Sept. 24, 1864, East Point, Ga.
Porcupile, James H. Age 18. Residence Butler County, nativity Ohio. Enlisted Oct. 10, 1864.
Mustered Oct. 10, 1864. Mustered out July 18, 1865, Louisville, Ky.
Powell, Jeremiah F. (Veteran.) Age 21. Residence New Oregon, nativity Illinois. Enlisted Aug.
17, 1861. Mustered Sept. 18, 1861. Re-enlisted and re-mustered Jan. 23, 1861. Promoted Fifth
Corporal May 1, 1865. Mustered out July 18, 1865, Louisville, Ky.
Powell, Thomas J. Age 19. Residence New Oregon, nativity Ireland. Enlisted Aug. 18, 1861, as
Third Corporal. Mustered Sept. 18, 1861. Discharged July 29, 1862, St. Louis, Mo.
Powers, Julius H. Residence New Hampton, nativity Vermont. Appointed Captain Aug. 17,
1861. Mustered Sept. 18, 1861. Resigned April 13, 1863, Young's Point, La.
Proctor, Uriah A. Age 29. Residence Osage, nativity Maine. Enlisted Aug. 20, 1861, as Fourth
Corporal. Mustered Sept. 18, 1861. Promoted Fifth Sergeant March 23, 1862. Wounded severely
in hip May 22, 1863, Vicksburg, Miss. Promoted Third Sergeant Dec. 10, 1863; First Sergeant
May 24, 1864. Mustered out July 18, 1865, Louisville, Ky.
COMPANY "K"
Painter, Robert M. Age 19. Residence Lee County, nativity Iowa. Enlisted Nov. 4, 1864.
Mustered Nov. 4, 1864. Mustered out July 18, 1865, Louisville, Ky.
Pratt, Sterns D. Age 27. Residence Cottage Hill, nativity New York. Enlisted Aug. 28, 1861.
Mustered Sept. 12, 1861. Promoted Fourth Corporal Oct. 12,

1862; Second Corporal March 3,
1864. Mustered out Sept. 23, 1864, East Point, Ga., expiration of term of service.

COMPANY "K"

Quick, Jacob. Age 18. Residence Keokuk, nativity Indiana. Enlisted Nov. 18, 1864. Mustered
Nov. 18, 1864. Mustered out July 18, 1865, Louisville, Ky.

COMPANY "A"

Ramsey, Morris A. (Veteran.) Age 23. Residence Spragueville, nativity Virginia. Enlisted Aug.
10, 1861. Mustered Sept. 24, 1861. Re-enlisted and re-mustered Jan. 23, 1864. Mustered out July
18, 1865, Louisville, Ky. 8 ' J0'0

Reyner, Franklin. Age 20. Residence Maquoketa, nativity Maryland. Enlisted July 29, 1861, as
Drummer. Mustered Sept. 24, 1861. Promoted Drum Major April 8, 1862. Mustered out.

Reyner, Henry C. Age 18. Residence South Fork, nativity Maryland. Enlisted Dec. 29, 1863.
Mustered Jan. 15, 1864. Mustered out July 18, 1865, Louisville, Ky.

105

Reyner, Marcus D. (Veteran.) Age 18. Residence Maquoketa, nativity Maryland. Enlisted Jan.
19, 1862, Mustered Jan. 19, 1862. Re-enlisted and re-mustered Jan. 23, 1864. Wounded in arm
slightly March 21, 1865, Bentonville, N. C. Mustered out July 18, 1865, Louisville, Ky.

Rhodes, Norman B. Rejected Aug. 8, 1861, by Mustering Officer.

Riley, Asher. Age 34. Residence Spragueville, nativity New York Enlisted July 29, 1861, as
First Sergeant. Mustered Sept. 1, 1861. Promoted Second Lieutenant Feb. 5, 1862; First
Lieutenant March 8, 1862; Captain May 27, 1863. Resigned Aug. 7, 1863.

Robinson, Whitman D. Age 21. Residence Spragueville, nativity

New York. Enlisted Aug. 8, 1861. Mustered Sept. 24, 1861. Discharged Feb. 28, 1863, Keokuk, Iowa.

Rowland, William G. Age 24. Residence Second Congressional District, nativity Canada. Enlisted Nov. 3, 1864. Mustered Nov. 3, 1864. Mustered out July 18, 1865, Louisville, Ky.

COMPANY "B"

Rich, Nelson. Age 18. Residence Wyoming, nativity Iowa. Enlisted Sept. 10, 1861. Mustered Sept. 24, 1861. Mustered out Sept. 24, 1864, East Point, Ga., expiration of term of service.

Roberts, Lyman A. (Veteran.) Age 31. Residence Walnut Fork, nativity New York. Enlisted Aug. 29, 1862. Mustered Aug. 29, 1862. Re-enlisted and re-mustered Jan. 23, 1864. Discharged for disability July 7, 1865, Louisville, Ky.

Robinson, Henry. (Veteran.) Age 23. Residence Hale, nativity Ohio. Enlisted Aug. 12, 1861, as Eighth Corporal. Mustered Sept. 24, 1861. Re-enlisted and re-mustered Jan. 23, 1864. Killed in battle June 23, 1864, Kenesaw Mountain, Georgia. Buried in National Cemetery, Marietta, Ga. Section A, grave 1016.

Robinson, Isaac B. (Veteran.) Age 18. Residence Onion Grove, nativity Iowa. Enlisted Aug. 30, 1861. Mustered Sept. 24, 1861. Re-enlisted and re-mustered Jan. 23, 1864. Wounded in thigh severely May 27, 1864, Dallas, Ga. Died of wounds Aug. 28, 1864, Rome, Ga.

Robinson, J. Age 28. Residence Jones County, nativity Indiana. Enlisted Dec. 20, 1861. No further record.

Robinson, Samuel. (Veteran.) Age 27. Residence Hale, nativity Ohio. Enlisted Aug. 1, 1861. Mustered Sept. 24, 1861. Promoted Eighth Corporal May 23,

1863; Seventh Corporal; Sixth
Corporal Dec. 1, 1863; Fourth Corporal May 27, 1864; Second
Sergeant April 6, 1865. Mustered
out July 18, 1865, Louisville, Ky.
Robinson, Samuel O. Age 30. Residence Walnut Fork, nativity
New York. Enlisted Dec. 19,
1861. Mustered Dec. 19, 1861. Discharged for disability Feb. 4,
1864, St. Louis, Mo.
106
Rudd, Harvey. Age 20. Residence Lee County, nativity Illinois.
Enlisted Nov. 1, 1864.
Mustered Nov. 1, 1861. Mustered out July 18, 1865, Louisville,
Ky.
Rummel, David E. Age 21. Residence Rome, nativity Ohio.
Enlisted Aug. 12, 1861. Mustered
Sept. 24, 1861. Promoted Eighth Corporal May 1, 1864; Seventh
Corporal May 7, 1864; First
Corporal April 6, 1865. Mustered out July 18, 1865, Louisville,
Ky.
COMPANY "C"
Redfield, Wallace. Age 18. Residence Fairbanks, nativity New
Jersey. Enlisted March 14, 1864,
as Drummer. Mustered March 23, 1864. Mustered out July 18,
1865, Louisville, Ky.
Reynolds, Henry. Age 21. Residence Center Point, nativity
Illinois. Enlisted Aug. 9, 1861.
Mustered Sept. 24, 1861. Promoted Wagoner. Discharged for
disability Nov. 10, 1861, Pacific
City, Mo.
Rice, Nathan. Age 22. Residence Vinton, nativity Tennessee.
Enlisted Aug. 3, 1861, as Second
Sergeant. Mustered Sept. 24, 1861. Promoted Second Lieutenant
Sept. 2, 1861; First Lieutenant
Jan. 29, 1862. Killed in action March 7, 1862, Pea Ridge, Ark.
Rich, Darwin. (Veteran.) Age 21. Residence Winthrop, nativity
Wisconsin. Enlisted Aug. 20,

1861. Mustered Sept. 24, 1861. Re-enlisted and re-mustered Jan. 23, 1864. Mustered out July 18, 1865, Louisville, Ky.

Ritterman, Philip. (Veteran.) Age 22. Residence Brandon, nativity Germany. Enlisted Aug. 13, 1861. Mustered Sept. 24, 1861. Wounded slightly in arm March 7, 1862, Pea Ridge, Ark. Reenlisted and re-mustered Jan. 23, 1864. Promoted Fifth Sergeant June 10, 1865. Mustered out July 18, 1865, Louisville, Ky.

Robbins, Aham K. Age 18. Residence Linn County, nativity Pennsylvania. Enlisted Aug. 3, 1861. Mustered Sept. 24, 1861. Discharged for disability Aug. 22, 1862, Davenport, Iowa. Reentered service Feb. 25, 1864. Mustered March 3, 1864. Deserted May 29, 1864, Dallas, Ga.

Robbins, Samuel. (Veteran.) Age 22. Residence Center Point, nativity Pennsylvania. Enlisted Aug. 17, 1861. Mustered Sept. 24, 1861. Wounded in knee slightly March 7, 1862, Pea Ridge, Ark. Re-enlisted and re-mustered Jan. 23, 1864. Mustered out June 9, 1865, New York City.

Rodgers, John. Age 28. Residence Dubuque, nativity England. Enlisted Sept. 12, 1861. Mustered Sept. 24, 1861. Discharged for disability April 2, 1862, Cassville, Mo.

Rouse, Reuben. (Veteran.) Age 20. Residence Independence, nativity Ohio. Enlisted Aug. 24, 1861. Mustered Sept. 24, 1861. Promoted First Corporal April 14, 1863. Wounded in thigh severely May 22, 1863, Vicksburg, Miss. Wounded slightly Nov. 27, 1863, Ringgold, Ga. Reenlisted and re-mustered Jan. 23, 1864.

Rouse, Russell. (Veteran.) Age 18. Residence Independence, nativity Ohio. Enlisted Aug. 13, 1861. Mustered Sept. 24, 1861. Wounded in thigh March 7, 1862,

Pea Ridge, Ark. Re-enlisted 107
and re-mustered Jan. 23, 1864. Wounded severely Aug. 24, 1864. Discharged for wounds July 2,
1865, Louisville, Ky.
Rust, Ezra T. Age 21. Residence Center Point, nativity Illinois. Enlisted Aug. 20, 1861, as
Fourth Corporal. Mustered Sept. 24, 1861. Promoted Third Corporal March 8, 1862. Died of
chronic diarrhea Oct. 20, 1863, Iuka, Miss.
Rust, George Q. Age 18. Residence Dubuque, nativity Illinois. Enlisted Aug. 28, 1861.
Mustered Sept. 24, 1861. Discharged for disability Feb. 28, 1863, Young's Point, La.
COMPANY "D"
Radden, Thomas. Age 38. Residence Jones County, nativity Ireland. Enlisted Nov. 3, 1864.
Mustered Nov. 3, 1864. Wounded at Kingston, N. C. Died of wounds March 13, 1865, Newbern,
N. C. Buried in Old Cemetery, Newbern, N. C. No. 59, plot 12, grave 2126.
Remington, Ewing. Age 18. Residence Jones County, nativity New York. Enlisted Feb. 29,
1864. Mustered March 17, 1864. Mustered out July 18, 1866, Louisville, Ky.
Remington, Newman. (Veteran.) Age 19. Residence Scotch Grove, nativity New York. Enlisted
Aug. 18, 1861. Mustered Sept. 2, 1861. Re-enlisted and re-mustered Jan. 23, 1864. Mustered out
July 18, 1865, Louisville, Ky.
Ridings, James. Age 35. Residence Monticello, nativity North Carolina. Enlisted Aug. 16, 1861.
Mustered Sept. 2, 1861. Discharged for disability Sept. 20, 1862, St. Louis, Mo.
Rippey, George. Age 20. Residence Monticello, nativity Illinois. Enlisted, Aug. 18, 1861.

Mustered Sept. 2, 1861. Transferred to Veteran Reserve Corps Feb. 29, 1864. No further record.

Ress, Franklin. (Veteran.) Age 21. Residence Castle Grove, nativity New York. Enlisted Aug. 16, 1861. Mustered Sept. 2, 1861. Re-enlisted and re-mustered Jan. 23, 1864. Mustered out July 18, 1865, Louisville, Ky.

COMPANY "E"

Reichart, John. Age 43. Residence Guttenburg, nativity Germany. Mustered Sept. 24, 1861. Killed in battle March 7, 1862, Pea Ridge, Ark.

Rice, Alexander. Age 34. Residence Elkader, nativity Pennsylvania. Mustered Sept. 24, 1861. Discharged for disability Jan. 8, 1862, Pacific, Mo. See company I, Eighth Cavalry.

Rossman, Noyes. Age 31. Residence Cox Creek, nativity Ohio. Enlisted Sept. 9, 1861. Mustered Sept. 24, 1861. Wounded severely in arm; arm amputated, March 7, 1862, Pea Ridge, Ark. Discharged for disability Nov. 5, 1862, St. Louis, Mo.

Roth, Henry Joseph. Age 42. Residence Dubuque, nativity Prussia. Mustered Sept. 24, 1861. Discharged Jan. 8, 1862, Pacific, Mo.

Rowley, John C. Age 43. Residence Chickasaw County, nativity New York. Enlisted Jan. 23, 1864. Mustered Jan. 23, 1864. Died of fever Aug. 28, 1864, Marietta, Ga. Buried in National Cemetery, Marietta, Ga. Section G, grave 1081.

Russell, James A. Age 18. Residence Cox Creek, nativity Canada. Enlisted Sept. 11, 1861. Mustered Sept. 24, 1861. Died of typhoid fever Jan. 13, 1862, Pacific, Mo.

COMPANY "F"

Richardson, Sargent H. Age 43. Residence Leo, nativity Vermont. Enlisted Feb. 29, 1864.

Mustered March 18, 1864. Mustered out July 18, 1865, Louisville, Ky.
Riley, Miles. (Veteran.) Age 18. Residence West Union, nativity Virginia. Enlisted Sept. 8,
1861. Mustered Sept. 12, 1861. Died April 4, 1864, West Union, Iowa.

COMPANY "G"

Rament, Albert. Age 26. Residence Black Hawk County, nativity Canada. Enlisted Feb. 29,
1864. Mustered March 7, 1864. Mustered out July 18, 1865, Louisville, Ky.
Renn, Benjamin F. Age 24. Residence Waverly, nativity Pennsylvania. Enlisted Aug. 10, 1861.
Mustered Sept. 24, 1861. Promoted Fourth Sergeant. Mustered out Sept. 24, 1864, East Point,
Ga., expiration of term of service.
Risdon, Daniel. Age 20. Residence Bremer County, nativity Vermont. Enlisted Jan. 4, 1864.
Mustered Feb. 3, 1864. Mustered out July 18, 1865, Louisville, Ky.
Robinson, William. Age 27. Residence Dubuque, nativity Indiana. Enlisted Sept. 18, 1861.
Mustered Sept. 24, 1861. Killed in battle March 7, 1862, Pea Ridge, Ark.

COMPANY "H"

Randall, Elias. Age 24. Residence Waukon, nativity New York. Enlisted Nov. 20, 1861.
Mustered Nov. 20, 1861. Discharged for disability Jan. 20, 1863, St. Louis, Mo.
Reynolds, Jonathan T. Age 24. Residence Decorah, nativity New York. Enlisted Sept. 22,
1861. Mustered Sept. 24, 1861. Discharged for disability Aug. 10, 1863, Davenport, Iowa.
Richmond, Robert. Age 18. Residence Decorah, nativity Ohio. Enlisted Aug. 21, 1861.
Mustered Sept. 24, 1861. Wounded severely in left arm May 22, 1863, Vicksburg, Miss. Died of

pneumonia Jan. 3, 1864, Keokuk, Iowa.
Roe, Barney. (Veteran.) Age 23. Residence Pacific City, Mo., nativity Ireland. Enlisted Nov. 15,
1861. Mustered Nov. 15, 1861. Re-enlisted and re-mustered Jan. 23, 1864. Mustered out July 18,
1865, Louisville, Ky.
109
Rotner, Martin V. (Veteran.) Age 26. Residence Decorah, nativity New York. Enlisted Sept.
10, 1861. Mustered Sept. 24, 1861. Wounded severely March 7, 1862, Pea Ridge, Ark. Promoted
Fourth Corporal April 2, 1863; Third Corporal Jan. 23, 1864. Re-enlisted and re-mustered Jan.
23, 1864. Wounded slightly in head July 28, 1864, Ezra Church, Ga. Mustered out July 18, 1865,
Louisville, Ky.
Ryan, Edward. Age 28. Residence Waukon, nativity Ireland. Enlisted Aug. 26, 1861. Mustered
Sept. 24, 1861. Promoted Sixth Corporal Feb. 10, 1862. Wounded severely in shoulder March 7,
1862, Pea Ridge, Ark. Promoted Fifth Corporal Jan. 1, 1863. Discharged for wounds Feb. 7,
1863, St. Louis, Mo. See company K, Ninth Cavalry.
COMPANY "I"
Ransom, William L. (Veteran.) Age 32. Residence New Oregon, nativity New York. Enlisted
Dec. 15, 1861. Mustered Dec. 15, 1861. Wounded severely in head March 7, 1862, Pea Ridge,
Ark. Wounded slightly Dec. 28, 1862, Chickasaw Bayou, Miss. Re-enlisted and re-mustered Jan.
23, 1864. Wounded Aug. 26, 1864, Atlanta, Ga. Mustered out July, 18. 1865. Louisville. Ky.
Reeve, Fernando T. Age 20. Residence Maysville, nativity Ohio. Enlisted Aug. 22, 1861.
Mustered Sept. 18, 1861. Wounded severely in head and thigh May 22, 1863. Taken prisoner

March 14, 1864, Claysville, Ala. Died Sept. 21, 1864, Andersonville, Ga. Buried in National Cemetery, Andersonville, Ga. Grave 9483.

Reeve, Theodore H. (Veteran.) Age 19. Residence Maysville, nativity Ohio. Enlisted Aug. 22, 1861. Mustered Sept. 2, 1861. Wounded in action Nov. 27, 1863, Ringgold, Ga. Re-enlisted and re-mustered Jan. 23, 1864. Mustered out July 18, 1865, Louisville, Ky.

Rexford, Dewitt C. Age 27. Residence Marshall County, nativity Illinois. Enlisted Nov. l, 1864. Mustered Nov. l, 1864. Mustered out July 18, 1865, Louisville, Ky.

Rice, George S. Age 26. Residence Postville, nativity Ohio. Enlisted Sept. 9, 1861. Mustered Sept. 18, 1861. Mustered out Sept. 24, 1864, East Point, Ga.

Riddle, James H. Age 32. Residence Chapin, nativity North Carolina. Enlisted Aug. 28, 1861. Mustered Sept. 2, 1861. Wounded in shoulder severely May 22, 1862, Vicksburg, Miss. Died of wounds June 3, 1863, Vicksburg, Miss.

Rome, Horace B. Age 20. Residence Howard Center, nativity New York. Enlisted Sept. 10, 1861. Mustered Sept. 18, 1861. Wounded severely in left thigh March 7, 1862, Pea Ridge, Ark. Discharged for wounds Aug. 27, 1862, Cairo, Ill. See company G, Ninth Cavalry.

Rupert, Jeremiah D. Age 23. Residence Fort Atkinson, nativity Pennsylvania. Enlisted Sept. 22, 1861. Mustered Sept. 22, 1861. Wounded in action Nov. 24, 1863, Lookout Mountain, Tenn. Mustered out Sept. 24, 1864, East Point, Ga., expiration of term of service.

COMPANY "K"
110

Ramsay, Thomas. Age 30. Residence Marion, nativity

Pennsylvania. Enlisted Sept. 14, 1861.
Mustered Sept. 24, 1861. Died Oct. 27, 1862, Helena, Ark. Buried in Mississippi River National
Cemetery, Memphis, Tenn. Section 3, grave 670.
Retter, Francis. Age 18. Residence Boone County, nativity Ohio. Enlisted Nov. 7, 1864.
Mustered Nov. 7, 1864. Mustered out July 18, 1865, Louisville, Ky.
Rhodes, Abraham. Age 44. Residence Boone County, nativity Ohio. Enlisted Oct. 27, 1864.
Mustered Oct. 27, 1864. Died March 28, 1865, Goldsburg, N. C.
Richmond, Miles W. Age 25. Residence Cottage Hill, nativity New York. Enlisted Aug. 3,
1861. Mustered Sept. 24, 1861. Discharged for disability Feb. 27, 1863, Young's Point, La.
Richmond, Royal H. Age 20. Residence Paris, nativity New York. Enlisted Sept. 21, 1861.
Mustered Sept. 24, 1861. Wounded severely in hand March 7, 1862, Pea Ridge, Ark. Discharged
for disability Jan. 26, 1863, Davenport, Iowa.
Riley, James A. Age 18. Residence Marion, nativity Iowa. Enlisted Sept. 14, 1861. Mustered
Sept. 14, 1861. Discharged for disability Jan. 10, 1862, Pacific City, Mo.
Robbins, Joseph. Age 18. Residence Des Moines County, nativity Iowa. Enlisted Jan. 13, 1865.
Mustered Jan. 13, 1865. Mustered out July 18, 1865, Louisville, Ky. See company G, Twentyfifth
Infantry.
Robertson, Robert A. Age 18. Residence Linn County, nativity Illinois. Enlisted Feb. 24, 1864.
Mustered Feb. 24, 1864. Mustered out May 26, 1865, Madison, Ind.
Rose, Joseph. Age 18. Residence Lee County, nativity Iowa. Enlisted Nov. 4, 1864. Mustered
Nov. 4, 1864. Mustered out July 15, 1865, Washington, D. C.

Ross, Henry A. Age 24. Residence Marion, nativity Ohio. Enlisted Sept. 21, 1861. Mustered
Sept. 24, 1861. Killed in battle March 7, 1862, Pea Ridge, Ark. Buried in National Cemetery,
Fayetteville, Ark. Section 2, grave 30.
Rutherford, Edgar D. Age 21. Residence Cottage Hill, nativity Illinois. Enlisted Sept. 6, 1861.
Mustered Sept. 24, 1861. Died March 24, 1862, Cassville, Mo.
COMPANY "A"
Sanburn, Henry C. (Veteran.) Age 18. Residence Sabula, nativity New York. Enlisted Aug. 12,
1861. Mustered Sept. 24, 1861. Re-enlisted and re-mustered Jan. 23, 1864. Taken prisoner May
27, 1864, Dallas, Ga. Discharged June 10, 1865, Clinton, Iowa.
Scott, Samuel S. (Veteran.) Age 27. Residence Andrew, nativity Pennsylvania. Enlisted July 29,
1861, as Fourth Corporal. Mustered Sept. 2, 1861. Promoted Third Corporal Dec. 19, 1861;
Second Corporal March 3, 1862; Fifth Sergeant March 10, 1862. Wounded slightly in leg June 7,
111
1863, Walnut Hills, Miss. Promoted Third Sergeant June 7, 1863; Second Sergeant Oct. 23,
1863. Re-enlisted and re-mustered Jan. 23, 1864. Mustered out July 18, 1865, Louisville, Ky.
Searle, George C. Age 18. Residence Iowa City, nativity Rhode Island. Enlisted Feb. 20, 1864.
Mustered March 17, 1864. Discharged for disability May 11, 1865, Fort Schuyler, New York
Harbor.
Seaward, William T. (Veteran.) Age 23. Residence Maquoketa, nativity Illinois. Enlisted Aug.
13, 1861. Mustered Sept. 24, 1861. Re-enlisted and re-mustered Jan. 23, 1864. Promoted
Sergeant Major Jan. 6, 1865. Mustered out July 18, 1865, Louisville, Ky.

Shepherd, Henry H. Age 21. Residence Maquoketa, nativity New York. Enlisted Aug. 13,
1861. Mustered Sept. 24, 1861. Mustered out Sept. 24, 1864, East Point, Ga., expiration of term
of service.
Shepherd, James A. Age 18. Residence Henry County, nativity Iowa. Enlisted Feb. 22, 1864.
Mustered March 5, 1864. Mustered out July 18, 1865, Louisville, Ky. See company K, Twentyfifth
Infantry.
Sloan, David Allen. Age 19. Residence Maquoketa, nativity Pennsylvania. Enlisted Sept. 24,
1861. Mustered Sept. 24, 1861. Mustered out Sept. 24, 1864, East Point, Ga., expiration of term
of service.
Spaulding, Warren. Age 20. Residence Maquoketa, nativity Iowa. Enlisted Aug. 8, 1861.
Mustered Sept. 24, 1861. Died Aug. 1, 1863, Vicksburg, Miss.
Spear, Henry F. Age 31. Residence Maquoketa, nativity Vermont. Enlisted Aug. 9, 1861.
Mustered Sept. 24, 1861. Discharged for disability Dec. 5, 1862, Memphis, Tenn.
Speith, William. Age 24. Residence South Fork, nativity Brunswick. Enlisted Feb. 20, 1864.
Mustered March 1, 1864. Mustered out July 18, 1865, Louisville, Ky.
Spellman, John P. Age 19. Residence Charlotte, nativity Vermont. Enlisted Aug. 15, 1861.
Mustered Sept. 24, 1861. Discharged for disability Feb. 15, 1863, St. Louis, Mo.
Stephens, Francis M. Age 19. Residence Maquoketa, nativity Ohio. Enlisted Sept. 11, 1861.
Mustered Sept. 24, 1861. Died Dec. 22, 1861, Pacific, Mo.
Sweet, Menzo. Age 18. Residence Jackson County, nativity New York. Enlisted Aug. 8, 1861.
Mustered Sept. 24, 1861. Killed in battle June 7, 1863, Vicksburg,

Miss. Buried in National Cemetery, Vicksburg, Miss. Section G, grave 90.
COMPANY "B"
Seeley, Norman. Age 21. Residence Rome, nativity Iowa. Enlisted Aug. 12, 1861. Mustered Sept. 24, 1861. Died April 20, 1864, Andersonville, Ga. Buried in Andersonville National Cemetery, Ga. Grave 641.
112
Seels, Amos. (Veteran.) Age 25. Residence Madison, nativity Indiana. Enlisted Oct. 9, 1861. Mustered Oct. 9, 1861. Re-enlisted and re-mustered Jan. 23, 1864. Taken prisoner May 27, 1864, Dallas, Ga. Mustered out July 18, 1865, Louisville, Ky.
Sherman, Benedict. Age 25. Residence Madison, nativity New York. Enlisted Sept. 24, 1861. Mustered Sept. 24, 1861. Discharged for disability Jan. 18, 1862, Hospital Pacific, Mo.
Soults, Joseph. Age 25. Residence Rome, nativity Pennsylvania. Enlisted Aug. 30, 1861, as Wagoner. Mustered Sept. 24, 1861. Discharged for disability Sept. 9, 1863, Black River, Miss.
Stall, Silas H. (Veteran.) Age 18. Residence Madison, nativity Ohio. Enlisted Aug. 12, 1861. Mustered Sept. 24, 1861. Wounded slightly in leg May 22, 1863, Vicksburg, Miss. Re-enlisted and re-mustered Jan. 23, 1864. Promoted Second Corporal April 16, 1865. Mustered out July 19, 1865, Louisville, Ky.
Starry, William. (Veteran.) Age 18. Residence Linn County, nativity Iowa. Enlisted Sept. 23, 1861. Mustered Sept. 24, 1861. Promoted Seventh Corporal Dec. 1, 1863; Fifth Corporal. Reenlisted and re-mustered Jan. 23, 1864. Promoted Fourth Sergeant April 6, 1865. Mustered out July 18, 1865, Louisville, Ky.

Stephens, James B. Age 24. Residence Greenfield, nativity Pennsylvania. Enlisted Aug. 23, 1861. Mustered Sept. 24, 1861. Promoted Second Corporal Dec. 28, 1861; Fifth Sergeant Nov. 1, 1862; Fourth Sergeant May 23, 1863; Third Sergeant Jan. 20, 1864. Mustered out Sept. 24, 1864, East Point, Ga., expiration of term of service.
Sterling, George G. Age 19. Residence Greenfield, nativity Ohio. Enlisted Sept. 13, 1861.
Mustered Sept. 13, 1861. Died of typhoid fever June 6, 1862, Forsyth, Mo.
Steward, Joshua. Age 24. Residence Rome, nativity Ohio. Enlisted Aug. 12, 1861. Mustered
Sept. 24, 1861. Discharged for disability Oct. 13, 1862, Memphis, Tenn.
Steward, William. Age 21. Residence Walnut Fork, nativity Ohio. Enlisted March 16, 1864.
Mustered March 16, 1864. Died of typhoid fever July 5, 1864, Rome, Ga. Buried in National
Cemetery, Marietta, Ga. Section C, grave 414.
Stewart, Charles F. (Veteran.) Age 18. Residence Rome, nativity Ohio. Enlisted Aug. 12, 1861.
Mustered Sept. 24, 1861. Wounded slightly in arm May 22, 1863, Vicksburg, Miss. Re-enlisted
and re-mustered Jan. 23, 1864. Wounded in action May 27, 1864, Dallas, Ga. Promoted Eighth
Corporal July 6, 1865. Mustered out July 18, 1865, Louisville, Ky.
Stewart, John A. Age 18. Residence Walnut Fork, nativity Ohio. Enlisted Feb. 29, 1864.
Mustered Feb. 29, 1864. Mustered out July 18, 1865.
Stillman, James R. (Veteran.) Age 31. Residence Bowen's Prairie, nativity Connecticut.
Enlisted Aug. 23, 1862. Mustered Aug. 23, 1862. Re-enlisted and re-mustered Jan. 23, 1864.
Mustered out July 18, 1865, Louisville, Ky.

COMPANY "C"
Sampson, Jacob P. Age 25. Residence Independence, nativity Pennsylvania. Enlisted Sept. 13,
1861. Mustered Sept. 24, 1861. Wounded slightly in head March 7, 1862, Pea Ridge, Ark.
Promoted First Sergeant Sept. 26, 1862; Second Lieutenant March 8, 1862; First Lieutenant July
18, 1862. Resigned to accept commission as First Lieutenant in Signal Corps Aug. 24, 1864,
Atlanta, Ga.
Sanders, Jacob D. Age 20. Residence Independence, nativity New Hampshire. Enlisted Aug.
14, 1861, as Sixth Corporal. Mustered Sept. 24, 1861. Wounded severely in ankle and thigh
March 7, 1862, Pea Ridge, Ark. Promoted Fifth Corporal March 8, 1862. Transferred to Invalid
Corps Dec. 1, 1863. No further record.
Sarchett, Charles W. (Veteran.) Age 18. Residence Center Point, nativity Ohio. Enlisted Aug.
10, 1861. Mustered Sept. 24, 1861. Promoted Eighth Corporal Jan. 21, 1862; Seventh Corporal
March 8, 1862; Fourth Corporal. Re-enlisted and re-mustered Jan. 23, 1864. Wounded severely
March 21, 1865, Bentonsville, N. C. Promoted Third Sergeant April 9, 1865. Mustered out July
18, 1865, Louisville, Ky.
Sayre, George W. (Veteran.) Age 22. Residence Buffalo Grove, nativity New York. Enlisted
Aug. 10, 1861. Mustered Sept. 24, 1861. Promoted Sixth Corporal. Re-enlisted and re-mustered
Jan. 23, 1864. Promoted Fourth Corporal June 10, 1865. Mustered out July 18, 1865, Louisville,
Ky.
Scott, William. Age 31. Residence Independence, nativity England. Appointed Second
Lieutenant Sept. 2, 1861. Mustered Sept. 2, 1861. Promoted First

Lieutenant and Adjutant Sept.
2, 1861. Wounded in leg March 7, 1862, Pea Ridge, Ark. Resigned Oct. 11, 1862, for disability.
Shafer, Henry L. (Veteran.) Age 22. Residence Hazelton, nativity Ohio. Enlisted Sept. 7, 1862.
Mustered Sept. 14, 1862. Mustered out July 18, 1865, Louisville, Ky.
Smith, John. Age 19. Residence Chickasaw County, nativity England. Enlisted Feb. 22, 1864.
Mustered Feb. 23, 1864. Mustered out July 18, 1865, Louisville, Ky.
Smith, Thomas. Age 22. Residence Dubuque, nativity England. Enlisted Sept. 12, 1861.
Mustered Sept. 24, 1861. Mustered out Sept. 25, 1864, East Point, Ga., expiration of term of
service.
Sparling, James M. Age 28. Residence Independence, nativity New York. Enlisted Aug. 3,
1861. Mustered Sept. 24, 1861. Mustered out July 18, 1865, Louisville, Ky.
Spragg, Charles. Age 28. Residence Independence, nativity New Brunswick. Enlisted Sept. 2,
1862. Mustered Sept. 2, 1862. Died June 1, 1863, Young's Point, La. Buried in National
Cemetery, Vicksburg, Miss. Section A, grave 221.
114
Steele, David. (Veteran.) Age 20. Residence Center Point, nativity Ohio. Enlisted Aug. 9, 1861.
Mustered Sept. 24, 1861. Promoted Sixth Corporal. Re-enlisted and re-mustered Jan. 23, 1864.
Killed in action May 15, 1864, Resaca, Ga. Buried in National Cemetery, Chattanooga, Tenn.
Section G, grave 319.
Steele, James M. (Veteran.) Age 25. Residence Independence, nativity Vermont. Enlisted Aug.
9, 1861. Mustered Sept. 24, 1861. Promoted Seventh Corporal.

Re-enlisted and re-mustered Jan.
23, 1864. Wounded slightly March 21, 1865, Bentonsville, N. C. Promoted Second Sergeant
June 10, 1865. Mustered out July 18, 1865, Louisville, Ky.
Sterns, Frederick. Age 28. Residence Benton County, nativity Pennsylvania. Enlisted Feb. 21,
1864. Mustered March 3, 1864. Wounded severely May 27, 1864, Dallas, Ga. Discharged for
wounds March 27, 1865, Palo, Iowa.
Stoneman, Rufus R. (Veteran.) Age 28. Residence Winthrop, nativity Ohio. Enlisted Aug. 26,
1861. Mustered Sept. 24, 1861. Re-enlisted and re-mustered Jan. 23, 1864. Mustered out July 18,
1865, Louisville, Ky.
Sutton, J. A. Age 29. Residence Dubuque, nativity Indiana. Enlisted Sept. 12, 1861. Mustered
Sept. 24, 1861. Discharged for disability April 4, 1862, St. Louis, Mo.

COMPANY "D"

Sanders, Michaels. Age 19. Residence Wyoming, nativity Pennsylvania. Enlisted Aug. 30,
1862. Mustered Aug. 30, 1862. Wounded in arm severely Dec. 29, 1862, Chickasaw Bayou,
Miss. Discharged for wounds April 22, 1863, St. Louis, Mo.
Schull, James B. Age 31. Residence Jones County, nativity Indiana. Enlisted Nov. 23, 1861.
Mustered Nov. 23, 1861. Killed in battle March 10, 1862, Pea Ridge, Ark. Buried at Pea Ridge,
Ark.
Schuster, Alfred E. Age 23. Residence Scotch Grove, nativity Iowa. Enlisted Aug. 16, 1861.
Mustered Sept. 2, 1861. Discharged for sickness Dec. 29, 1863, Memphis, Tenn.
Scott, George W. Age 21. Residence Pottawattamie County, nativity England. Enlisted Nov. 5,
1864. Mustered Nov. 5, 1864. Mustered out July 18, 1865,

Louisville, Ky.
Scott, Thomas. Age 25. Residence Monticello, nativity Ohio. Enlisted Aug. 16, 1861, as Sixth
Corporal. Mustered Sept. 2, 1861. disability April 22, 1862, Cross Timber, Mo.
Sheldon, George. Age 29. Residence Second Congressional District, nativity Germany. Enlisted
Nov. 17, 1864. Mustered Nov. 17, 1864. Mustered out July 18, 1865, Louisville, Ky.
Slaughter, George T. Age 18. Residence Allamakee County, nativity Illinois. Enlisted Jan. 14,
1865. Mustered Jan. 14, 1865. Mustered out July 18, 1865, Louisville, Ky.
115
Smith, Emory A. Age 18. Residence Monticello, nativity New York. Enlisted Sept. 17, 1861.
Mustered Sept. 17, 1861. Killed in battle March 7, 1862, Pea Ridge, Ark. Buried in National
Cemetery, Fayetteville, Ark. Section 2, grave 11.
Smith, George W. Age 23. Residence Monticello, nativity New York. Enlisted Aug. 16, 1861.
Mustered Sept. 2, 1861. Discharged for disability Aug. 22, 1862, Cairo, Ill.
Smith, James E. Age 18. Residence Pella, nativity Michigan. Enlisted Oct. 5, 1864. Mustered
Oct. 13, 1864. Mustered out July 18, 1865, Louisville, Ky. See company H, Twenty-fifth
Infantry.
Smith, James H. Age 22. Residence Monticello, nativity New York. Enlisted Sept. 12, 1861.
Mustered Sept. 12, 1861. Died April 25, 1863, St. Louis, Mo. Buried in National Cemetery,
Jefferson Barracks, St. Louis, Mo. Section 1, grave 81.
Smith, John Isaac. Age 36. Residence Monticello, nativity Pennsylvania. Enlisted Aug. 16,
1861. Mustered Sept. 2, 1861. Discharged June 29, 1862,

Jacksonport, Ark.
South, Franklin M. Age 20. Residence Monticello, nativity Iowa. Enlisted Aug. 19, 1861.
Mustered Sept. 2, 1861. Mustered out Sept. 26, 1864, East Point, Ga., expiration of term of
service.
Spates, Jacob R. Age 18. Residence Mahaska County, nativity Indiana. Enlisted Nov. 18, 1864.
Mustered Nov. 18, 1864. Mustered out July 18, 1865, Louisville, Ky.
Standish, William H. Age 21. Residence Wyoming, nativity Pennsylvania. Enlisted Aug. 26,
1861. Mustered Sept. 2, 1861. Died of diarrhea Feb. 25, 1862, on march in Missouri.
Steele, Harlan P. Age 21. Residence Andrew, nativity Ohio. Enlisted Aug. 16, 1861 Mustered
Sept. 24 1861. Promoted Fourth Corporal Jan. 24, 1863; Second Corporal April 29, 1863; First
Corporal Aug. 4, 1863. Died of chronic diarrhea Jan. 29, 1864, Mound City, Ill.
Stewart, Bradley. Age 43. Residence Monticello, nativity New York. Enlisted March 10, 1864.
Mustered March 17, 1864. Mustered out July 18, 1865, Louisville, Ky.
Stowell, Gershom R. C. Age 45. Residence Monticello, nativity New York. Enlisted Sept. 4,
1861. Mustered Sept. 4, 1861. Discharged for disability Aug. 2, 1862, St. Louis, Mo.
Stowell, Joseph G. (Veteran.) Age 18. Residence Jones County, nativity New York. Enlisted
Sept. 4, 1861. Re-enlisted and re-mustered Jan. 23, 1864. Transferred to Veteran Reserve Corps.
Mustered out July 22, 1865, Davenport, Iowa.
Sutherland, Adam. Age 26. Residence Jones County, nativity Canada. Enlisted Feb. 25, 1864.
Mustered March 17, 1864. Promoted Eighth Corporal June 20,

1865. Mustered out July 18,
1865, Louisville, Ky.
116
Sutherland, Donald. Age 30. Residence Scotch Grove, nativity Iowa. Enlisted Aug. 16, 1861.
Mustered Sept. 2, 1861. Wounded severely in leg March 9, 1862, Pea Ridge, Ark. Died of
wounds March 15, 1862, Pea Ridge, Ark.
Sutherland, John. Age 43. Residence Jones County, nativity Iowa. Enlisted Aug. 16, 1861, as
Third Sergeant. Mustered Sept. 2, 1861. Wounded slightly in face March 7, 1862, Pea Ridge,
Ark. Promoted First Sergeant; First Lieutenant March 15, 1863. Wounded severely in shoulder
May 22, 1863, Vicksburg, Miss. Discharged Jan. 2, 1865.
Sutherland, Morrison. Age 20. Residence Monticello, nativity Iowa. Enlisted Aug. 16, 1861.
Mustered Sept. 2, 1861. Wounded severely in shoulder March 7, 1862, Pea Ridge, Ark.
Discharged for wounds Aug. 28, 1862, Cairo, Ill.
Sweesey, Thomas W., Jr. Age 22. Residence Scotch Grove, nativity Pennsylvania. Enlisted
Aug. 16, 1861, as Fourth Sergeant. Mustered Sept. 2 1861. Wounded severely in wrist March 7,
1862, Pea Ridge, Ark. Died of wounds March 24, 1862, Cassville, Mo.
COMPANY "E"
Sarggent, Lyman. Age 43. Residence Cox Creek, nativity Vermont. Enlisted Sept. 9, 1861, as
Second Corporal. Mustered Sept. 24, 1861. Died Nov. 14, 1861, Pacific, Mo. Buried in National
Cemetery, Franklin, Mo.
Schell, Charles F. W. Age 18. Residence Burlington, nativity Germany. Enlisted Dec. 31, 1863.
Mustered Dec. 31, 1863. Mustered out July 18, 1865, Louisville, Ky. See company G, Twentyfifth

Infantry.
Schlagal, Michael. Age 40. Residence Dubuque, nativity Hungary. Enlisted July 30, 1861, as
Drummer. Mustered Sept. 24, 1861. Missing in battle March 7, 1862, Pea Ridge, Ark.
Discharged for disability Aug. 12, 1862, St. Louis, Mo.
Schmidt, William. Age 40. Residence Dubuque, nativity Germany. Enlisted Aug. 3, 1861.
Mustered Sept. 24, 1861. Discharged for disability Nov. 11, 1862, St. Louis, Mo.
Seeber, Timothy. Age 34. Residence Clayton County, nativity New York. Enlisted Sept. 9,
1861. Mustered Sept. 24, 1861. Killed in battle March 7, 1862, Pea Ridge, Ark.
Shaffer, Timothy. Age 22. Residence Clayton County, nativity Canada. Enlisted Feb. 1, 1865.
Mustered Feb. 1, 1865. Mustered out July 18, 1865, Louisville, Ky.
Sherman Edwin M. Age 20. Residence Clayton County, nativity New York. Enlisted Sept. 9,
1861. Mustered Sept. 24, 1861. Died of fever Oct. 12, 1863, Jefferson Barracks, Mo. Buried in
National Cemetery, Jefferson Barracks, St. Louis, Mo. Section 33, grave 72.
Smith, Frederick. Age 36. Residence Elkader, nativity Germany. Mustered Sept. 24, 1861.
Wounded in right lung severely March 7, 1862, Pea Ridge, Ark. Discharged for disability Oct. 4,
1862, St. Louis, Mo.
117
Stevens, Henry. Age 42. Residence Guttenburg, nativity Germany. Enlisted Sept. 9, 1861.
Mustered Sept. 24, 1861. Wounded in leg and left arm severely March 7, 1862, Pea Ridge, Ark.
Discharged for disability Aug. 15, 1862, St. Louis, Mo.
Strunk, Albert D. (Veteran.) Age 19. Residence Clayton County. Enlisted Sept. 23, 1861.

Mustered Sept. 24, 1861. Promoted Sixth Corporal March 10, 1862; Fourth Corporal Dec. 1,
1862. Re-enlisted and re-mustered Jan. 23,1864. Promoted Second Corporal; First Corporal Jan.
23, 1864; First Lieutenant Jan. 24, 1865. Mustered out July 18, 1865, Louisville, Ky.
COMPANY "F"
Sawyer, Charles N. (Veteran.) Age 18. Residence Auburn, nativity New Hampshire. Enlisted
Sept. 19, 1861. Mustered Sept. 24, 1861. Re-enlisted and re-mustered Jan. 23, 1864. Wounded
slightly in left knee May 15, 1864, Resaca, Ga. Wounded in wrist Aug. 31, 1864, Jonesboro, Ga.
Mustered out July 18, 1865, Louisville, Ky.
Searles, Orlando. (Veteran.) Age 18. Residence Taylorville, nativity Ohio. Enlisted Sept. 4,
1861. Mustered Sept. 14, 1861. Re-enlisted and re-mustered Jan. 23, 1864. Promoted Eighth
Corporal Jan. 23, 1864; Seventh Corporal Aug. 1, 1864; Fourth Sergeant April 1, 1865; Third
Sergeant June 6, 1865. Mustered out July 18, 1865, Louisville, Ky.
Seaton, Asa M. Age 40. Residence Manchester, nativity New York. Enlisted Sept. 13, 1861.
Mustered Sept. 14, 1861. Died of chronic diarrhea May 20, 1863, Young's Point, La.
Shepheard, Abram P. Age 18. Residence Brush Creek, nativity Iowa. Enlisted Feb. 29, 1864.
Mustered March 18, 1864. Died July 30, 1864, Rome, Ga. Buried in National Cemetery,
Marietta, Ga. Section C, grave 254.
Sherman, William R. Age 33. Residence Taylorville, nativity Vermont. Enlisted Sept. 5, 1861.
Mustered Sept. 14, 1861. Discharged for illness May 20, 1862, St. Louis, Mo.
Smith, Absalom C. (Veteran.) Age 20. Residence Bethel, nativity Indiana. Enlisted Sept. 8,

1861, as Fifth Corporal. Mustered Sept. 14, 1861. Wounded severely in knee March 7, 1862, Pea Ridge, Ark. Promoted First Corporal Aug. 27, 1862; Fourth Sergeant Oct. 6, 1863. Re-enlisted and re-mustered Jan. 23, 1864. Promoted First Sergeant May 11,1865. Mustered out July 18, 1865, Louisville, Ky.

Smith, James. Age 30. Residence Strawberry Point, nativity Ireland. Enlisted Sept. 7, 1861. Mustered Sept. 14, 1861. Killed in battle May 22, 1863, Vicksburg, Miss.

Smith, John. Age 28. Residence Windsor, nativity Germany. Enlisted Aug. 28, 1861. Mustered Sept. 12, 1861. Died Oct. 21, 1863, Windsor, Iowa.

Smith, John W. Age 18. Residence Fayette, nativity Michigan. Enlisted Feb. 27, 1864. Mustered March 18, 1864. Mustered out July 18, 1865, Louisville, Ky.

118

Snow, Grimes. (Veteran.) Age 18. Residence Strawberry Point, nativity Kentucky. Enlisted Sept. 5, 1861. Mustered Sept. 14, 1861. Re-enlisted and re-mustered Jan. 23, 1864. Mustered out July 18, 1865, Louisville, Ky.

Snyder, Daniel. Age 21. Residence West Union, nativity Canada. Enlisted Sept. 12, 1861. Mustered Sept. 12, 1861. Discharged for disability July 19, 1862, St. Louis, Mo.

Stout, Herbert G. Age 18. Residence Fredericksburg, nativity New York. Enlisted Feb. 27, 1864. Mustered March 18, 1864. Mustered out July 18, 1865, Louisville, Ky.

Strong, Frank. Age 18. Residence Leo, nativity Ohio. Enlisted Feb. 29, 1864. Mustered March 18, 1864. Promoted Seventh Corporal May 12, 1865. Mustered out July 18, 1865, Louisville, Ky.

COMPANY "G"

Sewell, Sylvester. (Veteran.) Age 18. Residence Janesville, nativity Indiana. Enlisted Sept. 15,
1861. Mustered Sept. 24, 1861. Re-enlisted and re-mustered Jan. 23, 1864. Wounded in left
breast and arm severely May 13, 1864. Promoted Sixth Corporal Jan. 1, 1865; Fifth Corporal
May 1, 1865. Mustered out July 18, 1865, Louisville, Ky.

Sharp, George B. (Veteran.) Age 24. Residence Wolf Creek, nativity England. Enlisted Sept.
18, 1861. Mustered Sept. 24, 1861. Re-enlisted and re-mustered Jan. 23, 1864. Promoted Eighth
Corporal Aug. 1, 1864; First Lieutenant Jan. 1, 1865. Mustered out July 18, 1865, Louisville, Ky.

Sharp, Samuel. (Veteran.) Age 20. Residence Wolf Creek, nativity New York. Enlisted Sept.
18, 1861. Mustered Sept. 24, 1861. Wounded slightly in arm March 7, 1862, Pea Ridge, Ark. Reenlisted
and re-mustered Jan. 23, 1864. Promoted Fourth Corporal Oct. 1, 1864; Fifth Sergeant
May 1, 1865. Mustered out July 18, 1865, Louisville, Ky.

Shaw, William W. Age 18. Residence Dubuque, nativity Iowa. Enlisted July 28, 1861. Mustered
Sept. 24, 1861. Mustered out Sept. 24, 1864, East Point, Ga., expiration of term of service.

Shrunk, Joseph. Age 18. Residence Colesburg, nativity Pennsylvania. Enlisted Sept. 24, 1861.
Mustered Sept. 24, 1861. Mustered out Sept. 24, 1864, East Point, Ga., expiration of term of
service.

St. John, Delos B. Age 18. Residence Dubuque, nativity New York. Enlisted Oct. 12, 1864.
Mustered Oct. 12, 1864. Mustered out July 18, 1865, Louisville, Ky.

St. John, James M. (Veteran.) Age 26. Residence Janesville, nativity New York. Enlisted Aug.

24, 1861. Mustered Sept. 24, 1861. Re-enlisted and re-mustered Jan. 23, 1864. Mustered out July
18, 1865, Louisville, Ky.
St. John, Johnnie G. Age 18. Residence Janesville, nativity New York. Enlisted Aug. 10, 1861.
Mustered Sept. 24, 1861. Discharged for disability July 15, 1863, Keokuk, Iowa.
119
Strow, Andrew J. Age 33. Residence Waverly, nativity Pennsylvania. Enlisted July 28, 1861,
as First Sergeant. Mustered Sept. 24, 1861. Discharged for disability July 16, 1862, Helena, Ark.
Sturdevant, Caleb J. Age 25. Residence Waverly, nativity Pennsylvania. Enlisted Aug. 10,
1861. Mustered Sept. 24, 1861. Promoted Fourth Corporal March 28, 1862; Third Corporal.
Died of chronic diarrhea Jan. 26, 1863, Vicksburg, Miss.
COMPANY "H"
Sallee, William G. (Veteran.) Age 26. Residence Decorah, nativity Illinois. Enlisted Aug. 21,
1861, as Fifth Corporal. Mustered Sept. 24, 1861. Wounded slightly in right thigh March 7,
1862, Pea Ridge, Ark. Promoted Fourth Corporal Jan. 1, 1863; Third Corporal; Fifth Sergeant
April 2, 1863. Wounded in leg and hip May 22, 1863, Vicksburg, Miss. Re-enlisted and remustered
Jan. 23, 1864. Mustered out July 18, 1865, Louisville, Ky.
Sanborn, John M. Age 26. Residence Decorah, nativity New York. Enlisted Aug. 21, 1861.
Mustered Sept. 24, 1861. Wounded severely in thigh June 27, 1864, Kenesaw Mountain, Ga.
Mustered out Sept. 24, 1864, East Point, Ga.
Scott, John. Age 24. Residence Janesville, nativity New York. Enlisted Sept. 23, 1861.
Mustered Sept. 24, 1861. Discharged for disability July 2, 1862, St. Louis, Mo.

Simenson, Hans. (Veteran.) Age 21. Residence Decorah, nativity Norway. Enlisted Aug. 26,
1861. Mustered Sept. 24, 1861. Re-enlisted and re-mustered Jan. 23, 1864. Promoted Seventh
Corporal June 1, 1865. Mustered out July 18, 1865, Louisville, Ky.
Smalley, Samuel C. Age 19. Residence Decorah, nativity Illinois. Enlisted Sept. 20, 1861.
Mustered Sept. 24, 1861. Mustered out Sept. 24, 1864, East Point, Ga., expiration of term of
service.
Smalley, Wesley D. Age 20. Residence Burr Oak, nativity Illinois. Enlisted Sept. 20, 1861.
Mustered Sept. 24, 1861. Discharged for disability March 19, 1862, St. Louis, Mo.
Smith, James S. Age 18. Residence Alamakee County, nativity New York. Enlisted Feb. 27,
1864. Mustered March 17, 1864. Promoted Eighth Corporal July 1, 1865. Mustered out July 18,
1865, Louisville, Ky.
Smith, William W. Age 25. Residence Decorah, nativity Vermont. Enlisted Sept. 24, 1861.
Mustered Sept. 24, 1861. Wounded severely in arm March 7, 1862, Pea Ridge, Ark. Died of
wounds March 21, 1862, Cassville, Mo.
Soper, David. Age 44. Residence Belleville, nativity Canada. Enlisted Aug. 26, 1861. Mustered
Sept. 24, 1861. Discharged for disability Feb. 27, 1863, Young's Point, La.
Stinson, James. Age 25. Residence Burlington, nativity Ireland. Enlisted Jan. 20, 1865.
Mustered Jan. 20, 1865. Mustered out July 18, 1865, Louisville, Ky. See company G, Twentyfifth
Infantry.
120
Supher, Jacob P. Age 29. Residence Dubuque, nativity Pennsylvania. Enlisted Oct. 2, 1861.

Mustered Oct. 2, 1861. Wounded severely March 7, 1862, Pea Ridge, Ark. Died of wounds,
April 8, 1862, Cassville, Mo.
Symons, Oliver E. (Veteran.) Age 23. Residence Cedar Falls, nativity Indiana. Enlisted Sept.
23, 1861. Mustered Sept. 24, 1861. Re-enlisted and re-mustered Jan. 23, 1864. Wounded in left
thigh March 15, 1864, Resaca, Ga. Transferred to Veteran Reserve Corps. Mustered out July 22,
1865, Davenport, Iowa.
COMPANY "I"
Scofield, Walter. Age 21. Residence New Oregon, nativity Pennsylvania. Enlisted Aug. 17,
1861, as First Corporal. Mustered Sept. 18, 1861. Wounded severely in side March 7, 1862, Pea
Ridge, Ark. Promoted Second Sergeant May 4, 1862. Discharged for wounds June 7, 1862, St.
Louis, Mo.
Serfoss, Hiram. Rejected Aug. 25, 1861, by Mustering Officer. See company B, Fifty-fifth
Infantry.
Sherman, Salisbury. Age 28. Residence Castalia, nativity Ohio. Enlisted Sept. 10, 1861.
Mustered Sept. 18, 1861. Wounded severely in thigh March 7, 1862, Pea Ridge, Ark. Discharged
for wounds Aug. 27, 1862, Cairo, Ill.
Smalley, William W. (Veteran.) Age 20. Residence Cedar, nativity Vermont. Enlisted Aug. 20,
1861. Mustered Sept. 18, 1861. Re-enlisted and re-mustered Jan. 23, 1864. Mustered out July 18,
1865, Louisville, Ky.
Sporling, Edwin R. Age 32. Residence Maysville, nativity New York. Enlisted Aug. 20, 1861,
as Third Sergeant. Mustered Sept. 18, 1861. Died of fever June 23, 1862, Batesville, Ark.
Stragher, Adolphus C. Age 27. Residence Foreston, nativity

Pennsylvania. Enlisted Aug. 19,
1861. Mustered Sept. 2, 1861. Wounded severely March 7, 1862, Pea Ridge, Ark. Died June 23,
1863, Vicksburg, Miss.
Stuart, John W. Age 30. Residence Deerfield, nativity Maine. Enlisted Aug. 21, 1861.
Mustered Sept. 18, 1861. Wounded severely in left foot; foot amputated March 7, 1862, Pea
Ridge, Ark. Died of wounds May 6, 1862, Cassville, Mo. Buried in National Cemetery,
Springfield, Mo. Section 10, grave 59.
Sutton, Samuel. Age 20. Residence New Hampton, nativity Illinois. Enlisted March 15, 1862.
Mustered March 15, 1862. Wounded severely in action Nov. 25, 1863, Missionary Ridge, Tenn.
Transferred to Invalid Corps April 10, 1864. No further record.
COMPANY "K"
121
Scott, Marquis M. Age 22. Residence Marion, nativity Ohio. Enlisted Sept. 14, 1861. Mustered
Sept. 24, 1861. Died of dysentery Oct. 29, 1861, Pacific City, Mo.
Sessions, Jerome H. Age 18. Residence Johnson County, nativity New York. Enlisted March
16, 1864. Mustered March 22, 1864. Mustered out June 10, 1865, Jeffersonville, Ind.
Slife, David M. Age 18. Residence Linn County, nativity Ohio. Enlisted Sept. 21, 1861.
Mustered Sept. 24, 1861. Died of scarlet fever April 28, 1863, on steamer "Crescent City."
Spanton, John. (Veteran.) Age 28. Residence Marion, nativity England. Mustered Sept. 24,
1861. Re-enlisted and re-mustered Jan. 23, 1864.
Spaulding, Warren. Age 20. Residence Linn County, nativity Iowa. Mustered Sept. 24, 1861.
Died of diarrhea Aug. 1, 1863, Vicksburg, Miss.
Straley, Joseph. Age 18. Residence Marion, nativity Ohio.

Mustered Sept. 24, 1861.
Discharged Sept. 23, 1864, East Point, Ga., expiration of term of service.
Sutton, Resin. Age 29. Residence Linn County, nativity Ohio. Enlisted Oct. 1, 1861. Mustered
Oct. 1, 1861. Died Dec. 16, 1863, Memphis, Tenn. Buried in Mississippi River National
Cemetery, Memphis, Tenn. Section 1, grave 203.
Sutzin, Henry B. Age 18. Residence Marion, nativity Ohio. Enlisted Sept. 14, 1861. Mustered
Sept. 24, 1861. Died Nov. 20, 1863, Memphis, Tenn. Buried in Mississippi River National
Cemetery, Memphis, Tenn. Section 1, grave 243.
Sutzin, Jacob. Age 18. Residence Linn County, nativity Ohio. Enlisted Feb. 22, 1864. Mustered
Feb. 22, 1864 Mustered out July 18, 1865, Louisville, Ky.
Sutzin, John G. (Veteran.) Age 19. Residence Marion, nativity Ohio. Re-enlisted and remustered
Jan. 23, 1864. Mustered out July 18, 1865, Louisville, Ky.
Swan, John. Age 18. Residence Linn County, nativity Iowa. Enlisted Feb. 15, 1864. Mustered
Feb. 15, 1864. Mustered out May 19, 1865, Davenport, Iowa.
COMPANY "A"
Taylor, Franklin D. Age 18. Residence Maquoketa, nativity New York. Enlisted July 28, 1861.
Mustered Sept. 24, 1861. Mustered out Sept. 24, 1864, East Point, Ga., expiration of term of
service.
Thompson, Robert S. (Veteran.) Age 19. Residence Andrew, nativity Pennsylvania. Enlisted
Sept. 22, 1862. Mustered Oct. 4, 1862. Re-enlisted and re-mustered Jan. 23, 1864. Promoted
Third Corporal Nov. 1, 1864; Fifth Sergeant May 1, 1865. Mustered out July 18, 1865,
Louisville, Ky.

Thompson, William M. Age 21. Residence Andrew, nativity Pennsylvania. Enlisted Aug. 15,
1861. Mustered Sept. 24, 1861. Wounded slightly in hand March 7, 1862, Pea Ridge, Ark. Died
Feb. 17, 1863, Vicksburg, Miss.
Tinker, George C. (Veteran.) Age 16. Residence Maquoketa, nativity New York. Enlisted Aug.
12, 1861, as Fifer. Mustered Sept. 24, 1861. Re-enlisted and re-mustered Jan. 23, 1864. Mustered
out July 18, 1865, Louisville, Ky.
Tollman, Edward A. (Veteran.) Age 21. Residence Sabula, nativity Massachusetts. Enlisted
Aug. 8, 1861. Mustered Sept. 24, 1861. Re-enlisted and re-mustered Jan. 23, 1864. Promoted
Sixth Corporal May 27, 1865. Mustered out July 18, 1865, Louisville, Ky.
Tompkins, Phineas H. Age 31. Residence Spragueville, nativity New York. Enlisted Oct. 7,
1861. Mustered Oct. 7, 1861. Mustered out Oct. 13, 1864, Rome, Ga., expiration of term of
service.
Townsend, Charles H. (Veteran.) Age 43. Residence Monmouth, nativity Ohio. Enlisted Sept.
10, 1861. Mustered Sept. 24, 1861. Promoted Fifth Corporal Dec. 19, 1861; Fourth Corporal;
Fifth Sergeant June 7, 1863; Fourth Sergeant Oct. 23, 1863. Re-enlisted and re-mustered Jan. 23,
1864. Promoted Third Sergeant Oct. 16, 1864; First Sergeant May 1, 1865. Mustered out July 18,
1865, Louisville, Ky.
Townsend, Samuel D. Age 31. Residence Monmouth. Mustered Sept. 24, 1861. Died of heart
disease March 3, 1862, Cross Hollows, Ark.
Trout, George. Age 19. Residence Maquoketa, nativity Ohio. Enlisted Aug. 10, 1861. Mustered
Sept. 24, 1861. Wounded slightly March 7, 1862, Pea Ridge, Ark.

Promoted Eighth Corporal
June 7, 1863; Seventh Corporal; Sixth Corporal Dec. 17, 1863. Discharged Dec. 24, 1864, East
Point, Ga., expiration of term of service.
Trout, William. (Veteran.) Age 20. Residence Maquoketa, nativity Pennsylvania. Enlisted May
1, 1862. Mustered May 1, 1862 . Re-enlisted and re-mustered Jan. 23, 1864. Promoted Eighth
Corporal Nov. 1, 1864; Seventh Corporal. Mustered out July 18, 1865, Louisville, Ky.
Tubbs, Daniel. Rejected Aug. 8, 1861, by Mustering Officer.
COMPANY "B"
Tarbox, Manville. Age 31. Residence Jackson, nativity New York. Enlisted Sept. 24, 1861.
Mustered Sept. 24, 1861. Discharged for disability Jan. 18, 1862, Pacific, Mo.
Taylor, Isum. Age 18. Residence Jamestown, nativity Wisconsin. Enlisted Aug. 28, 1861.
Mustered Sept. 24, 1861. Discharged for disability May 2, 1862, Springfield, Mo.
Thomas, John. Age 21. Residence Linn, nativity Pennsylvania. Enlisted Aug. 30, 1861.
Mustered Sept. 24, 1861. Mustered out Sept. 24, 1864, East Point, Ga., expiration of term of
service.
123
Torrance, Adam C. Age 22. Residence Rome, nativity Ohio. Enlisted Aug. 25, 1861. Mustered
Sept. 24, 1861. Mustered out Sept. 24, 1864, East Point, Ga., expiration of term of service.
Tourtellot, Lewis P. Age 21. Residence Wyoming, nativity Ohio. Enlisted Sept. 12, 1861.
Mustered Sept. 24, 1861. Promoted Third Corporal July 29, 1862; Second Corporal Nov. 1,
1862; First Corporal Dec. 8, 1862. Died of typhoid fever March 20, 1863, Memphis, Tenn.

Buried in National Cemetery, Jefferson Barracks, St. Louis, Mo. Section 38, grave 205.
COMPANY "C"
Taylor, Royal. Age 25. Residence Littleton, nativity Massachusetts. Enlisted Aug. 23, 1861.
Mustered Sept. 24, 1861. Mustered out Sept. 24, 1864, Davenport, Iowa, expiration of term of
service.
Thayer, William D. (Veteran.) Age 22. Residence Independence, nativity New York. Enlisted
Sept. 12, 1861. Mustered Sept. 24, 1861. Promoted Principal Musician Sept. 1, 1863. Re-enlisted
and re-mustered Jan. 23, 1864. Mustered out July 18, 1865, Louisville, Ky.
Turner, George A. Age 19. Residence Fairbanks, nativity Illinois. Enlisted Aug. 20, 1861.
Mustered Sept. 24, 1861. Died Feb. 14, 1864, Paducah, Ky. Buried in National Cemetery,
Mound City, Ill. Section D, grave 4150.
COMPANY "D"
Tate, Daniel H. Age 21. Residence South Fork, nativity Illinois. Enlisted Feb. 26, 1864.
Mustered March 17, 1864. Promoted Fifth Corporal June 20, 1865. Mustered out July 18, 1865,
Louisville, Ky.
Thompson, John. Age 19. Residence Boone County, nativity Ohio. Enlisted Nov. 7, 1864.
Mustered Nov. 7, 1864. Mustered out July 18, 1865, Louisville. Ky.
Tompkins, Amos S. Age 21. Residence Monticello, nativity New York. Enlisted Aug. 26, 1861.
Mustered Sept. 2, 1861. Missing in battle March 7, 1862, Pea Ridge, Ark. Died Jan. 31, 1863,
Jefferson Barracks, St. Louis, Mo. Buried in National Cemetery, Jefferson Barracks, St. Louis,
Mo. Section 38, grave 268.

COMPANY "E"
Tisdale, Gilbert J. Age 26. Residence New Hampton, nativity Ohio. Enlisted July 8, 1861.
Mustered July 24, 1861. Promoted First Sergeant Jan. 1, 1862. Wounded in left thigh severely
March 7, 1862, Pea Ridge, Ark. Promoted First Lieutenant March 8, 1862. Mustered out Jan. 2,
1865, expiration of term of service. See Seventh Infantry; also company F of this regiment.
Towsley, Charles H. Age 18. Residence West Union, nativity New York Enlisted Sept. 12,
1861. Mustered Sept. 24, 1861. Died of chronic diarrhea Nov. 18, 1863, Memphis, Tenn.
124
Truman, Cyrus L. Age 21. Residence Volga City, nativity Ohio. Enlisted Sept. 12, 1861.
Mustered Sept. 24, 1861. Discharged for disability Jan. 8, 1862, Franklin, Mo.
Truman, Henry J. Age 35. Residence Volga City, nativity New York. Mustered Sept. 24, 1861.
Discharged for disability Jan. 8, 1862, Pacific, Mo.
COMPANY "F"
Thompson, Andrew P. Age 24. Residence Eldorado, nativity Canada. Enlisted Sept. 3,1861.
Mustered Sept. 12,1861. Discharged for disability Feb. 15, 1862, St. Louis, Mo.
Thompson, John B. Age 33. Residence Eldorado, nativity Canada. Enlisted Sept. 6, 1861.
Mustered Sept. 12, 1861. Mustered out Sept. 24, 1864, East Point, Ga.
Thorp, Elbridge W. Age 18. Residence Lima, nativity Illinois. Enlisted Aug. 28, 1861.
Mustered Sept. 12, 1861. Discharged April 24, 1862, St. Louis, Mo.
Tisdale, Edgar. Age 23. Residence Dubuque, nativity Ohio. Appointed Second Lieutenant Sept.

14,1861. Mustered Sept. 14, 1861. Promoted First Lieutenant March 11, 1862; Captain Jan. 31,
1863. Resigned July 23,1863, Vicksburg, Miss.
Tisdale, Gilbert J. Age 26. Residence New Hampton, nativity Ohio. Enlisted July 8, 1861.
Mustered July 24, 1861. Transferred to company E, Jan. 1, 1862. See company B, Seventh
Infantry, and company E of this regiment.
Tollifson, Lewis. Age 20. Residence Clermont, nativity Norway. Enlisted Sept. 10, 1861.
Mustered Sept. 12, 1861. Died of typhoid fever Dec. 4,1864, Pacific, Mo.
Towner, James W. Age 37 Residence West Union, nativity New York. Appointed Captain Sept.
14, 1861. Mustered Sept. 14, 1861. Wounded severely in head March 7, 1862, Pea Ridge, Ark.
Resigned Jan. 30, 1863, Young's Point, La.
Tyrrell, Daniel W. Age 19. Residence West Union, nativity Michigan. Enlisted Sept. 8, 1861, as
Fifth Sergeant. Mustered Sept. 12, 1861. Promoted Second Sergeant March 12, 1863; Sergeant
Major Sept. 4, 1863. Mustered out Sept. 21, 1864, East Point, Ga., expiration of term of service.
COMPANY "G"
Taber, Silas. (Veteran.) Age 21. Residence Jamesville, nativity Pennsylvania. Enlisted Aug. 15,
1861. Mustered Sept. 24, 1861. Promoted Second Sergeant March 28, 1862. Died of chronic
diarrhea Aug. 19,1864, Rome, Ga.
Tanner, William. (Veteran.) Age I8. Residence Martinsburg, nativity Pennsylvania. Enlisted
Sept. 13, 1861. Mustered Sept. 24, 1861. Promoted Seventh Corporal May 1, 1865. Mustered out
July 18,1865. Louisville, Ky.
125
Thornsbrue, Asaheal. (Veteran.) Age 20. Residence Jamesville,

nativity Illinois. Enlisted Aug.
10, 1861, as Fifth Corporal. Mustered Sept. 24, 1861. Promoted Fourth Corporal Dec. 6, 1862;
Third Corporal. Re-enlisted and re-mustered Jan. 23, 1864. Fourth Sergeant Jan. 5, 1865;
Commissary Sergeant April 28, 1865. Mustered out July 18, 1865, Louisville, Ky.

True, Samuel W. Age 37. Residence Jamesville, nativity Pennsylvania. Enlisted Aug. 15, 1861.
Mustered Sept. 24, 1861. Promoted Sixth Corporal May 12, 1862; Fourth Corporal. Wounded in
right arm May 22, 1863, Vicksburg, Miss. Mustered out Sept. 24, 1864, East Point, Ga.,
expiration of term of service.

Tyrell, Edward. Age 40. Residence Waverly, nativity Ireland. Enlisted July 28, 1861. Mustered
Sept. 24, 1861. Promoted First Corporal; First Lieutenant March 11, 1862. Killed in battle May
22, 1863, Vicksburg, Miss.

COMPANY "H."

Teefle, Stephen. (Veteran.) Age 28. Residence Freeport, nativity Canada. Enlisted Nov. 23,
1861. Mustered Jan. 10, 1862. Re-enlisted and re-mustered Jan. 23, 1864. Wounded in left knee
severely March 21, 1865, Bentonville, N. C. Died of wounds May 1, 1865, Newbern, N. C.

Thompson, Orfin. Age 24. Residence Decorah, nativity Norway. Enlisted Aug. 26 1861.
Mustered Sept. 24, 1861. Wounded slightly in foot March 7, 1862, Pea Ridge, Ark. Discharged
for disability Aug. 26, 1862, St. Louis, Mo.

COMPANY "I"

Thompson, Abel. Age 43. Residence Albia, nativity New York. Enlisted Aug. 15, 1861, as
Fifer. Mustered Sept. 18, 1861. Transferred to Invalid Corps Sept. 1, 1863. No further record.

Townsend, David N. Age 19. Residence Castalia, nativity Indiana. Enlisted Sept. 13, 1861.
Mustered Sept. 18, 1861. Wounded severely in hand March 7, 1862, Pea Ridge, Ark. Discharged
for wounds Oct. 16, 1862, Keokuk, Iowa.
Townsend, Hiram M. Age 21. Residence Castalia, nativity Indiana. Enlisted Sept. 13, 1861.
Mustered Sept. 18, 1861. Wounded severely in arm; arm amputated March 7, 1862, Pea Ridge,
Ark. Died of wounds April 23, 1862, Cassville, Mo. Buried in National Cemetery, Springfield,
Mo. Section 10, grave 54.
COMPANY "K"
Tincher, Joseph. Age 29. Residence Marion. Mustered Sept. 24, 1861. Discharged Sept. 23,
1864, East Point, Ga.
COMPANY "A"
Updegraft, Jesse. Age 19. Residence Maquoketa, nativity Indiana. Enlisted Aug. 10, 1861.
Mustered Sept. 7, 1861. Killed March 7, 1862, Pea Ridge, Ark. Buried in National Cemetery,
Fayetteville, Ark. Section 2, grave 31.
126
Updegraft, Joseph. Age 22. Residence Maquoketa, nativity Ohio. Enlisted Sept. 7, 1861.
Mustered Sept. 24, 1861. Discharged for disability July 22, 1862, Helena, Ark.
COMPANY "C"
Utterbeck, Albert. (Veteran.) Age 18. Residence Buchanan County, nativity Ohio. Enlisted
Aug. 26, 1861. Mustered Sept. 24, 1861. Promoted Eighth Corporal; Sixth Corporal June 10,
1865. Mustered out July 18, 1865, Louisville, Ky.
COMPANY "A"
Van Orsdol, Alexander G. (Veteran.) Age 18. Residence Maquoketa, nativity Illinois. Enlisted

Aug. 10, 1861. Mustered Sept. 24, 1861. Re-enlisted and re-mustered Jan. 23, 1864. Promoted
Eighth Corporal Sept. 23, 1864; Second Corporal Nov. 1, 1864; First Corporal May 27, 1865.
Mustered out July 18, 1865, Louisville, Ky.
Vaughan, Bailey. Age 19. Residence Muscatine, nativity Iowa. Enlisted Feb. 20. 1864.
Mustered March 1, 1864. Mustered out July 18, 1865, Louisville, Ky.
Vickery, Frederick R. Age 23. Residence Maquoketa, nativity England. Enlisted Sept. 15,
1861. Mustered Sept. 24, 1861. Died March 22, 1863, St. Louis, Mo. Buried in National
Cemetery, Jefferson Barracks, Mo. Section 38, grave 204.
COMPANY "B"
Vaughn, Samuel J. Age 18. Residence Madison, nativity Illinois. Enlisted March 18, 1864.
Mustered March 18, 1864. Wounded in hand May 28, 1864, Dallas, Ga. Mustered out July 18,
1865, Louisville, Ky.
Volle, John. (Veteran.) Age 24. Residence Madison, nativity Germany. Enlisted Aug. 12, 1861.
Mustered Sept. 24, 1861. Re-enlisted and re-mustered Jan. 23, 1864. Promoted Seventh Corporal
July 5, 1865. Mustered out July 18, 1865, Louisville, Ky.
COMPANY "C"
Vanderbilt, Philetus. (Veteran.) Age 21. Residence Buffalo Grove, nativity New York. Enlisted
Aug. 10, 1861. Mustered Sept. 24, 1861. Re-enlisted and re-mustered Jan. 23, 1864. Wounded
slightly July 28, 1864, Atlanta, Ga. Mustered out July 18, 1865, Louisville, Ky.
Vanguson, John N. Age 20. Residence Independence, nativity Michigan. Enlisted Sept. 21,
1862. Mustered Sept. 21, 1862. Mustered out July 18, 1865, Louisville, Ky.

Van Wie, Henry. Age 23. Residence Black Hawk County, nativity New York. Enlisted Feb. 22,
1864. Mustered Feb. 23, 1864. Mustered out May 27, 1865, Davenport, Iowa.
Van Wie, John. Age 20. Residence Black Hawk County, nativity New York. Enlisted Dec. 14,
1863. Mustered Feb. 23, 1864. Mustered out July 18, 1865, Louisville, Ky.

COMPANY "D"

Van Sant, Leroy J. Age 18. Residence Monticello. nativity Iowa. Enlisted Aug. 16, 1861.
Mustered Sept. 2, 1861. Died July 14, 1862, Helena, Ark.
Vanvolkingburgh, Vincent. Age 18. Residence Wyoming, nativity Indiana. Enlisted Sept. 2,
1861. Mustered Sept. 12, 1861. Deserted Oct. 14, 1861, Dubuque, Iowa.

COMPANY "G"

Vankleeck, David. (Veteran.) Age 28. Residence Waverly, nativity New York. Enlisted Aug.
10, 1861, as Seventh Corporal. Mustered Sept. 24, 1861. Promoted Fifth Corporal. Re-enlisted
and re-mustered Jan. 23, 1864. Promoted First Corporal Oct. 1, 1864. Mustered out July 18,
1865, Louisville, Ky.
Vincent, Joseph. Age 18. Residence Wolf Creek, nativity Pennsylvania. Enlisted Aug. 18, 1861.
Mustered Sept. 24, 1861. Killed in battle March 7, 1862, Pea Ridge, Ark.
Van Leuven, Alonzo C. Age 23. Residence Decorah, nativity New York. Enlisted Oct. 25,
1861. Mustered Oct. 25, 1861. Promoted Fourth Corporal July 19, l862; Third Corporal Jan. 3
1863. Killed in battle May 22,1863, Vicksburg, Miss.
Van Leuven, Henry C. Age l8. Residence Howard County, nativity New York. Enlisted Oct.

25, 1861. Discharged for disability April 4, 1862, St. Louis, A10.
COMPANY "I"
Vance, Adam. Age 36. Residence Castalia, nativity Ohio. Enlisted Oct. 21, 1861. Mustered Oct.
21, 1861. Discharged for disability July 29, 1862, St. Louis, Mo.
COMPANY "K"
Van Dyke, Peter H. Age 12. Residence Marion, nativity Indiana. Enlisted Sept. 14, 1861.
Mustered Sept. 21, 1861. Died of chronic diarrhea May 29, 1863, Hospital Boat.
Vorman, John. (Veteran.) Age 18. Residence Pacific, Mo., nativity Virginia. Mustered Dec. 27,
1861. Re-enlisted and re-mustered Jan. 23, 1864. Mustered out July 18, 1865, Louisville, Ky.
COMPANY "A"
Wait, Lewis M. Age 18. Residence Jackson County, nativity Michigan. Enlisted Feb. 27, 1864.
Mustered Feb. 27, 1864. Wounded in side May 13, 1864, Resaca, Ga. Died of wounds May 25,
1864, Resaca, Ga.
128
Wait, Willett R. (Veteran.) Age 19. Residence Maquoketa, nativity New York. Enlisted Aug.
12, 1861. Mustered Sept. 24, 1861. Re-enlisted and re-mustered Jan. 23, 1864. Joined from
company K. Mustered out July 18, 1865, Louisville, Ky. See company K.
West, James. Age 25. Residence Dubuque, nativity Canada. Enlisted Sept. 24, 1861. Mustered
Sept. 24, 1861. Wounded slightly in knee March 7, 1862, Pea Ridge, Ark. Mustered out July 24,
1864, East Point, Ga., expiration of term of service.
White, Norman C. Age 24. Residence Sabula, nativity Ohio. Enlisted Nov. 19, 1861. Mustered
Nov. 19, 1861. Mustered out Jan. 12, 1865, St. Louis, Mo.
White, Samuel W. Age 27. Residence Montgomery County,

nativity Indiana. Enlisted Nov. 5, 1864. Mustered Nov. 5, 1864. Mustered out July 18, 1865, Louisville, Ky.
Wicking, John. Age 20. Residence Maquoketa, nativity New York. Enlisted Aug. 14, 1861.
Mustered Sept. 24, 1861. Transferred to Invalid Corps May 15, 1864. Mustered out Sept. 24,
1864, East Point, Ga., expiration of term of service.
COMPANY "B"
Wade, Aaron L. Age 21. Residence Hale, nativity Ohio. Enlisted Aug. 12, 1861. Mustered Sept.
24, 1861. Discharged for disability July 24, 1862, St. Louis, Mo.
Walker, Isaac. Age 20. Residence Rome, nativity Indiana. Enlisted Aug. 12, 1861. Mustered
Sept. 24, 1861. Promoted Eighth Corporal March 11, 1862; Seventh Corporal Aug. 1, 1862;
Sixth Corporal Nov. 1, 1862; Fifth Corporal Dec. 8, 1862; Fourth Corporal March 20, 1863.
Killed in battle May 22, 1863, Vicksburg, Miss.
Warner, James M. (Veteran.) Age 24. Residence Hale, nativity New York. Enlisted Aug. 12,
1861. Mustered Sept. 24, 1861. Promoted Eighth Corporal Aug. 12, 1862; Seventh Corporal
Nov. 1, 1862. Re-enlisted and re-mustered Jan. 23, 1864. Mustered out July 18, 1865, Louisville, Ky.
Weaver, Francis. (Veteran.) Age 20. Residence Rome, nativity Indiana. Enlisted Aug. 12,1861.
Mustered Sept. 24,1861. Promoted Wagoner. Re-enlisted and re-mustered Jan. 23, 1864.
Mustered out July 18, 1865, Louisville, Ky.
Weeks, Stephen M. Age 19. Residence Oxford, nativity Ohio. Enlisted Aug. 30, 1861. Mustered
Sept. 24, 1861. Died of chronic diarrhea Oct. 15, 1864, Rome, Ga. Buried in National
Cemetery, Marietta, Ga. Section C, grave 133.

Welch, James M. Age 19. Residence Fairview, nativity New York. Enlisted Aug. 12, 1861. Mustered Sect. 24, 1861. Wounded in right leg Oct. 29, 1863, Cherokee, Ala. Discharged Sept. 24, 1864, Paducah, Ky., expiration of term of service.
Wells, Ely V. (Veteran.) Age 20. Residence Linn, nativity Pennsylvania. Enlisted Aug. 30, 1861. Mustered Sept. 24, 1861. Re-enlisted and re-mustered Jan. 23, 1864. Mustered out June 26, l865.
129
Whitney, John H. Age 27. Residence Hale, nativity New York. Enlisted Aug. 12, 1861. Mustered Sept. 24, 1861. Discharged for disability May 13, 1862, Batesville, Ark.
Winn, Welcome B. Age 23. Residence Fairview, nativity Ohio. Enlisted Aug. 23, 1861. Mustered Sept. 24, 1861. Discharged for chronic diarrhea Dec. 6. 1862, St. Louis, Mo.
Works, Joseph S. Age 18. Residence Paris, nativity Wisconsin. Enlisted Aug. 29, 1861. Mustered Sept. 24, 1861. Discharged for disability Aug. 9, 1862, St. Louis, Mo. See Ninth Cavalry.
Walton, Pierce. Age 21. Residence Spring Grove, nativity Ohio. Enlisted Aug. 23, 1861. Mustered Sept. 24, 1861. Discharged for disability April 2, 1862, Cassville, Mo.
Way, James. Age 18. Residence Muscatine, nativity Iowa. Enlisted Feb. 25, 1864. Mustered March 3, 1864. Mustered out July 18, 1865, Louisville, Ky.
Whisnand, William. Age 19. Residence Spring Grove, nativity Indiana. Enlisted Aug. 23, 1861. Mustered Sept. 24, 1861. Wounded in thigh March 7, 1862, Pea Ridge, Ark. Died of wounds March 27, 1862, Cassville, Mo.
Whitlock, Rinaldo M. (Veteran.) Age 21. Residence Jessup,

nativity Vermont. Enlisted Aug.
25, 1861. Mustered Sept. 24, 1841. Promoted Fifth Corporal;
Third Corporal; Second Corporal
June 14, 1865. Mustered out July 18, 1865, Louisville, Ky.
Wilbur, Frederick M. Age 22. Residence Littleton, nativity
Massachusetts. Enlisted Aug. 23,
1861. Mustered Sept. 24, 1861. Promoted Sixth Corporal March 8, 1862; Fourth Corporal.
Mustered out Sept. 25, 1864, East Point, Ga., expiration or term of service.
Wilbur, Henry P. Age 23. Residence Alton, nativity
Massachusetts. Enlisted Aug. 23, 1861.
Mustered Sept. 24, 1861. Promoted First Sergeant; Second
Lieutenant March 8, 1863. Wounded
mortally while on picket guard May 18, 1863, Vicksburg, Miss. Died of wounds May 2, 1863,
Walnut Hills, Miss.
Willey, William. Age 21. Residence Fairbanks, nativity Iowa. Enlisted Aug. 10, 1861. Mustered
Sept. 24, 1861. Wounded slightly May 22, 1863, Vicksburg, Miss. Mustered out Sept. 25, 1864,
East Point, Ga., expiration of term of service.
Windsor, Adonin J. Age 27. Residence Independence, nativity
New York. Enlisted Aug. 25,
1861. Mustered Sept. 24, 1861. Wounded severely in leg March 7, 1862, Pea Ridge, Ark. Died
of wounds March 13, 1862, Pea Ridge, Ark.
Wright, Robert W. Age 33. Residence Independence, nativity
England. Enlisted July 20, 1861,
as First Sergeant. Mustered Sept. 24, 1861. Promoted Hospital Steward Sept. 26, 1862; Second
Lieutenant Jan. 29, 1862; First Lieutenant March 8, 1862; Captain July 18, 1862. Re-signed
March 7, 1863, Young's Point, La.
130
COMPANY "D"

Wagner, John. Age 21. Residence Jefferson County, nativity Canada. Enlisted Nov. 12, 1864.
Mustered Nov. 12, 1864. Mustered out July 18, 1865, Louisville, Ky.
Waldron, James C. Age 20. Residence Monticello, nativity Indiana. Enlisted Aug. 16, 1861.
Mustered Sept. 2, 1861. Discharged Jan. 18, 1862, Camp Heron, Mo.
White, Isaac. Age 40. Residence Monticello, nativity Ohio. Enlisted Aug. 16, 1861, as Eighth
Corporal. Mustered Sept. 2, 1861. Discharged July 3, 1862, St. Louis, Mo. Re-entered service
Feb. 29, 1864. Mustered March 17, 1864. Mustered out July 18, 1865, Louisville, Ky. See
company H, Twenty-fifth Infantry.
White, Joseph L. Age 18. Residence Monticello, nativity Ohio. Enlisted Aug. 16, 1861.
Mustered Sept. 2, 1861. Wounded slightly in hand March 7, 1862, Pea Ridge, Ark. Died April
22, 1862, Bowen's Prairie, Iowa.
Winslow, Amos. Age 27. Residence Monticello, nativity New York. Enlisted Aug. 16, 1861.
Mustered Sept. 2, 1861. Died of typhoid fever Oct. 12, 1861, General Hospital, St. Louis, Mo.
Buried in National Cemetery, Jefferson Barracks, Mo. Section 38, grave 227.
Wood, William. Age 35. Residence Monticello, nativity Ireland. Enlisted Feb. 29, 1864.
Mustered March 17, 1864. Mustered out July 18, 1865, Louisville, Ky.
Wright, James C. Age 21. Residence Wyoming, nativity Illinois. Enlisted Aug. 16, 1861.
Mustered Sept. 2, 1861. Wounded slightly in arm March 7, 1862, Pea Ridge, Ark. Discharged
Sept. 24, 1864, East Point, Ga., expiration of term of service.
COMPANY "E"

Walter, John. Age 43. Residence Guttenburg, nativity Germany. Enlisted Sept. 9, 1861.
Mustered Sept. 24, 1861. Wounded May 22, 1863, Vicksburg, Miss. Died of wounds May 24,
1863, Walnut Hills, Miss.
Wasmer, Franz. Age 36. Residence Alamakee County, nativity Switzerland. Enlisted March 7,
1864. Mustered March 19, 1864. Died of fever June 3, 1865, Alexandria, Va. Buried in National
Cemetery, Alexandria, Va. Grave 3196.
Webber, Frank. Age 36. Residence Guttenburg, nativity Germany. Mustered Sept. 24, 1861.
Discharged for disability Jan. 8, 1862, Pacific, Mo.
Weseman, Charles. Age 33. Residence Guttenburg, nativity Germany. Mustered Sept. 24, 1861.
Killed in battle March 7, 1862, Pea Ridge, Ark.
Wilson. James. (Veteran.) Age 21. Residence Farmersburg, nativity New York. Enlisted Sept.
12, 1861, as Fifth Sergeant. Mustered Sept. 24, 1861. Reduced to ranks. Re-enlisted and remustered
Jan. 23, 1864. Promoted Sixth Corporal Jan. 23, 1864; Fifth Corporal May 27, 1864;

Third Corporal Jan. 4, 1865; Fifth Sergeant Jan. 24, 1865. Mustered out July 18, 1865,
Louisville, Ky.
Wragg, Josiah L. Age 23. Residence Farmersburg, nativity Pennsylvania. Enlisted Sept. 13,
1861. Mustered Sept. 24, 1861. Promoted Fifth Corporal March 10, 1862; Third Corporal;
Second Lieutenant April 16, 1863. Wounded in back May 27, 1864, Dallas, Ga. Died of wounds
June 9, 1864, Atlanta, Ga. Buried in National Cemetery, Atlanta, Ga.
Wright, Joseph M. (Veteran.) Age 18. Residence Elkader, nativity New York. Mustered Sept.

24, 1861. Re-enlisted and re-mustered Jan. 23, 1864. Promoted Sixth Corporal Jan. 24, 1865.
Mustered out July 18, 1865, Louisville, Ky.
Company "F"
Walsh, Charles J. Age 21. Residence Decorah, nativity Massachusetts. Enlisted Dec. 14, 1861.
Mustered Jan. 7, 1862. Wounded in leg severely March 7, 1862, Pea Ridge, Ark. Discharged for
wounds June 10, 1863, Chicago, Ill.
Ward, Edward. Age 18. Residence Des Moines, nativity Iowa. Enlisted Feb. 24, 1864.
Mustered Sept. 24, 1864. Mustered out July 18, 1865, Louisville, Ky. See company G, Twentyfifth
Infantry.
Ward, George W. Age 37. Residence Lima, nativity New York. Enlisted Feb. 29, 1864.
Mustered March 18, 1864. Promoted Drummer. Died Aug. 19, 1864, Rome, Ga. Buried in
National Cemetery, Marietta, Ga. Section C, grave 169.
Watrous, Levi. W. Age 36. Residence Albany, nativity Canada. Enlisted Aug. 28, 1861, as
Wagoner. Mustered Sept. 12, 1861. Discharged for disability June 8, 1862, St. Louis, Mo.
Webster, William B. Age 20. Residence West Union, nativity Indiana. Enlisted Sept. 12, 1861.
Mustered Sept. 14, 1861. Mustered out Sept. 24, 1864, East Point, Ga., expiration of term of
service.
White, George W. Age 18. Residence Fayette, nativity Maine. Enlisted Feb. 22, 1864. Mustered
Feb. 22, 1864. Wounded in right forearm severely Sept. 1, 1864, Jonesboro, Ga. Discharged
March 25, 1864, Davenport, Iowa.
Wigorn, John J. (Veteran.) Age 18. Residence Deborah, nativity Norway. Enlisted Nov. 21,
1861. Mustered Jan. 7, 1862. Re-enlisted and re-mustered Jan. 23,

1864. Mustered out July 18,
1865, Louisville, Ky.
Wilcox, Hiram R. Age 22. Residence Jones County, nativity New York. Enlisted Sept. 8, 1861.
Mustered Sept. 14, 1861. Died of fever May 5,1862, Forsyth, Mo.
Wood, Alfred C. Age 28. Residence Mount Pleasant, nativity Indiana. Enlisted Oct. 16, 1862.
Mustered Oct. 16, 1862. Mustered out July 18,1865, Louisville, Ky. See company G, Twentyfifth
Infantry.
132
COMPANY "G"
Walker, Charles. Age 18. Residence Hudson, nativity Massachusetts. Enlisted Sept. 15, 1861.
Mustered Sept. 24, 1861. Killed in battle March 7,1862, Pea Ridge, Ark.
Washburn, Frederick S. Age 38. Residence Waterloo, nativity New Hampshire. Appointed
Captain Sept. 16, 1861. Mustered Sept. 16, 1861. Wounded in face and neck May 22, 1863,
Vicksburg, Miss. Died of wounds June 16,1863, Vicksburg, Miss.
Waters, Asa. Age 23. Residence Delaware County, nativity Illinois. Enlisted July 28,1861.
Mustered Sept. 24,1861. Killed in battle March 7, 1862, Pea Ridge, Ark. Buried in National
Cemetery, Fayetteville, Ark. Section 2, grave 27.
Waters, John H. Age 23. Residence Colony, nativity Illinois. Mustered Sept. 24, 1861.
Mustered out July 18, 1865, Louisville, Ky.
Watson, Andrew. Age 37. Residence Burlington, nativity New York. Enlisted Oct. 5, 1864.
Mustered Oct. 5, 1864. Mustered out July 18, 1865, Louisville, Ky. See company C, Twentyfifth
Infantry.
Wells, Truman T. (Veteran.) Age 22. Residence Colesburg, nativity Ohio. Enlisted Sept. 18,

1861. Mustered Sept. 24 , 1861. Re-enlisted and re-mustered Jan. 23,1864. Promoted Fifth
Sergeant Jan. 5, 1865; Fourth Sergeant May 1, 1865. Mustered out July 18, 1865, Louisville, Ky.
West, Errich. Age 28. Residence Burlington, nativity Sweden. Enlisted Oct. 6, 1864. Mustered
Oct. 8, 1864. Mustered out July 18, 1865, Louisville, Ky. See company G, Twenty-fifth Infantry.
COMPANY H
Waggoner, Frederick. Age 44. Residence Deborah, nativity France. Enlisted Oct. 25, 1861.
Mustered Oct. 25, 1861. Discharged for disability Feb. 27, 1863.
Walters, Joseph B. Age 24. Residence Burr Oak, nativity Pennsylvania. Enlisted Aug. 26, 1861.
Mustered Sept. 24, 1861. Promoted Wagoner. Discharged for disability Aug. 29, 1862, Helena, Ark.
Ward, Charles G. (Veteran.) Age 19. Residence Burr Oak, nativity Canada. Enlisted Aug. 21, 1861, as Second Corporal. Mustered Sept. 24, 1861. Wounded in right arm slightly March 7, 1862, Pea Ridge, Ark. Promoted First Corporal March 14, 1863. Re-enlisted and re-mustered Jan. 23, 1864. Promoted Third Sergeant Jan. 23, 1864. Mustered out July 18, 1865, Louisville, Ky.
Ward, Henry P. Age 20. Residence Burr Oak, nativity Canada. Enlisted Sept. 24, 1861.
Mustered Sept. 24, 1861. Killed in battle March 7, 1862, Pea Ridge, Ark.
133
Warner, George R. Age 18. Residence Decorah, nativity Ohio. Enlisted Aug. 21, 1861.
Mustered Sept. 24, 1861. Discharged for disability July 1, 1865, Louisville, Ky.
Webber, August. Age 33. Residence Decorah, nativity Germany. Enlisted Aug. 21, 1861.
Mustered Sept. 24, 1861. Discharged for disability April 26, 1863, Milliken's Bend, La.

Wellington, Cyrus. Age 20. Residence Decorah, nativity New York. Enlisted Aug. 21, 1861.
Mustered Sept. 24, 1861. Promoted Eighth Corporal July 19, 1862. Wounded Aug. 18, 1864,
Atlanta, Ga. Mustered out Sept. 24, 1864, expiration of term of service.
West, Nelson. (Veteran.) Age 21. Residence Burr Oak, nativity New York. Enlisted Aug. 26,
1861, as Sixth Corporal. Mustered Aug. 26, 1861. Re-enlisted and re-mustered Jan. 23, 1864.
Mustered out July 18, 1865, Louisville, Ky.
Willsie, Henry. Age 20. Residence Burr Oak, nativity Canada Enlisted Sept. 24, 1861. Mustered
Sept. 24, 1861. Promoted Fourth Corporal Oct. 12, 1861. Wounded slightly in right leg March 7,
1862, Pea . Ridge, Ark. Discharged for wounds Oct. 24, 1862, Keokuk, Iowa.
Willsie, Myron. Age 22. Residence Burr Oak, nativity Canada. Enlisted Aug. 26, 1861, as Fifth
Sergeant. Mustered Sept. 24, 1861. Discharged for disability Aug. 19, 1862, Keokuk, Iowa.
COMPANY "I"
Walker, Nathan A. Age 24. Residence Fort Atkinson, nativity Vermont. Enlisted Aug. 12,
1861. Mustered Sept. 18, 1861. Wounded severely in leg March 7, 1862, Pea Ridge, Ark. Died
of wounds April 2, 1862, Cassville, Mo.
Webster, Baker. Age 18. Residence Webster County, nativity New Hampshire. Enlisted Oct. 1,
1864. Mustered Oct. 1, 1864. Mustered out July 18, 1865, Louisville, Ky.
Webster, George W. Age 28. Residence Howard Center, nativity New York. Enlisted Aug. 19,
1861, as Seventh Corporal. Mustered Sept. 18, 1861. Promoted First Sergeant June 13, 1862;
Second Lieutenant Nov. 11, 1862; Captain April 14, 1863.

Resigned Aug. 10, 1863, Black River Bridge, Miss.

Wells, Martin M. Age 30. Residence Lime Springs, nativity New York. Enlisted Dec. 1, 1861. Mustered Dec. 1, 1861. Discharged for disability Oct. 16, 1862, Hospital, St. Louis, Mo.

Wentworth, Lorenzo. Age 23. Residence New Oregon, nativity New York. Enlisted Aug. 17, 1861. Mustered Sept. 18, 1861. Wounded in right hand Jan. 1, 1863, Vicksburg, Miss. Discharged for wounds Feb. 18, 1863, St. Louis, Mo.

White, Elisha C. Age 21. Residence Jacksonville, nativity Pennsylvania. Enlisted Aug. 22, 1861. Mustered Sept. 18, 1861. Transferred to company B, Seventh Infantry. Discharged for disability Aug. 9, 1862, St. Louis, Mo. See company B, Seventh Infantry.

Wilder, Charles L. Age 18. Residence Vernon Springs, nativity Pennsylvania. Enlisted Aug. 17, 1861. Mustered Sept. 18, 1861. Wounded slightly June 28, 1864, Kenesaw Mountain, Ga. Mustered out Sept. 24, 1864, East Point, Ga., expiration of term of service.

Woodworth, Sylvanus. (Veteran.) Age 23. Residence Osage, nativity Ohio. Enlisted Jan. 3, 1863. Mustered Jan. 24, 1863. Re-enlisted and re-mustered Jan. 23, 1864. Wounded in action severely March 21, 1865, Bentonsville, N. C. Mustered out July 18, 1865, Louisville, Ky.

COMPANY "K"

Wait, Willett R. Age 19. Residence Maquoketa, nativity New York. Enlisted Aug. 12, 1861. Mustered Sept. 24, 1861. Transferred to company A. See company A.

Warner, George S. (Veteran.) Age 27. Residence Cedar Rapids, nativity Vermont. Enlisted

Sept. 14, 1861. Mustered Sept. 24, 1861. Promoted Third Corporal Jan. 1, 1865. Mustered out
July 18, 1865, Louisville, Ky.
Warren, Elijah. Age 28. Residence Dubuque, nativity Ohio. Enlisted Aug. 10, 1861. Mustered
Sept. 24, 1861. Discharged for disability July 22, 1862, St. Louis, Mo.
West, Alexander M. (Veteran.) Age 22. Residence Pacific, Mo., nativity Ohio. Mustered Nov.
16, 1861. Re-enlisted and re-mustered Jan. 23, 1864. Mustered out July 18, 1865, Louisville, Ky.
West, James K. (Veteran.) Age 18. Residence Cedar Rapids, nativity Indiana. Enlisted Sept. 14,
1861. Mustered Sept. 24, 1861. Promoted Second Corporal. Wounded slightly in leg March 7,
1862, Pea Ridge, Ark. Re-enlisted and re-mustered Jan. 23, 1864. Wounded slightly in arm Sept.
3, 1864, Jonesboro, Ga. Promoted Fifth Sergeant April 17, 1865. Mustered out July 18, 1865,
Louisville, Ky.
White, Charles C. Age 20. Residence Marion, nativity Ohio. Mustered Sept. 24, 1861. Died of
chronic diarrhea Feb. 2, 1864, Marion, Iowa.
White, Franklin. Age 18. Residence Marion, nativity Pennsylvania. Enlisted Sept. 14, 1861.
Mustered Sept. 24, 1861. Died of typhoid fever Aug. 8, 1863, Black River, Miss.
White, Hezekiah. Age 19. Residence Marion, nativity Pennsylvania. Enlisted Sept. 14, 1861.
Mustered Sept. 24, 1861. Wounded severely in head May 22, 1863, Vicksburg, Miss. Died of
wounds May 27, 1863, Walnut Hills, Vicksburg, Miss.
Whitenack, Andrew R. Age 20. Residence Marion, nativity Indiana. Enlisted Sept. 14, 1861.
Mustered Sept. 24, 1861. Wounded slightly in thigh March 7, 1862, Pea Ridge, Ark. Wounded

severely in breast May 22, 1863, Vicksburg, Miss. Promoted Fourth Corporal July 17, 1863.
Taken prisoner Feb. 13, 1864, Claysville, Ala. Died in prison June 20, 1864, Andersonville, Ga.
Buried in Andersonville National Cemetery, Georgia. Grave 2213.
Whitenack, George W. Age 20. Residence Marion, nativity Ohio. Enlisted Sept. 14, 1861.
Mustered Sept. 24, 1861. Discharged for disability April 12, 1862, Pacific City, Mo.
Williams, John M. Age 36. Residence Marion, nativity Pennsylvania. Enlisted Sept. 14, 1861,
as Second Sergeant. Mustered Sept. 24, 1861. Discharged for disability May 22, 1862, Pacific
City, Mo. See company K, Sixth Cavalry.
Windsor, Charles. (Veteran.) Age 21. Residence Marion, nativity Canada. Mustered Sept. 24,
1861. Reenlisted and re-mustered Jan. 23, 1864. Mustered out July 18, 1865, Louisville, Ky.
Wing, Alvah S. Age 20. Residence Paris, nativity New York. Enlisted Sept. 21, 1861. Mustered
Sept. 24, 1861. Wounded severely in ankle March 7, 1862, Pea Ridge, Ark. Died of wounds Feb.
3, 1863, Hospital Boat.
Wright, Daniel L. (Veteran.) Age 20. Residence Marion, nativity New York. Mustered Sept. 24,
1861. Re-enlisted and re-mustered Jan. 23, 1864. Mustered out July 18, 1865, Louisville, Ky.
COMPANY A
Young, Charles C. Age 21. Residence Maquoketa, nativity New York. Enlisted Sept. 10, 1861.
Mustered Sept. 24, 1861. Wounded severely in leg and thigh March 7, 1862, Pea Ridge, Ark.
Discharged for disability Aug. 18, 1862, St. Louis, Mo.
COMPANY B
Yeager, Harvey B. Age 19. Residence Louisa County, nativity

Ohio. Enlisted Feb. 29, 1864.
Mustered March 3, 1864. Mustered out July 18, 1865, Louisville,
Ky. See company I, Twentyfifth
Infantry.
COMPANY C
Young, John H. (Veteran.) Age 39. Residence Independence,
nativity New York. Enlisted June
25, 1861. Mustered Sept. 24, 1861. Promoted Hospital Steward
April 1, 1862. Returned to
company. Re-enlisted and re-mustered Jan. 23, 1864. Died Oct.
13, 1864, Marietta, Ga.
Young, Warren H. Age 18. Residence Black Hawk County,
nativity New York. Enlisted Feb. 8,
1864. Mustered Feb. 23, 1864. Mustered out July 18, 1865,
Louisville, Ky.

COMPANY G

Young, James T. Age 26. Residence Delaware County, nativity
Indiana. Enlisted July 28, 1861. Mustered Sept. 24, 1861.
Wounded slightly in leg March 7, 1862, Pea Ridge, Ark. Died of
chronic diarrhea Nov. 24, 1863, Memphis, Tenn.

COMPANY I

Yantz, Joseph. Age 21. Residence Castalia, nativity New York.
Enlisted Sept. 11, 186].
Mustered Sept. 18, 1861. Wounded severely in leg March 7, 1862,
Pea Ridge, Ark. Died of
wounds March 12, 1862, Pea Ridge, Ark. Buried in National
Cemetery, Fayetteville, Ark.
Section 2, grave 12.

Yantz, Levi. (Veteran.) Age 18. Residence Castalia, nativity
Wisconsin. Enlisted Sept. 10, 1861. Mustered Sept. 18, 1861.
Wounded slightly in hand March 7, 1863, Pea Ridge, Ark.

Promoted Fifth Corporal Dec. 20, 1862; Fourth Corporal. Wounded slightly in breast May 22, 1863,
Vicksburg, Miss. Promoted Second Corporal July 1, 1863; First Corporal Oct. 6, 1864; Fifth Sergeant Sept. 16, 1864; Fourth Sergeant Jan. l, 1865. Mustered out July 18, 1865, Louisville, Ky.

COMPANY K

Yambert, Moses. Age 22. Residence Marion, nativity Ohio. Enlisted Sept. 14, 1861. Mustered Sept. 24, 1861. Died July 15, 1863, Jackson, Miss.

Young, Amos S. Age 25 Residence Castalia, nativity New York. Enlisted Oct. 1, 1861. Wounded severely in face march 7, 1862, Pea Ridge, Ark. Transferred to Invalid Corps Sept. l, 1863. No further record

Bibliography

IA 9th Infantry Regiment

Annual reunions of the 9th infantry and 3d battery light artillery. *1st (1883). Independence, 1883. 65 p. 8°. (In Contributiontoward a . . . bibliography ... of Iowa . . . Torchpress bookshop. Cedar Rapids, Iowa. Catalogue no. 10, May, 1910.)

Color guard of the 9th Iowa. The "Pea Ridge flag" at Vicksburg. By Otis Crawford. (In National tribune. July 16, 1903.)

Dyer, Frederick H. A Compendium of the War of the Rebellion. Vol. 2. Powder Springs, GA: Eastern Digital Resources, 1998. Ref. See p. 1168 (1 photocopied page) for a concise summary of the regiment's service.

Ingersoll, Lurton D. Iowa and the Rebellion.... Cartersville, GA: Eastern Digital Resources, 2010. E507I47. See pp. 731-36 (4 photocopied pages) for a brief history of the regiment.

Iowa. AGO. Roster and Records of Iowa Soldiers in the War of the Rebellion Together With Historical Sketches of Volunteer Organizations, 1861-1865. Vol. 1. Cartersville, GA: Eastern Digital Resources, 2011.. UA43I82v1.

Serle, C. P. "Personal Reminiscences of Shiloh." In War Sketches and Incidents (MOLLUS, IA, Vol. 1). Des Moines, IA: Kenyon, 1893. pp. 326-39 (7 photocopied pages). E464M5.1991v55.

Stuart, Addison. Iowa Colonels and Regiments.... Cartersville, GA: Eastern Digital Resources, 2012. E507S92. See pp. 179-94 (9 photocopied pages) for biographical sketches of the unit commander(s).

Index

Abbe, Augustus W. ~ Co. K
Abbe, William. ~ Co. K
Abbott, George M. ~ Co. C
Abernethy, Alonzo. ~ Co. F
Able, Joseph. ~ Co. H
Acker, John. (Veteran.) ~ Co. A
Ackerman, John A. ~ Co. H
Adam, George Gordon. ~ Co. H
Adams, Horace N. ~ Co. C
Adams, John. (Veteran.) ~ Co. A
Adams, William. ~ Co. C
Aiken, Eslie. ~ Co. H
Ailer, George F. ~ Co. B
Albright, Benjamin. ~ Co. D
Alexander, Alpheus. ~ Co. A
Alexander, Austin. (Veteran.) ~ Co. A
Alexander, John W. ~ Co. A
Alexander, Martin. ~ Co. G
Alexander, Samuel M. ~ Co. K

Allen, Charles A. ~ Co. E
Allen, Edwin J. ~ Co. C
Allen, Marsena. ~ Co. C
Allen, Nathan B. ~ Co. I
Allison, William. ~ Co. C
Allman, James B. ~ Co. G
Allspraugh, Perry. ~ Co. C
Anderson, James C. ~ Co. K
Andress, William. ~ Co. F
Andrew, Hanson. ~ Co. H
Andrus, Daniel P. ~ Co. F
Andrus, Horace J. (Veteran.) ~ Co. F
Anway, Charles. ~ Co. H
Armstrong, Isaac. ~ Co. C
Arnold, Riley. ~ Co. B
Arwine, Isaac. ~ Co. C
Ashley, Charles B. (Veteran.) ~ Co. I
Atchinson, John. ~ Co. H
Austin, William A. ~ Co. K
Averill, Lariston. ~ Co. I
Avery, John T. (Veteran.) ~ Co. F
Axtel, William C. ~ Co. K
Axtell, Francis M. ~ Co. I
Ayres, Harvey L. ~ Co. I
Bachtell, John A. ~ Co. E

Appendix

Bailey, Simeon. (Veteran.) ~ Co. H
Bain, Robert Y. ~ Co. C
Baker, DeWitt C. ~ Co. E
Baker, John S. ~ Co. K
Bakerman, Lewis. ~ Co. E
Baldwin, George W. ~ Co. E
Baldwin, Marcellus O. ~ Co. B
Balkcom, Dexter E. ~ Co. G
Ballou, Almon C. ~ Co. E
Bancroft, Ormus D. ~ Co. A
Baninger, James M. ~ Co. G
Barber, Alanson. ~ Co. F
Barber, Alfred. ~ Co. H
Barber, Thomas J. ~ Co. C
Barker, Usual. ~ Co. B
Barlow, Charles H. ~ Co. K
Barnes, Hilon M. ~ Co. E
Barnes, Sherman W. ~ Co. I
Barnett, Jesse. ~ Co. C
Barnett or Barrett, Daniel W. ~ Co. H
Barnhouse, Henry Milton. ~ Co. F
Barnhouse, James M. (Veteran.) ~ Co. E
Barnhouse, John M. ~ Co. E
Barnhouse, John. (Veteran.) ~ Co. F
Barns, Addison W. ~ Co. A
Barr, James M. (Veteran.) ~ Co. H
Barr, Samuel. ~ Co. H
Barr, William. ~ Co. F
Barrick, John. ~ Co. G
Bartholomew, Andrew J. (Veteran.) ~ Co. E
Bartholomew, Jacob W. ~ Co. H
Bartholomew, William. ~ Co. E
Bartlett, John W. ~ Co. F
Baskins, Clark J. ~ Co. G
Bates, Charles. ~ Co. B
Beaman, Daniel. ~ Co. B
Bean, Rinaldo P. ~ Co. K
Beatty, Alexander. ~ Co. D
Beckwith, Emanuel. ~ Co. A
Beckwith, Oliver. (Veteran.) ~ Co. A
Beckwith, Samuel. ~ Co. A
Beebe, Hinkly F. ~ Co. G
Beebe, Organ A. ~ Co. G
Bellus, Adelbert C. (Veteran.) ~ Co. C
Benedict, David L. ~ Co. F
Benedict, George M. ~ Co. F

Appendix

Benedict, Myron R. (Veteran.) ~ Co. F
Benham, Richard. ~ Co. K
Bennett, Charles N. (Veteran.) ~ Co. C
Bennett, Lucius. (Veteran) ~ Co. A
Bentley, William A. ~ Co. H
Berg, Peter. ~ Co. K
Beswick, William P. (Veteran.) ~ Co. K
Bevins, Alva. ~ Co. E
Bice, Isaac. ~ Co. K
Bigger, Wm. T. ~ Co. K
Billups, John S. (Veteran.) ~ Co. A
Binehart, David. ~ Co. H
Bird, John. ~ Co. G
Bishop, John R. ~ Co. A
Bishop, Thompson. ~ Co. E
Bishop, William. ~ Co. E
Blackman, Elmer L. ~ Co. H
Blair, James. (Veteran.) ~ Co. H
Blaisdell, Bogardus A. ~ Co. D
Blake, Edward A. (Veteran.) ~ Co. H
Blake, George W. ~ Co. H
Blakely, Nelson D. (Veteran.) ~ Co. B
Blass, Benoni H. ~ Co. H
Bledsoe, William J. ~ Co. D
Bliss, John S. (Veteran.) ~ Co. K
Bliss, Orlando M. ~ Co. H
Blizzard, Thomas W. ~ Co. B
Blodgett, Austin. ~ Co. K
Blondin, Samuel. ~ Co. H
Bloodsworth, John H. ~ Co. G
Blue, Calvin C. (Veteran.) ~ Co. D
Bouck, William. (Veteran.) ~ Co. E
Bower, John H. ~ Co. C
Bowers, George H. ~ Co. B
Bowman, Abraham. ~ Co. K
Bowman, David. (Veteran.) ~ Co. K
Bowman, John P. ~ Co. G
Bowsman, Jacob. (Veteran.) ~ Co. K
Boyd, Alexander. ~ Co. E
Boyer, Isaiah C. ~ Co. D
Boyles, Luther. ~ Co. D
Bradley, John. ~ Co. F
Bradshaw, Joseph. ~ Co. E
Brammer, Jahill. (Veteran.) ~ Co. C
Braninger, Henry L. (Veteran.) ~ Co. G

Appendix

Breen, Michael. (Veteran.) ~ Co. D
Brees, Silas F. (Veteran.) ~ Co. H
Brewer, William W. ~ Co. F
Brewster, James P. (Veteran.) ~ Co. G
Brewster, James T. ~ Co. H
Brickley, James T. ~ Co. B
Bridenthall, Henry N. ~ Co. K
Bridges, Thomas J. ~ Co. I
Briggs, George S. ~ Co. F
Briggs, George S. ~ Co. I
Briggs, Orion. ~ Co. F
Briney, Andrew J. ~ Co. I
Brisco, Hezekiah. ~ Co. H
Broadbent, George M. (Veteran.) ~ Co. F
Broadbent, Robert A. ~ Co. F
Brock, William. ~ Co. A
Bromwell, William H. (Veteran.) ~ Co. K
Brooks, Franklin. ~ Co. E
Brooks, John. (Veteran.) ~ Co. E
Brown, Andrew H. ~ Co. A
Brown, Charles. ~ Co. K
Brown, Henry. ~ Co. A
Brown, James J. ~ Co. B
Brown, James M. ~ Co. B
Brown, James. ~ Co. G
Brown, John A. (Veteran.) ~ Co. F
Brown, John C. ~ Co. C
Brown, Josiah. ~ Co. A
Brown, Milton. ~ Co. D
Brown, Sylvester D. (Veteran.) ~ Co. A
Brown, Thomas W. ~ Co. G
Brown, Volney N. (Veteran.) ~ Co. F
Brown, William L. (Veteran.) ~ Co. K
Bryan, Benjamin. ~ Co. K
Bryan, Isaac. (Veteran.) ~ Co. I
Bryan, William C. (Veteran.) ~ Co. I
Bryan, William J. ~ Co. B
Bucher, Eli. (Veteran.) ~ Co. D
Buchman, Amos. ~ Co. G
Buckingham, Frederick S. ~ Co. C
Buckmaster, James F. ~ Co. G
Bugh, Alexander. (Veteran.) ~ Co. B
Bull, Hiram C. ~ Co. C
Bumgardner, Morgan. ~ Co. B
Bumgardner, Samuel V. ~ Co. K
Bump, George M. (Veteran.) ~ Co. A
Bunce, Frank. ~ Co. I

Appendix

Bunce, Theodore L. ~ Co. B
Bunt, Eli. ~ Co. H
Bunt, James. (Veteran.) ~ Co. H
Burch, Hiram. ~ Co. I
Burdick, Joseph A. ~ Co. D
Burdick, Lavern W. ~ Co. E
Burdine, Thomas B. ~ Co. E
Burk, William. (Veteran.) ~ Co. H
Burke, Daniel B. ~ Co. I
Burkhart, John H. (Veteran.) ~ Co. K
Burnett, John R. ~ Co. K
Burns, John. ~ Co. G
Burtis, James S. ~ Co. K
Bush, Henry. ~ Co. H
Button, William. ~ Co. D
Byres, Jacob L. ~ Co. D
Cady, James D. ~ Co. A
Calaway, Jacob. ~ Co. D
Calhoun, Jasper. ~ Co. G
Calkins, Edward A. ~ Co. H
Capler, Joseph. (Veteran.) ~ Co. I
Carlton, Lorenzo D. ~ Co. B
Carmichael, William H. ~ Co. F
Carnahan, Christopher. ~ Co. K
Carnes, John. ~ Co. C
Carnes, Robert. (Veteran.) ~ Co. H
Carpenter, Don A. ~ Co. B
Carpenter, George. (Veteran.) ~ Co. E
Carskaddon, David. ~ Co. K
Carson, Daniel. ~ Co. C
Carter, Andrew J. ~ Co. D
Cartwright, John. ~ Co. C
Cass, Wallace. ~ Co. H
Cassady, Jackson E. (Veteran.) ~ Co. D
Cassady, James P. ~ Co. D
Cates, Valentine. (Veteran.) ~ Co. C
Cave, Philip. (Veteran.) ~ Co. G
Chaffee, Daniel. ~ Co. C
Chambers, William. ~ Co. G
Channel, Daniel. ~ Co. K
Chapel, Edwin. (Veteran.) ~ Co. I
Chapman, James M. ~ Co. E
Charles, Isaac N. ~ Co. D
Chase, Harvey. ~ Co. C
Chase, Isaac. (Veteran.) ~ Co. C
Chase, William H. ~ Co. E

Appendix

Claflin, Norman W. ~ Co. K
Clark, Albert. ~ Co. D
Clark, Francis J. ~ Co. G
Clark, Hiram. ~ Co. H
Clark, James D. ~ Co. I
Clark, William. ~ Co. D
Clark, William. ~ Co. G
Cleveland, Richard J. ~ Co. B
Cline, William. ~ Co. E
Coe, David V. ~ Co. C
Coenen, Joseph. (Veteran.) ~ Co. K
Coenen, William. (Veteran.) ~ Co. K
Coggswell, Frederick A. (Veteran.) ~ Co. A
Colby, Charles. ~ Co. B
Colby, David. ~ Co. B
Colby, Whitman N. ~ Co. I
Cole, Ezra M. ~ Co. I
Coleman, Hiram. ~ Co. A
Collins, John H. ~ Co. D
Colyer, Charles C. ~ Co. D
Cone, John. (Veteran.) ~ Co. K
Cone, Oliver B. ~ Co. K
Conklin, James W. ~ Co. D
Connable, Edgar W. ~ Co. I
Consadine, Patrick. ~ Co. I
Converse, Stillman A. (Veteran) ~ Co. I
Cook, Arthur J. (Veteran.) ~ Co. H
Cook, David F. ~ Co. D
Cook, Edward C. ~ Co. D
Cook, George G. (Veteran.) ~ Co. F
Cook, Thomas G. ~ Co. K
Cook, Wesley D. ~ Co. H
Coon, Isaac H. (Veteran.) ~ Co. F
Corbet, C. Sylvanus. (Veteran.) ~ Co. C
Corbin, George W. ~ Co. I
Corbin, Levi M. (Veteran.) ~ Co. E
Cornell, Thomas J. ~ Co. A
Cornwell, John or Jacob L. ~ Co. B
Costello, Thomas. (Veteran.) ~ Co. G
Countryman, Jacob. ~ Co. A
Covert, Alonzo W. ~ Co. B
Cowley, Abraham. ~ Co. K
Cox, Albert L. ~ Co. B
Cox, Joshua S. ~ Co. D
Craig, James E. ~ Co. H
Craig, Thomas. ~ Co. B
Crane, Carson. ~ Co. D
Crane, Earl. ~ Co. G

Appendix

Crane, Edgar. ~ Co. E
Crane, George C. ~ Co. B
Crane, John H. ~ Co. A
Crane, Morgan. ~ Co. B
Crane, Webster J. (Veteran.) ~ Co. F
Crane, Winfield S. ~ Co. D
Crary, Elisha A. ~ Co. E
Crawford, Henry D. (Veteran.) ~ Co. H
Crawford, Otis. ~ Co. A
Cress, Thomas. (Veteran.) ~ Co. C
Crook, William C. H. ~ Co. B
Crook, William C. H. ~ Co. K
Crow, Aquilla B. (Veteran.) ~ Co. B
Culver, Elmer R. ~ Co. H
Cuppet, David L. (Veteran.) ~ Co. G
Curtis, Charles G. ~ Co. C
Curtis, Lewis D. ~ Co. C
Curtis, Orin G. ~ Co. C
Curtis, Wesley. ~ Co. C
Curtiss, James R. (Veteran.) ~ Co. F
Cutter, Edwin G. ~ Co. A
Cutts, Levi. ~ Co. G
Dale, James J. ~ Co. D
Daniel, Andrew L. ~ Co. G
Daniels, Francis A. ~ Co. I
Darling, Benjamin F. ~ Co. A
Darling, Edwin. (Veteran.) ~ Co. A
Darling, Edwin. (Veteran.) ~ Co. K
Darrow, Daniel L. ~ Co. K
Dart, Lyman A. ~ Co. C
Davis, Billings. ~ Co. C
Davis, Clark H. ~ Co. H
Davis, Ezra. ~ Co. E
Davis, John S. ~ Co. D
Davis, Joseph A. ~ Co. A
Day, Otis G. ~ Co. G
Dean, John S. ~ Co. B
Dean, William H. ~ Co. D
Debold, Joseph. ~ Co. G
Decker, William. (Veteran.) ~ Co. C
DeGrush, Frederick J. (Veteran.) ~ Co. A
Delano, Smith. (Veteran.) ~ Co. A
DeMott, Isaac. ~ Co. I
Dempsy, Thomas. (Veteran.) ~ Co. H
Denny, Ebenezer. ~ Co. B
Desart, Wesley. ~ Co. E
Devore, William. ~ Co. D
Dickey, Charles H. ~ Co. D
Dickey, Fred N. ~ Co. D

Appendix

Dickinson, Samuel P. ~ Co. A
Diffendorffer, James. ~ Co. D
Dildine, James. ~ Co. F
Dingman, Wilson S. ~ Co. K
Ditmore, Conrad. (Veteran.) ~ Co. H
Dixon, Thomas C. ~ Co. D
Dixon, William H. (Veteran.) ~ Co. D
Dockendorf, Nicholas. ~ Co. E
Dockstadter, Charles R. ~ Co. D
Dorland, Clement. (Veteran.) ~ Co. E
Dorland, George. (Veteran.) ~ Co. E
Dorlond, James. (Veteran.) ~ Co. E
Doty, Thomas. (Veteran.) ~ Co. E
Doty, William. ~ Co. E
Douglass, Robert R. ~ Co. I
Downey, Ira. (Veteran.) ~ Co. A
Downs, David H. ~ Co. F
Drake, Zephaniah, L. ~ Co. H
Dreibelbis, John A. ~ Co. D
Dresser, Ezra. ~ Co. K
Drips, Andrew W. ~ Co. A
Drips, John F. ~ Co. A
Dubois, Everitt. (Veteran.) ~ Co. D
Dunahe, Cyrus. (Veteran.) ~ Co. D
Dunahoo, Andrew J. (Veteran.) ~ Co. G
Dunham, David W. ~ Co. B
Dunham, Hazle. ~ Co. A
Dunton, John. ~ Co. E
Dunton, John. (Veteran.) ~ Co. G
Dupray, William. ~ Co. A
Durham, Levi. ~ Co. H
Eagan, Michael. ~ Co. I
East, Wiley H. ~ Co. D
Eastburn, Charles. ~ Co. B
Easterly, Charles. ~ Co. B
Eaton, Edwin. ~ Co. F
Eaton, John C. ~ Co. F
Eby, James B. (Veteran.) ~ Co. A
Edgington, Thomas J. ~ Co. D
Eggan, Nelson S. ~ Co. F
Eggleston, Orson F. ~ Co. I
Eilorck, Joseph. ~ Co. E
Eldredge, James R. ~ Co. G
Eldredge, James R. ~ Co. H

Appendix

Eller, Daniel. ~ Co. E
Ellingson, Lois A. ~ Co. H
Elliott, Joel B. (Veteran.) ~ Co. I
Ellis, George W. (Veteran.) ~ Co. G
Elson, James M. ~ Co. C
Elson, Jerry E. ~ Co. C
Emmitt, George W. ~ Co. K
England, Titus. (Veteran.) ~ Co. F
Engle, Alonso K. ~ Co. C
Engreman, John. ~ Co. C
Eno, Joseph H. ~ Co. E
Ensign, Devolso. ~ Co. B
Eriksen, Edward. ~ Co. F
Erwin, George W. ~ Co. K
Espy, Robert J. ~ Co. D
Estell, Hiram. ~ Co. G
Evans, Rufus. ~ Co. K
Evans, S. Hamilton. ~ Co. K
Everingham, William. ~ Co. I
Ewing, Joseph. ~ Co. E
Ewing, Milligan. (Veteran.) ~ Co. D
Farley, Owen. ~ Co. B
Farnsworth, James B. ~ Co. F
Farrington, Thomas A. (Veteran.) ~ Co. UNK
Fary, Edwin. ~ Co. C

Fary, Enoch. ~ Co. C
Fellows, Samuel. ~ Co. UNK
Fenton, Joseph H. ~ Co. UNK
Figg, Lewis M. (Veteran.) ~ Co. G
Filley, William. ~ Co. H
Fillson, Robert F. ~ Co. D
Finch, Elkanah D. ~ Co. B
Finch, Irwin. (Veteran.) ~ Co. B
Finch, Laben. ~ Co. F
Finney, William H. ~ Co. F
Fisher, Ira. ~ Co. A
Fisher, Jonathan C. ~ Co. B
Fisher, Thomas. ~ Co. E
Flannagan, James. ~ Co. E
Fletcher, Thomas J. ~ Co. C
Flick, William H. ~ Co. UNK
Fobes, Warren S. ~ Co. E
Fontz, Asbury. ~ Co. UNK
Foos, William. ~ Co. H
Ford, George W. ~ Co. E
Ford, John H. ~ Co. C
Fordney, Francis. ~ Co. G
Foster, Floyd W. ~ Co. A
Foster, Floyd W. ~ Co. G
Fowler, James T. ~ Co. G

Appendix

Fowler, Milton F. (Veteran.) ~ Co. G
Fox, Thomas. ~ Co. A
Francis, Daniel A. ~ Co. UNK
Franey, William. ~ Co. H
Franklin, James L. ~ Co. F
Fraser, Francis P. (Veteran.) ~ Co. D
Freeburn, John P. ~ Co. UNK
Freeman, Reuben E. ~ Co. C
Freeman, Robert E. ~ Co. E
Freyberthauser, George. ~ Co. C
Fry, Enoch. (Veteran.) ~ Co. B
Fuller, Charles. ~ Co. D
Fuller, David C. ~ Co. E
Fuller, Eleazer. (Veteran.) ~ Co. E
Fuller, Oliver N. ~ Co. B
Fuller, William. ~ Co. D
Fulton, Joseph. ~ Co. A
Fultz, Thomas E. ~ Co. UNK
Furcht, Julius. ~ Co. C
Gager, Edward L. ~ Co. E
Gale, Luther H. ~ Co. F
Gale, William L. ~ Co. D
Gannon, Thomas. (Veteran.) ~ Co. E
Gard, Isaac. ~ Co. C

Gardner, Andrew J. ~ Co. F
Gardner, Edwin. ~ Co. K
Gardner, Joseph J. (Veteran.) ~ Co. F
Gardner, Ralph B. (Veteran.) ~ Co. E
Gardner, William G. ~ Co. F
Garretson, John H. (Veteran.) ~ Co. E
Garretson, Joseph. (Veteran.) ~ Co. E
Garver, David. (Veteran.) ~ Co. I
Gates, Ambrose H. (Veteran.) ~ Co. H
Gates, Martin. ~ Co. I
Gault, Moses. ~ Co. UNK
Gay, Kingsbury. ~ Co. H
Gee, George W. (Veteran.) ~ Co. F
Gemmill, John. ~ Co. I
German, David. ~ Co. F
Gibbs, Cyrus C. ~ Co. H
Gibson, Hiram H. ~ Co. D
Gibson, James M. ~ Co. G
Gibson, Victor. ~ Co. K
Gieger, Arthur O. ~ Co. G
Gieger, Lewis P. ~ Co. K
Gilbert, Amos D. ~ Co. D
Gilbert, Fred D. ~ Co. D
Gilham, Jordan. (Veteran.) ~ Co. G

Appendix

Gilham, William. ~ Co. G
Gillan, Zachariah. ~ Co. H
Gillaspie, Henry. ~ Co. D
Gillum, William C. ~ Co. C
Gilmore, Charles. ~ Co. UNK
Gipe, James H. ~ Co. G
Gipert, Jacob. ~ Co. UNK
Glass, Ole. ~ Co. F
Glenn, William C. M. ~ Co. D
Godfrey, Door E. ~ Co. C
Goesen, Lars. ~ Co. F
Goodenough, John. ~ Co. I
Gorsuch, Andrew F. ~ Co. UNK
Gragg, Thomas J. (Veteran.) ~ Co. E
Graham, Henry R. ~ Co. H
Graham, William J. (Veteran.) ~ Co. UNK
Granger, Albert E. ~ Co. K
Granger, George. ~ Co. K
Gray, Henry H. (Veteran.) ~ Co. K
Gray, John W. ~ Co. K
Gray, Thomas. ~ Co. UNK
Greek, David. ~ Co. C
Greeley, Albert. ~ Co. E
Green, Abijah B. (Veteran.) ~ Co. G
Green, Albert. ~ Co. UNK
Green, Benton. ~ Co. UNK
Green, George. ~ Co. E
Green, Jasper. ~ Co. UNK
Green, John H. ~ Co. UNK
Green, Joseph E. ~ Co. D
Green, Levi A. (Veteran.) ~ Co. H
Green, Nimrod A. (Veteran.) ~ Co. C
Greenly, George. ~ Co. K
Greenly, William. ~ Co. K
Gregory, Nathan. ~ Co. H
Gridley, Charles. (Veteran.) ~ Co. D
Griffin, Daniel P. ~ Co. I
Grindrod, Joshua. (Veteran.) ~ Co. UNK
Groat, Thomas P. (Veteran.) ~ Co. UNK
Gross, Henry. ~ Co. D
Grote, Henry A. ~ Co. UNK
Groves, James. ~ Co. D
Grundy, Henry. ~ Co. H
Grupe, Durbin. ~ Co. E
Guenther, Jacob H. ~ Co. UNK
Guin, James W. (Veteran.) ~ Co. F

Appendix

Guist, William H. H. (Veteran.) ~ Co. UNK
Gulford, Richard. ~ Co. E
Gunn, John A. (Veteran.) ~ Co. K
Gunsaulus, Alfred C. (Veteran.) ~ Co. F
Hagaman, William E. ~ Co. K
Hageman, Isaac A. ~ Co. E
Hager, Horace. ~ Co. B
Hall, Andrew H. (Veteran.) ~ Co. B
Hall, Eugene G. ~ Co. F
Hall, Garret N. ~ Co. D
Hall, George W. (Veteran.) ~ Co. K
Hall, Henry E. ~ Co. H
Hall, Ralph R. ~ Co. H
Hallsted, James. ~ Co. K
Hamilton, Andrew. ~ Co. H
Hamilton, James S. ~ Co. A
Hammond, George. ~ Co. B
Handy, Edward H. ~ Co. B
Hansen, Hans. ~ Co. D
Hanstet or Hemstead, Herman. ~ Co. E
Harkness, David. ~ Co. G
Harper, David. ~ Co. D
Harper, George W. (Veteran.) ~ Co. F
Harper, James L. ~ Co. F
Harris, George H. ~ Co. I
Harris, William R. (Veteran.) ~ Co. K
Harrison, Albertus U. (Veteran.) ~ Co. B
Harrison, Benjamin F. ~ Co. B
Hart, James T. ~ Co. B
Harter, Matthias. (Veteran.) ~ Co. C
Hartwell, Franklin G. ~ Co. F
Harvey, James T. ~ Co. A
Harwood, Nathan S. ~ Co. G
Haskett, Eli. ~ Co. G
Hathaway, Lewis Henry. ~ Co. E
Haven, George R. ~ Co. G
Haven, James H. (Veteran.) ~ Co. G
Havens, Romanzo. ~ Co. D
Hawthorn, John. ~ Co. F
Haylan, Isaiah. ~ Co. K
Hays, John. ~ Co. D
Healis, William. ~ Co. G
Heath, Franklin H. ~ Co. G
Hendricks, Levi. ~ Co. E
Herrick, Emerson E. ~ Co. E
Herriman, Cal C. (Veteran.) ~ Co. F

Appendix

Herriman, Charles. (Veteran.) ~ Co. E
Herriman, Samuel K. ~ Co. E
Herrington, George. ~ Co. C
Hidinger, William A. ~ Co. D
Hightman, Charles H. ~ Co. C
Hill, Darwin. ~ Co. E
Hill, George. (Veteran.) ~ Co. F
Hill, James G. ~ Co. G
Hill, William O. ~ Co. C
Himebaugh, George. ~ Co. D
Hines, Alfred C. ~ Co. D
Hinkley, Albert. (Veteran.) ~ Co. H
Hobert, Charles A. (Veteran.) ~ Co. C
Hobson, Nicholas J. ~ Co. F
Hodge, Jonathan D. ~ Co. A
Hofer, Andrew F. ~ Co. E
Hogan, Thomas J. ~ Co. H
Hogeboom, William. (Veteran.) ~ Co. D
Holes, George. ~ Co. F
Holland, Eli. (Veteran.) ~ Co. C
Hollman, Benjamin. ~ Co. H
Holloway, Daniel. ~ Co. A
Hollridge, Hira. ~ Co. C
Holman, Isaac N. ~ Co. C
Holman, Stephen. ~ Co. C
Holman, Sylvester F. ~ Co. D
Holman, Vinson. ~ Co. C
Holsted, Amos S. ~ Co. I
Holton, Miles. (Veteran.) ~ Co. F
Hooker, Adam. ~ Co. K
Hoousky, Albert. (Veteran.) ~ Co. E
Hopkins, William H. ~ Co. A
Hord, Jared M. ~ Co. C
Horn, Daniel. ~ Co. K
Horning, David C. (Veteran.) ~ Co. I
Hornsby, Marion. ~ Co. B
Hough, Edgar G. (Veteran.) ~ Co. F
House, Marshall. (Veteran.) ~ Co. F
Hovey, Nelson. (Veteran.) ~ Co. C
Howard, George. ~ Co. D
Howard, John L. (Veteran.) ~ Co. E
Howe, Warrington P. ~ Co. C
Huff, Abel M. ~ Co. H
Huff, Abram C. ~ Co. H
Huff, George W. ~ Co. F

Appendix

Huffnie, John. ~ Co. E
Hughes, Aaron. ~ Co. K
Hughes, Francis M. ~ Co. E
Hughes, Hezekiah R. ~ Co. E
Hughes, Simon. ~ Co. I
Hull, Benjamin E. ~ Co. B
Hull, Perry. ~ Co. E
Humphrey, John. ~ Co. I
Humphrey, Oscar L. ~ Co. H
Hunter, William H. (Veteran.) ~ Co. D
Huntsinger, Joseph B. ~ Co. F
Hurd, William H. (Veteran.) ~ Co. E
Hurlbut, Samuel B. (Veteran.) ~ Co. G
Hurley, Lewellin. ~ Co. I
Hurley, Robert. ~ Co. I
Hutton, Philander. ~ Co. D
Hyde, Theodore W. ~ Co. C
Ingels, William B. ~ Co. D
Inglebritson, Hartvig. ~ Co. G
Inglebritson, Inglebright. ~ Co. F
Inman, Chester W. ~ Co. I
Inman, Daniel W. ~ Co. I
Inman, Franklin E. ~ Co. I

Inman, Joseph G. ~ Co. I
Irwin, Hugh. ~ Co. H
Irwin, Isaac. ~ Co. B
Irwin, James A. ~ Co. C
Irwin, John C. ~ Co. D
Irwin, Thomas. ~ Co. D
Isabel, Jones. ~ Co. B
Jacobs, Henry. ~ Co. K
Jacoby, Elias. ~ Co. H
Jacoby, James. ~ Co. H
Jacoby, John S. ~ Co. I
James, Walter. (Veteran.) ~ Co. B
Jenkins, John. ~ Co. B
Jennings, William L. ~ Co. B
Jenson, Loren P. ~ Co. D
Johnson, Abram C. (Veteran.) ~ Co. I
Johnson, Calvin. ~ Co. D
Johnson, Clark. ~ Co. I
Johnson, James M. (Veteran.) ~ Co. I
Johnson, Joseph. ~ Co. G
Johnson, Samuel. ~ Co. E
Johnson, Thomas. ~ Co. I
Johnston, Noah R. ~ Co. I
Jolly, Beaden B. ~ Co. K
Jones, Aaron B. ~ Co. E
Jones, Edward P. ~ Co. I
Jones, Henry. ~ Co. C
Jones, Jacob. ~ Co. B
Jones, John. ~ Co. D
Jones, Jonathan, Jr. ~ Co. B

Appendix

Jones, Martin B. (Veteran.) ~ Co. I
Jones, Thomas J. ~ Co. D
Jones, William A. ~ Co. C
Jones, William H. ~ Co. H
Jordon, Michael L. (Veteran.) ~ Co. G
Justin, Charles F. ~ Co. K
Justin, Marion. ~ Co. K
Kahoe, Edward. (Veteran.) ~ Co. D
Kaiser, Christian. ~ Co. E
Karker, John. ~ Co. G
Karst, George. ~ Co. D
Kearney, Isaac. (Veteran.) ~ Co. F
Keasey, William B. ~ Co. F
Keller, David. ~ Co. E
Kelley, James H. (Veteran.) ~ Co. A
Kelley, Samuel P. ~ Co. A
Kelly, William. ~ Co. H
Kelsey, Florilla M. ~ Co. A
Kemery, Charles. ~ Co. I
Kernes, Daniel. ~ Co. K
Kerr, Samuel P. (Veteran.) ~ Co. B
Ketsinger, Michael. ~ Co. E
Keys, Samuel R. ~ Co. D
Kidder, Ezra. ~ Co. K
Kilbourn, Hiram. ~ Co. G
Kile, Martin. (Veteran.) ~ Co. I
King, John M. (Veteran.) ~ Co. C
King, John S. ~ Co. D
King, Silas E. ~ Co. C
King, Wildu B. (Veteran.) ~ Co. E
Kinney, John. ~ Co. A
Kinsey, David. ~ Co. F
Kinsey, Isaac M. ~ Co. G
Kirchner, Henry. ~ Co. E
Kirk, William H. ~ Co. G
Kirkwood, James C. (Veteran.) ~ Co. D
Klinger, Henry L. (Veteran.) ~ Co. A
Klock, George. (Veteran.) ~ Co. G
Klopp, Benjamin. (Veteran.) ~ Co. C
Knapp, Edward A. ~ Co. E
Knight, Benjamin F. ~ Co. I
Knight, John F. ~ Co. I
Knight, John S. ~ Co. F
Knowlton, Alfred. (Veteran.) ~ Co. H
Knudsen, Trow. ~ Co. B
Kraft, Oscar. ~ Co. A
Kriger, August. ~ Co. K
Lackey, Augustus. ~ Co. F
LaMont, Joseph. ~ Co. H
Lampert, Joseph. ~ Co. E
Lamson, James H. ~ Co. G

Appendix

Landers, Jonas W. ~ Co. H
Lane, Clement H. ~ Co. B
Lane, William. ~ Co. I
Langstaff, Enoch. ~ Co. D
Larabee, Franklin L. ~ Co. F
Larimore, John. ~ Co. D
Larson, Hans. (Veteran.) ~ Co. F
Larue, Francis. ~ Co. G
Laumsden, John A. (Veteran.) ~ Co. F
Lawrence, John. (Veteran.) ~ Co. I
Lawson, Frank. (Veteran.) ~ Co. C
Leatherman, James or John. ~ Co. C
Lee, Albert. ~ Co. F
Lee, Israel. ~ Co. D
Lee, Jasper. ~ Co. F
Lee, Martin. ~ Co. F
Leggett, Herman C. ~ Co. I
Lenhart, John. ~ Co. E
Lest, Daniel. ~ Co. A
Leverich, Asbury. ~ Co. G
Leverich, Willard. ~ Co. G
Levy, Frederick. ~ Co. I
Lichtenheim, Lavine A. (Veteran.) ~ Co. D
Lightly, David. ~ Co. G
Lines, Nelson. ~ Co. C
Linsey, James S. ~ Co. G
Littell, George W. ~ Co. A
Littell, Hiram B. ~ Co. A
Little, Edmund C. ~ Co. C
Little, John. ~ Co. H
Little, Sardis. ~ Co. G
Livingston, William H. (Veteran.) ~ Co. A
Lockard, Robert W. ~ Co. E
Lockerly, Nelson. ~ Co. G
Lockwood, Charles U. ~ Co. I
Logan, Lyman B. ~ Co. E
Logue, John. (Veteran.) ~ Co. I
Long, Daniel R. (Veteran.) ~ Co. B
Long, George W. ~ Co. B
Long, James P. ~ Co. H
Long, Joel. ~ Co. B
Long, John. ~ Co. I
Long, William. (Veteran.) ~ Co. E
Longneckhard, Henry. ~ Co. E
Losey, Alpheus. (Veteran.) ~ Co. C
Lott, Thomas B. ~ Co. E
Lough, John B. ~ Co. H
Love, Daniel. ~ Co. E
Lovesee, Isaac A. ~ Co. E
Lowbower, John C. ~ Co. D

Appendix

Lowe, Christian. ~ Co. D
Lucas, Alexander J. ~ Co. G
Lucky, Orlando F. (Veteran.) ~ Co. C
Lukscart, James. ~ Co. B
Lutes, Osborn. (Veteran.) ~ Co. I
Luther, Jonathan. ~ Co. B
Lutz, Joseph W. ~ Co. K
Lyle, Josiah A. ~ Co. A
Lyman, Charles H. (Veteran.) ~ Co. A
Lyon, Alfred P. ~ Co. F
Mabin, Harrison. ~ Co. D
Machett, Joseph R. ~ Co. H
Mackenzie, Charles. ~ Co. H
Magee, David F. ~ Co. D
Magee, Francis A. ~ Co. D
Magee, John C. ~ Co. D
Mahony, Michael. ~ Co. D
Malony, William H. ~ Co. A
Malory, Charles W. (Veteran.) ~ Co. G
Manka, Gottleib. ~ Co. E
Mann, Garrison C. ~ Co. H
Manwarin, Emery. ~ Co. D
Marcelles, Charles. ~ Co. D
Marcelles, John. (Veteran.) ~ Co. D
Maricle, Joel G. ~ Co. H
Maricle, Justus. (Veteran.) ~ Co. H
Markle, John R. ~ Co. A
Markle, Joseph. ~ Co. A
Marsh, William A. ~ Co. D
Martin, David I. ~ Co. G
Martin, Leonard L. ~ Co. A
Martin, Stephen R. ~ Co. A
Martinson, Christian. ~ Co. H
Masley, Charles. ~ Co. E
Mason, John M. ~ Co. B
Mather, Esquire. ~ Co. I
Mather, John S. (Veteran.) ~ Co. I
Matteson, Abel. ~ Co. H
Matteson, Daniel M. (Veteran.) ~ Co. B
Matteson, Elisha C. ~ Co. B
Matthew, Lewis. (Veteran.) ~ Co. D
McAlavay, Charles. ~ Co. F
McAlpin, Benjamin F. ~ Co. G
McCabe, William. (Veteran.) ~ Co. E
McCaffery, John. ~ Co. E
McCalla, George. ~ Co. C

Appendix

McCardoe, James. ~ Co. B
McCarty, Charles. ~ Co. B
McComb, Samuel. ~ Co. A
McCoy, James K. ~ Co. K
McCrea, Charles. ~ Co. A
McCrea, William. ~ Co. I
McCuin, James B. ~ Co. H
McCullough, William. ~ Co. D
McCurniff, Thomas. ~ Co. C
McDaniel, Orlando. ~ Co. D
McDavitt, Martin S. ~ Co. D
McFerren, Jacob. (Veteran.) ~ Co. K
McGaffee, John S. ~ Co. A
McGowan, Calvin. ~ Co. B
McGuigan, Thomas. ~ Co. B
McGuigan, William H. ~ Co. G
McGuire, Henry O. ~ Co. C
McIntosh, Andrew. (Veteran.) ~ Co. I
McIntosh, James F. ~ Co. D
McKean, Francis C. ~ Co. D
McKee, John S. ~ Co. K
McKinney, James R. ~ Co. B
McKinnis, Robert. ~ Co. G
McKisson, Martin V. B. ~ Co. C
McLavy, Allen. ~ Co. E
McLavy, William E. ~ Co. E
McManus, John. ~ Co. A
McMartin, Daniel A. ~ Co. I
McMeans, Andrew. ~ Co. A
McMeans, John W. ~ Co. A
McMellen, James. ~ Co. B
McNally, James. ~ Co. A
McQuay, Thomas. ~ Co. H
McQuillan, William H. ~ Co. F
McRoberts, Alonzo. ~ Co. G
McSweeney, Paul. ~ Co. B
McVerts, Lewis C. ~ Co. E
McVey, James D. ~ Co. I
McVey, William H. ~ Co. D
Mead, Charles W. ~ Co. F

Appendix

Mead, Harrison H. ~ Co. I
Meader, Charles E. ~ Co. H
Means, Jasper. ~ Co. G
Meisner, Fred. (Veteran.) ~ Co. E
Meligan, Alfred. ~ Co. G
Melot, Benjamin. ~ Co. H
Merrett, Horatio M. ~ Co. B
Merrill, James H. ~ Co. C
Merry, Ezra H. ~ Co. F
Merry, Jeremiah. (Veteran.) ~ Co. F
Merwin, Byron W. ~ Co. D
Metcalf, Arthur. (Veteran.) ~ Co. B
Metcalf, Michael. ~ Co. E
Metz, Silas. ~ Co. G
Michaels, Aaron. ~ Co. G
Milhausen, Henry H. P. (Veteran.) ~ Co. A
Millar, Charles H. ~ Co. F
Miller, Andrew. ~ Co. I
Miller, David E. ~ Co. B
Miller, Edwin A. ~ Co. I
Miller, Isaac A. ~ Co. D
Miller, James J. (Veteran.) ~ Co. D
Miller, James. ~ Co. D
Miller, John B. ~ Co. D
Miller, John. ~ Co. D
Miller, Peter J. (Veteran.) ~ Co. A

Miller, Philip A. (Veteran.) ~ Co. A
Miller, Robert H. ~ Co. B
Miller, Samuel. ~ Co. A
Milliken, Henry. ~ Co. H
Milliken, John. ~ Co. C
Mills, Marvin. ~ Co. K
Minnard, James. ~ Co. I
Mintey, Walter. ~ Co. I
Mitchell, Charles A. ~ Co. G
Mitchell, John G. ~ Co. I
Mitts, Jesse B. ~ Co. D
Moats, John S. ~ Co. E
Monroe, Eugene B. ~ Co. H
Monroe, Jonathan W. (Veteran.) ~ Co. K
Monroe, Samuel. ~ Co. C
Montgomery, Hugh H. ~ Co. K
Montgomery, Joseph. ~ Co. K
Moore, James. ~ Co. B
Moore, John D. ~ Co. B
Moore, Martin A. ~ Co. H
Moore, William H. ~ Co. H
Moore, William. ~ Co. A
Moore, Zadoc. (Veteran.) ~ Co. D
Moran, John. ~ Co. E
More, Robert. ~ Co. G
Morehead, James C. ~ Co. K

Appendix

Morgan, Edwin. (Veteran.) ~ Co. I
Morgan, Franklin. ~ Co. D
Moriarty, Miletus E. ~ Co. K
Morley, William R. ~ Co. F
Morrison, John. ~ Co. E
Morton, Franklin A. ~ Co. G
Morton, Thomas J. ~ Co. K
Moulton, Jasper N. (Veteran.) ~ Co. H
Mower, James E. ~ Co. I
Mower, Nathan A. ~ Co. D
Moyer, Emanuel. ~ Co. K
Muline, Elmer. ~ Co. E
Munger, Charles E. ~ Co. F
Munger, William H. ~ Co. F
Murphy, Albert. ~ Co. H
Murphy, Michael. ~ Co. F
Murphy, William L. ~ Co. D
Murray, William. ~ Co. I
Musser, James P. (Veteran.) ~ Co. G
Myers, Cyrus. ~ Co. D
Myers, George W. ~ Co. F
Myers, George. ~ Co. E
Myers, John C. ~ Co. F
Myers, John M. ~ Co. G

Myers, Philip B. (Veteran.) ~ Co. G
Nackey, Frederick. ~ Co. G
Neff, Abner G. M. ~ Co. F
Neff, Cyrenus D. (Veteran.) ~ Co. G
Nelson, John G. ~ Co. H
Newman, James H. ~ Co. G
Newton, James. ~ Co. H
Nichols, George. ~ Co. F
Nichols, John C. (Veteran.) ~ Co. D
Nichols, Otho D. ~ Co. D
Nicholson, Thomas P. ~ Co. K
Niles, John W. ~ Co. B
Niles, Sylvester J. ~ Co. I
Nixon, Herbert E. ~ Co. A
Norton, Alfred M. ~ Co. A
Norton, John W. ~ Co. K
Nuckolls, Ezra. ~ Co. D
Nutt, Cyrus E. ~ Co. K
Nutting, Lucien H. C. ~ Co. K
Oakly, Peter W. ~ Co. F
Oats, James A. ~ Co. D
Oberholzer, John. ~ Co. E
Obert, Lewis. (Veteran.) ~ Co. H
O'Brien, Michael. ~ Co. F
Obrihan, Edwin C. (Veteran.) ~ Co. H

Appendix

Odell, Hiram A. ~ Co. H
O'Donnell, Joseph D. ~ Co. I
Ogden, Henry T. ~ Co. A
Oliver, John H. ~ Co. K
Older, Augustus H. ~ Co. H
Oleson, Jacob. ~ Co. H
O'Morrow, William. (Veteran.) ~ Co. A
Oren, John. (Veteran.) ~ Co. I
Ort, John. (Veteran.) ~ Co. F
Osborne, John V. ~ Co. B
Osgood, Levi A. (Veteran.) ~ Co. F
Overacker, Horace T. ~ Co. B
Overly, Henry. ~ Co. D
Overly, James F. ~ Co. D
Owen, George A. ~ Co. I
Owens, James, Jr. ~ Co. D
Padden, Loron. ~ Co. F
Painter, Robert M. ~ Co. K
Palmer, Henry C. ~ Co. B
Palmer, Leroy. ~ Co. D
Pangburn, Daniel D. (Veteran.) ~ Co. C
Parker, Joseph. ~ Co. G
Parker, William B. ~ Co. F
Parker, William H. ~ Co. G
Parr, Philemon. ~ Co. H

Partch, Wilbur V. ~ Co. E
Patchen, Eugene U. ~ Co. C
Patter, Alphonso. ~ Co. A
Patterson, David B. ~ Co. A
Peacock, Henry L. ~ Co. G
Pearce, George C. ~ Co. A
Peddler, Philip. ~ Co. H
Peet, William T. ~ Co. B
Pelton, William A. (Veteran.) ~ Co. G
Penrod, Franklin. ~ Co. F
Pepin, Francis J. ~ Co. I
Perdue, Isaiah. ~ Co. C
Perkins, George. ~ Co. H
Perry, Alvin M. ~ Co. H
Perry, John. ~ Co. E
Perry, Wesley D. ~ Co. H
Persall, Lewis A. ~ Co. C
Peters, John F. ~ Co. F
Peters, Silas G. W. (Veteran.) ~ Co. I
Peters, William R. ~ Co. F
Peterson, Thomas. ~ Co. F
Phelps, John. ~ Co. D
Phillips, Alexander. ~ Co. D
Phillips, Hugh K. ~ Co. H
Phillips, John W. ~ Co. H
Phipp, James T. ~ Co. B
Pieper, Joseph. ~ Co. E

Appendix

Pierce, Finley D. (Veteran.) ~ Co. I
Pierce, George W. ~ Co. D
Pierce, Levi L. ~ Co. A
Piggott, John W. ~ Co. G
Platt, Enoch. ~ Co. C
Platt, Jacob. (Veteran.) ~ Co. G
Plein, Alexander. ~ Co. E
Polley, Charles W. (Veteran.) ~ Co. I
Polley, David C. ~ Co. I
Pope, William. ~ Co. C
Porcupile, James H. ~ Co. I
Porter, George. ~ Co. B
Potter, Benjamin B. ~ Co. F
Potts, Samuel K. ~ Co. E
Powell, Jeremiah F. (Veteran.) ~ Co. I
Powell, Joseph. ~ Co. D
Powell, Thomas J. ~ Co. I
Powers, Benjamin W. ~ Co. C
Powers, John M. ~ Co. H
Powers, Wilbur F. ~ Co. H
Pratt, Elvin L. ~ Co. F
Pratt, Sterns D. ~ Co. K
Pregler, George. (Veteran.) ~ Co. G
Price, Anthony. ~ Co. G
Price, John N. ~ Co. B
Price, Samuel. ~ Co. D

Proctor, Samuel O. ~ Co. E
Proctor, Uriah A. ~ Co. I
Purcell, Garrett. ~ Co. H
Putnam, Henry. ~ Co. E
Quick, Jacob. ~ Co. K
Radden, Thomas. ~ Co. D
Rament, Albert. ~ Co. G
Ramsay, Thomas. ~ Co. K
Ramsey, Morris A. (Veteran.) ~ Co. A
Randall, Elias. ~ Co. H
Ransom, William L. (Veteran.) ~ Co. I
Redfield, Wallace. ~ Co. C
Reeve, Fernando T. ~ Co. I
Reeve, Theodore H. (Veteran.) ~ Co. I
Reichart, John. ~ Co. E
Remington, Ewing. ~ Co. D
Remington, Newman. (Veteran.) ~ Co. D
Renn, Benjamin F. ~ Co. G
Ress, Franklin. (Veteran.) ~ Co. D
Retter, Francis. ~ Co. K
Rexford, Dewitt C. ~ Co. I
Reyner, Franklin. ~ Co. A
Reyner, Henry C. ~ Co. A
Reyner, Marcus D. (Veteran.) ~ Co. A

Appendix

Reynolds, Henry. ~ Co. C
Reynolds, Jonathan T. ~ Co. H
Rhodes, Abraham. ~ Co. K
Rice, Alexander. ~ Co. E
Rice, George S. ~ Co. I
Rice, Nathan. ~ Co. C
Rich, Darwin. (Veteran.) ~ Co. C
Rich, Nelson. ~ Co. B
Richardson, Sargent H. ~ Co. F
Richmond, Miles W. ~ Co. K
Richmond, Robert. ~ Co. H
Richmond, Royal H. ~ Co. K
Riddle, James H. ~ Co. I
Ridings, James. ~ Co. D
Riley, Asher. ~ Co. A
Riley, James A. ~ Co. K
Riley, Miles. (Veteran.) ~ Co. F
Rippey, George. ~ Co. D
Risdon, Daniel. ~ Co. G
Ritterman, Philip. (Veteran.) ~ Co. C
Robbins, Aham K. ~ Co. C
Robbins, Joseph. ~ Co. K
Robbins, Samuel. (Veteran.) ~ Co. C
Roberts, Lyman A. (Veteran.) ~ Co. B
Robertson, Robert A. ~ Co. K
Robinson, Henry. (Veteran.) ~ Co. B
Robinson, Isaac B. (Veteran.) ~ Co. B
Robinson, J. ~ Co. B
Robinson, Samuel O. ~ Co. B
Robinson, Samuel. (Veteran.) ~ Co. B
Robinson, Whitman D. ~ Co. A
Robinson, William. ~ Co. G
Rodgers, John. ~ Co. C
Roe, Barney. (Veteran.) ~ Co. H
Rome, Horace B. ~ Co. I
Rose, Joseph. ~ Co. K
Ross, Henry A. ~ Co. K
Rossman, Noyes. ~ Co. E
Roth, Henry Joseph. ~ Co. E
Rotner, Martin V. (Veteran.) ~ Co. H
Rouse, Reuben. (Veteran.) ~ Co. C
Rouse, Russell. (Veteran.) ~ Co. C
Rowland, William G. ~ Co. A
Rowley, John C. ~ Co. E
Rudd, Harvey. ~ Co. B
Rummel, David E. ~ Co. B

Appendix

Rupert, Jeremiah D. ~ Co. I
Russell, James A. ~ Co. E
Rust, Ezra T. ~ Co. C
Rust, George Q. ~ Co. C
Rutherford, Edgar D. ~ Co. K
Ryan, Edward. ~ Co. H
Sallee, William G. (Veteran.) ~ Co. H
Sampson, Jacob P. ~ Co. C
Sanborn, John M. ~ Co. H
Sanburn, Henry C. (Veteran.) ~ Co. A
Sanders, Jacob D. ~ Co. C
Sanders, Michaels. ~ Co. D
Sarchett, Charles W. (Veteran.) ~ Co. C
Sarggent, Lyman. ~ Co. E
Sawyer, Charles N. (Veteran.) ~ Co. F
Sayre, George W. (Veteran.) ~ Co. C
Schell, Charles F. W. ~ Co. E
Schlagal, Michael. ~ Co. E
Schmidt, William. ~ Co. E
Schull, James B. ~ Co. D
Schuster, Alfred E. ~ Co. D
Scofield, Walter. ~ Co. I
Scott, George W. ~ Co. D
Scott, John. ~ Co. H
Scott, Marquis M. ~ Co. K
Scott, Samuel S. (Veteran.) ~ Co. A
Scott, Thomas. ~ Co. D
Scott, William. ~ Co. C
Searle, George C. ~ Co. A
Searles, Orlando. (Veteran.) ~ Co. F
Seaton, Asa M. ~ Co. F
Seaward, William T. (Veteran.) ~ Co. A
Seeber, Timothy. ~ Co. E
Seeley, Norman. ~ Co. B
Seels, Amos. (Veteran.) ~ Co. B
Sessions, Jerome H. ~ Co. K
Sewell, Sylvester. (Veteran.) ~ Co. G
Shafer, Henry L. (Veteran.) ~ Co. C
Shaffer, Timothy. ~ Co. E
Sharp, George B. (Veteran.) ~ Co. G
Sharp, Samuel. (Veteran.) ~ Co. G
Shaw, William W. ~ Co. G
Sheldon, George. ~ Co. D
Shepheard, Abram P. ~ Co. F
Shepherd, Henry H. ~ Co. A
Shepherd, James A. ~ Co. A
Sherman, Benedict. ~ Co. B

Appendix

Sherman, Salisbury. ~ Co. I
Sherman, William R. ~ Co. F
Shrunk, Joseph. ~ Co. G
Simenson, Hans. (Veteran.) ~ Co. H
Slaughter, George T. ~ Co. D
Slife, David M. ~ Co. K
Sloan, David Allen. ~ Co. A
Smalley, Samuel C. ~ Co. H
Smalley, Wesley D. ~ Co. H
Smalley, William W. (Veteran.) ~ Co. I
Smith, Absalom C. (Veteran.) ~ Co. F
Smith, Emory A. ~ Co. D
Smith, Frederick. ~ Co. E
Smith, George W. ~ Co. D
Smith, James E. ~ Co. D
Smith, James H. ~ Co. D
Smith, James S. ~ Co. H
Smith, James. ~ Co. F
Smith, John Isaac. ~ Co. D
Smith, John W. ~ Co. F
Smith, John. ~ Co. C
Smith, John. ~ Co. F
Smith, Thomas. ~ Co. C
Smith, William W. ~ Co. H

Snow, Grimes. (Veteran.) ~ Co. F
Snyder, Daniel. ~ Co. F
Soper, David. ~ Co. H
Soults, Joseph. ~ Co. B
South, Franklin M. ~ Co. D
Spanton, John. (Veteran.) ~ Co. K
Sparling, James M. ~ Co. C
Spates, Jacob R. ~ Co. D
Spaulding, Warren. ~ Co. A
Spaulding, Warren. ~ Co. K
Spear, Henry F. ~ Co. A
Speith, William. ~ Co. A
Spellman, John P. ~ Co. A
Sporling, Edwin R. ~ Co. I
Spragg, Charles. ~ Co. C
St. John, Delos B. ~ Co. G
St. John, James M. (Veteran.) ~ Co. G
St. John, Johnnie G. ~ Co. G
Stall, Silas H. (Veteran.) ~ Co. B
Standish, William H. ~ Co. D
Starry, William. (Veteran.) ~ Co. B
Steele, David. (Veteran.) ~ Co. C
Steele, Harlan P. ~ Co. D

Appendix

Steele, James M. (Veteran.) ~ Co. C
Stephens, Francis M. ~ Co. A
Stephens, James B. ~ Co. B
Sterling, George G. ~ Co. B
Sterns, Frederick. ~ Co. C
Stevens, Henry. ~ Co. E
Steward, Joshua. ~ Co. B
Steward, William. ~ Co. B
Stewart, Bradley. ~ Co. D
Stewart, Charles F. (Veteran.) ~ Co. B
Stewart, John A. ~ Co. B
Stillman, James R. (Veteran.) ~ Co. B
Stinson, James. ~ Co. H
Stoneman, Rufus R. (Veteran.) ~ Co. C
Stout, Herbert G. ~ Co. F
Stowell, Gershom R. C. ~ Co. D
Stowell, Joseph G. (Veteran.) ~ Co. D
Stragher, Adolphus C. ~ Co. I
Straley, Joseph. ~ Co. K
Strong, Frank. ~ Co. F
Strow, Andrew J. ~ Co. G
Strunk, Albert D. (Veteran.) ~ Co. E
Stuart, John W. ~ Co. I
Sturdevant, Caleb J. ~ Co. G
Supher, Jacob P. ~ Co. H
Sutherland, Adam. ~ Co. D
Sutherland, Donald. ~ Co. D
Sutherland, John. ~ Co. D
Sutherland, Morrison. ~ Co. D
Sutton, J. A. ~ Co. C
Sutton, Resin. ~ Co. K
Sutton, Samuel. ~ Co. I
Sutzin, Henry B. ~ Co. K
Sutzin, Jacob. ~ Co. K
Sutzin, John G. (Veteran.) ~ Co. K
Swan, John. ~ Co. K
Sweesey, Thomas W., Jr. ~ Co. D
Sweet, Menzo. ~ Co. A
Symons, Oliver E. (Veteran.) ~ Co. H
Taber, Silas. (Veteran.) ~ Co. G
Tanner, William. (Veteran.) ~ Co. G
Tarbox, Manville. ~ Co. B
Tate, Daniel H. ~ Co. D
Taylor, Franklin D. ~ Co. A
Taylor, Isum. ~ Co. B
Taylor, Royal. ~ Co. C
Teefle, Stephen. (Veteran.) ~ Co. H

Appendix

Thayer, William D. (Veteran.) ~ Co. C
Thomas, John. ~ Co. B
Thompson, Abel. ~ Co. I
Thompson, Andrew P. ~ Co. F
Thompson, John B. ~ Co. F
Thompson, John. ~ Co. D
Thompson, Orfin. ~ Co. H
Thompson, Robert S. (Veteran.) ~ Co. A
Thompson, William M. ~ Co. A
Thornsbrue, Asaheal. (Veteran.) ~ Co. G
Thorp, Elbridge W. ~ Co. F
Tincher, Joseph. ~ Co. K
Tinker, George C. (Veteran.) ~ Co. A
Tisdale, Edgar. ~ Co. F
Tisdale, Gilbert J. ~ Co. E
Tisdale, Gilbert J. ~ Co. F
Tollifson, Lewis. ~ Co. F
Tollman, Edward A. (Veteran.) ~ Co. A
Tompkins, Amos S. ~ Co. D
Tompkins, Phineas H. ~ Co. A
Torrance, Adam C. ~ Co. B
Tourtellot, Lewis P. ~ Co. B
Towner, James W. ~ Co. F
Townsend, Charles H. (Veteran.) ~ Co. A
Townsend, David N. ~ Co. I
Townsend, Hiram M. ~ Co. I
Townsend, Samuel D. ~ Co. A
Towsley, Charles H. ~ Co. E
Trout, George. ~ Co. A
Trout, William. (Veteran.) ~ Co. A
True, Samuel W. ~ Co. G
Truman, Cyrus L. ~ Co. E
Truman, Henry J. ~ Co. E
Turner, George A. ~ Co. C
Tyrell, Edward. ~ Co. G
Tyrrell, Daniel W. ~ Co. F
Updegraft, Jesse. ~ Co. A
Updegraft, Joseph. ~ Co. A
Utterbeck, Albert. (Veteran.) ~ Co. C
Van Dyke, Peter H. ~ Co. K
Van Leuven, Alonzo C. ~ Co. G
Van Leuven, Henry C. ~ Co. G
Van Orsdol, Alexander G. (Veteran.) ~ Co. A

Appendix

Van Sant, Leroy J. ~ Co. D
Van Wie, Henry. ~ Co. C
Van Wie, John. ~ Co. C
Vance, Adam. ~ Co. I
Vanderbilt, Philetus. (Veteran.) ~ Co. C
Vanguson, John N. ~ Co. C
Vankleeck, David. (Veteran.) ~ Co. G
Vanvolkingburgh, Vincent. ~ Co. D
Vaughan, Bailey. ~ Co. A
Vaughn, Samuel J. ~ Co. B
Vickery, Frederick R. ~ Co. A
Vincent, Joseph. ~ Co. G
Volle, John. (Veteran.) ~ Co. B
Vorman, John. (Veteran.) ~ Co. K
Wade, Aaron L. ~ Co. B
Waggoner, Frederick. ~ Co. UNK
Wagner, John. ~ Co. D
Wait, Lewis M. ~ Co. A
Wait, Willett R. (Veteran.) ~ Co. A
Wait, Willett R. ~ Co. K
Waldron, James C. ~ Co. D
Walker, Charles. ~ Co. G
Walker, Isaac. ~ Co. B
Walker, Nathan A. ~ Co. I
Walsh, Charles J. ~ Co. F
Walter, John. ~ Co. E
Walters, Joseph B. ~ Co. UNK
Walton, Pierce. ~ Co. B
Ward, Charles G. (Veteran.) ~ Co. UNK
Ward, Edward. ~ Co. F
Ward, George W. ~ Co. F
Ward, Henry P. ~ Co. UNK
Warner, George R. ~ Co. UNK
Warner, George S. (Veteran.) ~ Co. K
Warner, James M. (Veteran.) ~ Co. B
Warren, Elijah. ~ Co. K
Washburn, Frederick S. ~ Co. G
Wasmer, Franz. ~ Co. E
Waters, Asa. ~ Co. G
Waters, John H. ~ Co. G
Watrous, Levi. W. ~ Co. F
Watson, Andrew. ~ Co. G
Way, James. ~ Co. B
Weaver, Francis. (Veteran.) ~ Co. B
Webber, August. ~ Co. UNK
Webber, Frank. ~ Co. E
Webster, Baker. ~ Co. I
Webster, George W. ~ Co. I

Appendix

Webster, William B. ~ Co. F
Weeks, Stephen M. ~ Co. B
Welch, James M. ~ Co. B
Wellington, Cyrus. ~ Co. UNK
Wells, Ely V. (Veteran.) ~ Co. B
Wells, Martin M. ~ Co. I
Wells, Truman T. (Veteran.) ~ Co. G
Wentworth, Lorenzo. ~ Co. I
Weseman, Charles. ~ Co. E
West, Alexander M. (Veteran.) ~ Co. K
West, Errich. ~ Co. G
West, James K. (Veteran.) ~ Co. K
West, James. ~ Co. A
West, Nelson. (Veteran.) ~ Co. UNK
Whisnand, William. ~ Co. B
White, Charles C. ~ Co. K
White, Elisha C. ~ Co. I
White, Franklin. ~ Co. K
White, George W. ~ Co. F
White, Hezekiah. ~ Co. K
White, Isaac. ~ Co. D
White, Joseph L. ~ Co. D
White, Norman C. ~ Co. A
White, Samuel W. ~ Co. A
Whitenack, Andrew R. ~ Co. K
Whitenack, George W. ~ Co. K
Whitlock, Rinaldo M. (Veteran.) ~ Co. B
Whitney, John H. ~ Co. B
Wicking, John. ~ Co. A
Wigorn, John J. (Veteran.) ~ Co. F
Wilbur, Frederick M. ~ Co. B
Wilbur, Henry P. ~ Co. B
Wilcox, Hiram R. ~ Co. F
Wilder, Charles L. ~ Co. I
Willey, William. ~ Co. B
Williams, John M. ~ Co. K
Willsie, Henry. ~ Co. UNK
Willsie, Myron. ~ Co. UNK
Windsor, Adonin J. ~ Co. B
Windsor, Charles. (Veteran.) ~ Co. K
Wing, Alvah S. ~ Co. K
Winn, Welcome B. ~ Co. B
Winslow, Amos. ~ Co. D
Wood, Alfred C. ~ Co. F
Wood, William. ~ Co. D
Woodworth, Sylvanus. (Veteran.) ~ Co. I

Appendix

Works, Joseph S. ~ Co. B
Wragg, Josiah L. ~ Co. E
Wright, Daniel L. (Veteran.) ~ Co. K
Wright, James C. ~ Co. D
Wright, Joseph M. (Veteran.) ~ Co. E
Wright, Robert W. ~ Co. B
Yambert, Moses. ~ Co. UNK
Yantz, Joseph. ~ Co. UNK
Yantz, Levi. (Veteran.) ~ Co. UNK
Yeager, Harvey B. ~ Co. UNK
Young, Amos S. ~ Co. UNK
Young, Charles C. ~ Co. UNK
Young, James T. ~ Co. UNK
Young, John H. (Veteran.) ~ Co. UNK
Young, Warren H. ~ Co. UNK

Appendix

For Further Research

The website links referenced in this appendix change periodically. Check our website for updates.

http://www.researchonline.net/linkupdates.htm

National Archives and Records Administration

http://www.archives.gov/research/order/order-vets-records.html

Confederate Records

http://www.archives.gov/research/military/civil-war/

For Confederate army soldiers, there are two major record collections in the National Archives and Records Administration that provide information on military service:

(1) compiled military service record (CMSR) and

(2) records reproduced in microfilm publication M861, *Compiled Records Showing Service of Military Units in Confederate Organizations* (74 rolls). Records relating to Confederate soldiers are typically less complete than those relating to Union soldiers because many Confederate records did not survive the war. These records

Appendix

are now available on CD-ROM by state. They may be ordered from our website for $35.00 per state.

http://www.researchonline.net/catalog/service.htm

NARA does not have pension files for Confederate soldiers. Pensions were granted to Confederate veterans and their widows and minor children by the States of Alabama, Arkansas, Florida, Georgia, Kentucky, Louisiana, Mississippi, Missouri, North Carolina, Oklahoma, South Carolina, Tennessee, Texas, and Virginia; these records are in the state archives or equivalent agency.

NARA records are available from the Family History Library in Salt Lake City Utah. You can order them at your local Family History Center (FHC) (Mormon Church). The centers should have a Research Outline on Military Records which should cost about a dollar. Also there is a good book out on Military Records (NARA) by James Neagle. It should be in most FHC. In the card catalog on microfiche, you can go to the Author/Title section, look under Author = National Archives. All their film is there listed by NARA # (sample - M530. LDS microfilm is quicker and cheaper than requesting from NARA}.

Appendix

To obtain Civil War military service and pension records by mail

Paper copies of Civil War military service and pension records can be ordered by mail using one NATF Form 80 for **each soldier** and **each type of file**.

You can obtain the NATF Form 80 by providing your name and mailing address to inquire@nara.gov. Be sure to specify "Form 80" and the number of forms you need.

You can also obtain the NATF Form 80 by writing to:

National Archives and Records Administration
Attn: NWDT1
700 Pennsylvania Avenue, NW
Washington, DC 20408-0001

The Cost of this type of lookup is $45.00.

CONFEDERATE SERVICE AND PENSION RECORDS

The agencies listed below are repositories for Confederate pension records. The veteran was eligible to apply for a pension to the State in which he lived, even if he served in a unit from a different State. Generally, an applicant was eligible for a pension

Appendix

only if he was indigent or disabled. In your letter to the repository, state the Confederate veteran's name, his widow's name, the unit(s) in which he served, and the counties in which he and his widow lived after the Civil War. Some repositories also have records of Confederate Homes (for veterans, widows, etc.), muster rolls of State Confederate militia, and other records related to the war. For information on procedures and fees for requesting copies of records, contact the appropriate repository. Also See Online Pension Indexes for Florida, Georgia, Tennessee, Texas and Virginia

ALABAMA

Alabama Department of Archives and History –

http://www.archives.state.al.us/index.html

624 Washington Avenue
Montgomery, AL 36130-0100
Telephone: 334-242-4363

A Guide to Alabama Civil War Research is available in EBOOK and paper formats. 211 pgs.

http://www.researchonline.net/catalog/110601.htm

In 1867 Alabama began granting pensions to Confederate veterans who had lost arms or legs. In

Appendix

1886 the State began granting pensions to veterans' widows. In 1891 the law was amended to grant pensions to indigent veterans or their widows.

Service records of Alabama soldiers may be viewed on line:

http://archives.state.al.us/civilwar/search.cfm

ARKANSAS

Arkansas History Commission and State Archives

http://www.ark-ives.com/

1 Capitol Mall
Little Rock, AR 72201
Telephone: 501-682-6900

In 1891 Arkansas began granting pensions to indigent Confederate veterans. In 1915 the State began granting pensions to their widows and mothers.

Two published indexes are available in many libraries:

Appendix

Allen, Desmond Walls. Index to Confederate Pension Applications (Conway, Ark.: Arkansas Research, 1991).

Ingmire, Frances Terry. Arkansas Confederate Veterans and Widows Pensions Applications (St. Louis, MO: F.T. Ingmire, 1985).

FLORIDA

Florida State Archives –

http://dlis.dos.state.fl.us/index_researchers.cfm
R. A. Gray Building
500 South Bronough Street
Tallahassee, FL 32399-0250
Telephone: 850.245.6700

In 1885 Florida began granting pensions to Confederate veterans. In 1889 the State began granting pensions to their widows.

A published index, which provides each veteran's pension number, is available in many libraries:

White, Virgil. Register of Florida CSA Pension Applications (Waynesboro, TN: National Historical Publishing Co., 1989).

GEORGIA

Appendix

Georgia Department of Archives and History –

http://www.georgiaarchives.org/

Georgia State Archives
5800 Jonesboro Rd.
Morrow, GA 30260
Telephone: 678-364-3700

A Guide to Georgia Civil War Research is available in EBOOK and paper formats. 211 pgs.

http://www.researchonline.net/catalog/090801.htm

In 1870 Georgia began granting pensions to soldiers with artificial limbs. In 1879 the State began granting pensions to other disabled Confederate veterans or their widows who then resided in Georgia. By 1894 eligible disabilities had been expanded to include old age and poverty.

A published index is available in many libraries:

> *White, Virgil D.* Index to Georgia Civil War Confederate Pension Files (Waynesboro, TN: National Historical Publishing Co., 1996). and online:

KENTUCKY

Kentucky State Archives –
http://www.kdla.ky.gov/

Appendix

Research Room
300 Coffee Tree Road
Frankfort, KY 40601
Telephone: 502-564-8300

In 1912, Kentucky began granting pensions to Confederate veterans or their widows. The records are on microfilm. A published index is available in many libraries:

> Simpson, Alicia. Index of Confederate Pension Applications, Commonwealth of Kentucky (Frankfort, KY: Division of Archives and Records Management, Department of Library and Archives, 1978).

LOUISIANA

Louisiana State Archives –

http://www.sos.la.gov/Pages/default.aspx
3851 Essen Lane
Baton Rouge, LA 70809-2137
Telephone: 225-922-1000

In 1898 Louisiana began granting pensions to indigent Confederate veterans or their widows.

MISSISSIPPI

Mississippi State Archives –

Appendix

http://www.mdah.state.ms.us/
> Mississippi Department of Archives and History
> P.O. Box 571
> Jackson, MS 39205
> Telephone: 601- 576-6850

In 1888 Mississippi began granting pensions to indigent Confederate veterans or their widows. A published index is available in many libraries:

> *Wiltshire, Betty C.* Mississippi Confederate Pension Applications (Carrollton, MS: Pioneer Publishing Co., 1994).

MISSOURI

> Missouri State Archives –
> http://www.sos.mo.gov/archives/
> State Information Center
> 300 West Main Street
> P.O. Box 1747
> Jefferson City, MO 65102
> Telephone: 573-751-3280

In 1911 Missouri began granting pensions to indigent Confederate veterans only; none were granted to widows. Missouri also had a home for disabled Confederate veterans. The pension and veterans' home applications are interfiled and

Appendix

arranged alphabetically. Typically, the pension file is small, perhaps four to eight pages, containing a standard application form and may include letters of recommendation from family members or others.

NORTH CAROLINA

North Carolina Department of Cultural Resources

Division of Archives and History –

http://www.ah.dcr.state.nc.us/
>109 East Jones Street
>Raleigh, NC 27601-2807
>Telephone: 919-733-7305

In 1867 North Carolina began granting pensions to Confederate veterans who were blinded or lost an arm or leg during their service. In 1885 the State began granting pensions to all other disabled indigent Confederate veterans or widows.

OKLAHOMA

Archives and Records Management Divisions –
http://www.odl.state.ok.us/oar/archives/collections.htm
>200 Northeast 18th Street
>Oklahoma City, OK 73105
>Telephone: (405) 522-3579

Appendix

In 1915 Oklahoma began granting pensions to Confederate veterans or their widows. A published index is available in many libraries:

Oklahoma Genealogical Society. Index to Applications for Pensions from the State of Oklahoma, Submitted by Confederate Soldiers, Sailors, and Their Widows (Oklahoma City, OK: Oklahoma Genealogical Society Projects Committee, 1969)

SOUTH CAROLINA

South Carolina Department of Archives and History
http://scdah.sc.gov/
8301 Parklane Road
Columbia, SC 29223
Telephone: 803-896-6100

A Guide to South Carolina Civil War Research is available in EBOOK and paper formats. 200 pgs.

http://www.researchonline.net/catalog/scresearch.htm

A state law enacted December 24, 1887, permitted financially needy Confederate veterans and widows to apply for a pension; however, few applications survive from the 1888-1918 era. Beginning in 1889, the

Appendix

SC Comptroller began publishing lists of such veterans receiving pensions in his Annual Report. To obtain a copy of the pension application from the 1888-1918 era, the researcher needs to know the exact year in which the veteran or widow applied for a pension. From 1919 to 1925, South Carolina granted pensions to Confederate veterans and widows regardless of financial need. These files are arranged alpha-betically. Pension application files are typically one sheet of paper with writing on both sides. Also available are Confederate Home applications and inmate records for veterans (1909-1957), and applications of wives, widows, sisters, and daughters (1925-1955).

TENNESSEE

Tennessee State Library and Archives –
http://sos.tn.gov/tsla

Public Service Division
403 Seventh Avenue North
Nashville, TN 37243-0312
Telephone: 615-741-2764

A Guide to Tennessee Civil War Research is available in EBOOK and paper formats. 180 pgs.

http://www.researchonline.net/catalog/110801.htm

Appendix

In 1891 Tennessee began granting pensions to indigent Confederate veterans. In 1905 the State began granting pensions to their widows. The records are on microfilm.

A published index is available in many libraries:

Sistler, Samuel. Index to Tennessee Confederate Pension Applications (Nashville, TN: Sistler & Assoc., 1995).

Confederate Home records are also available, and there is an online index:

Index to Tennessee Confederate Soldiers' Home Applications

http://www.tennessee.gov/tsla/history/military/pension.htm

TEXAS

Texas State Library and Archives Commission –

http://www.tsl.state.tx.us/

P.O. Box 12927
Austin, TX 78711
Telephone: 512-463-5480

Appendix

In 1881 Texas set aside 1,280 acres for disabled Confederate veterans. In 1889 the State began granting pensions to indigent Confederate veterans and their widows. Muster rolls of State militia in Confederate service are also available.

A published index is available in many libraries:

White, Virgil D. Index to Texas CSA Pension Files (Waynesboro, TN: National Historical Publishing Co., 1989).

An online Index:

Index to Texas Confederate Pension Applications, 1899-1975

http://www.tsl.state.tx.us/arc/pensions/introcpi.html

VIRGINIA

Library of Virginia –

http://www.lva.lib.va.us

Archives Division
800 East Broad Street
Richmond, VA 23219
Telephone: 804-692-3500

Appendix

In 1888 Virginia began granting pensions to Confederate veterans or their widows. The records are on microfilm. Two indexes are available online:

Virginia Confederate Pension Rolls (Veterans and Widows) Database

http://lva1.hosted.exlibrisgroup.com/F/?file_name=find-b-clas10&func=file&local_base=CLAS10

Appendix

The Historical Sketch & Roster Series

These books contain information for researching the men who served in a particular unit. The focus is for genealogical rather than historical research. More than 1100 volumes are currently available. For a complete listing see our website:

For Confederate Titles by State

http://www.researchonline.net/catalog/crhmast.htm

For Union Titles by State

http://www.researchonline.net/catalog/urhmast.htm

TABLE OF CONTENTS:

List of Officers with biographical sketches
List of companies and the counties where formed
Officers of each company
Military assignments
Battles engaged in the war
Historical sketch of the regiment's service
Rosters / compiled service records of each company
Bibliography of sources

Appendix

Paperback - $25.00 (Selected larger volumes are more expensive.)
CD-ROM - $15.00
EBOOK - $9.49 – PDF format of the book delivered by EMAIL – NO SHIPPING CHARGE

Shipping is $6.00 per order regardless of the number of titles ordered.

Order From:
Eastern Digital Resources
31 Bramblewood Drive SW
Cartersville, GA 30120
(678) 739-9177
Order on Line
http://www.researchonline.net/catalog/crhmast.htm
Sales@researchonline.net

Made in the USA
Coppell, TX
13 June 2021